THE Permaculture Home Garden

LINDA WOODROW

VIKING

VIKING

Published by the Penguin Group
Penguin Group (Australia)
250 Camberwell Road, Camberwell, Victoria 3124, Australia
(a division of Pearson Australia Group Pty Ltd)
Penguin Group (USA) Inc.
375 Hudson Street, New York, New York 10014, USA
Penguin Group (Canada)
90 Eglinton Avenue East, Suite 700, Toronto, ON M4P 2Y3, Canada
(a division of Pearson Penguin Canada Inc.)
Penguin Books Ltd
80 Strand, London WC2R 0RL, England
Penguin Ireland
25 St Stephen's Green, Dublin 2, Ireland
(a division of Penguin Books Ltd)
Penguin Books India Pvt Ltd
11, Community Centre, Panchsheel Park, New Delhi – 110 017, India
Penguin Group (NZ)
Cnr Airborne and Rosedale Roads, Albany, Auckland, New Zealand
(a division of Pearson New Zealand Ltd)
Penguin Books (South Africa) (Pty) Ltd
24 Sturdee Avenue, Rosebank, Johannesburg 2196, South Africa

Penguin Books Ltd, Registered Offices: 80 Strand, London WC2R ORL, England

First published by Penguin Books Australia Ltd 1996

18 17 16 15 14 13

Typeset in Novarese by Post Pre-press Group, Brisbane, Queensland
Illustrations by Michelle Ryan
Diagrams by Alan Laver
Printed and bound in Australia by McPherson's Printing Group, Maryborough, Victoria

National Library of Australia
Cataloguing-in-Publication data:

Woodrow, Linda, 1957– .
The permaculture home garden.

Includes index.
ISBN 0 670 86599 0.

1. Organic gardening. I. Title.

635.987

www.penguin.com.au

FOREWORD

Permaculture ('permanent agriculture') is a word I coined in the 1970s. It means the conscious design and maintenance of agriculturally productive ecosystems that have the diversity, stability and resilience of natural ecosystems. It is the harmonious integration of landscape and people, providing their food, energy, shelter, and other material and non-material needs in a sustainable way. Without permanent agriculture there is no possibility of a stable social order.

The philosophy behind permaculture is one of working with, rather than against, nature; of protracted and thoughtful observation rather than protracted and thoughtless action; of looking at systems in all their functions, rather than asking only one yield of them; and of allowing systems to demonstrate their own evolutions.

Linda Woodrow studied permaculture intensively, and has written a fresh and lively book based on her wide experience. Her careful and intensive designs minimise work but allow nature to exist while encouraging natural controls. She includes personal self-management, time-and-motion studies and a variety of findings suited to our Australian climates, including the subtropical. I think Linda conveys, in detail, all the essentials for good gardening or mini-farming. There is very little derivative material, and the text has a first-hand and authentic ring to it, a feeling for soil and plants.

I can only recommend this book to all home gardeners who respect good soil husbandry, nutrition and design.

Bill Mollison

CONTENTS

PREFACE

Some who read this book will say, 'It's easy for you. You live in northern New South Wales where the climate is mild and the growing season long.' And it's true. I live quite close to the Border Ranges World Heritage Area, a wonderful natural garden with productivity unmatched by anything humans have ever created.

But I haven't always lived here. I have established gardens on windswept desert land in Western Australia, with local bush goats who thought it was too good to be true, and on an old schoolyard in Darwin. I have gardened in tiny courtyards and on a scale large enough to supply a Brisbane organic greengrocer. I have created a vegie garden out of the overgrown backyard of a squat in the inner-city Melbourne suburb of St Kilda. I have taught gardening in Glen Innes, where the first frost can be expected around Anzac Day and the last around Melbourne Cup Day. I am convinced that it is possible to grow most of your own food anywhere, under any circumstances.

I don't come from a gardening family. My mother still waits for the day when I will put my degree to 'proper' use. In the heady 1970s, when it seemed that turning the whole world into paradise was a perfectly reasonable goal, I decided that food production was the place to start, and I've stayed with it ever since. Some hippies never give up.

But I must admit that these days I do have it easy. For the last twelve years I have lived with my partner and our two children in a very beautiful valley near the Queensland/NSW border. My site is high, sloping, windy, and beloved by the local wallabies. The virgin soil is what is locally known as 'black pug' – a very heavy clay that cracks when dry and swallows gumboots whole when wet. For most of the last four years my area has been drought-declared. But it is also pretty nearly frost-free, faces north-east, and is surrounded by a forest that harbours over eighty species of birds.

Lately I have scaled back from commercial production to allow time for teaching and writing, keeping my garden just large enough to supply my family and community. But much of the credit for this book goes to my former partners in commercial gardening at different times. Allison Gillies tackled my Virgo insistence on use, and taught me that flowers, smells and contemplative time are as vital to farming as they are to gardening. Mark 'Carrot' Garrett taught me to have fun, exercise my curiosity, and examine and question what I do.

While I am on credits I must mention Bill Mollison, founder of the permaculture philosophy, whose works have influenced and informed me more than any other literature on gardening. My community at Black Horse Creek has supplied endless cups of coffee, listening ears and inspiration. And of course thanks go to my partner, Peter Lewis, without whom, as they say, none of this would be possible.

Linda Woodrow

INTRODUCTION

This is a book about saving the planet and living to be a hundred, while throwing very impressive dinner parties and organising other creatures to do most of the work. It is a book about a very different style of growing food.

I am a passionate gardener. I can't imagine not having a garden. I would feel both deprived and irresponsible. To me, gardening for the joy of it is for everyone who eats. My aims are very ordinary: good, healthy, unpoisoned food that tastes like it should; a bit of stretch to the household budget; work that feels like play, and not too much of it; greenery and bird calls and flower smells around the house; and a world that is fit for my grandchildren. The trouble is that no conventional system of gardening – or farming either – has it all.

If you follow conventional gardening systems, growing your own food is a very expensive hobby. It is a full-time job, and not exactly an inspiring one, just to provide *some* of your family's food. If you account for the cost of your own labour, those supermarket beans begin to look very cheap. Conventional farming systems can produce cheap beans, but by using poisons, drudgery and mined resources – and they taste like it! Neither system even aspires to the aesthetic and creative satisfaction of a landscaped garden, and both involve making enemies of almost every other creature.

I could never decide which of my aims to sacrifice, so I have had to develop an unconventional style of gardening. I like sensory delight. Not just in taste – that is an obvious one for gardeners. No bought food is a patch on food you grow yourself for taste. If I could find a way to persuade earthworms to wash the dishes, restaurants would lose their last attraction. But I like many other sensory delights too – weekends at the beach, long hot baths with a glass of wine, a good book. I don't mind physical work, but I hate drudgery. There are too many things to fit into life for anything as boring as weeding or driving a tractor back and forth, back and forth. There are simply not enough hours in the day for me to fit in gardening by any conventional system. The ratio of output to effort is too low.

The trick to doing less is doing more of what we humans do best: use our intelligence to see patterns, create designs and invent things – activities that come so naturally they feel like play. The other side of the coin is to do less of what we do worst. Humans make hard work of digging, but for worms it is fun.

I also believe that the best flavours come from the most seductive garden. A garden has to be an art form to be really productive. It has to feed the eyes and ears and nose as well. It has to be a refuge, a place of reflection, creation and enchantment to produce peas that can be used to bribe children. That late, tired dash through bedlam with a shopping trolley compares very badly with a stroll through a seductive garden, not least because you can leave your purse behind.

The worst part of supermarket shopping is that agricultural chemicals don't even appear as numbers on the packages. I am very dubious about the idea of a clandestine cocktail of chemicals in every mouthful. The human body can cope with a good deal of toxic abuse before it overloads, but there are quite enough poisons around already without adding to them. In any case, I would rather spend my quota on good red wine and blackforest cake.

I also like to visit, and keep for my children to visit, the kinds of gardens that humans have nothing to do with creating. To me, it is important to use the minimum amount of land so as to leave as much as possible for wallabies and snakes to find their livelihood in. I want to use the minimum water, fossil fuel and machinery, and to create nothing that someone else will have to clean up.

I can't help thinking that developing systems of clean, ethical agriculture is the most important step towards making sure this earth survives. Really clean, ethical agriculture can only be done by gardeners, in small intensive plots for very local consumption. Gardening is a way of doing something significant about the greenhouse effect, soil degradation, the ozone layer, fossil fuel depletion, genetic diversity, wilderness preservation, recycling – just about everything from Star Wars to saving whales. The wonder of it is that it is a step I can take individually, in my own backyard. It is almost indecent that being such an effective environmental activist can be so much fun!

This book is a recipe for the system of gardening that suits me, and if you share my aims and likes it may well suit you too. It is a recipe that can be scaled up or down. It works just as well for a backyard garden for a small family as for a full-scale commercial operation. Like all good recipes, if you follow it exactly, it will turn out well. Then you can adapt, experiment and substitute with impunity. If you are experienced, you are probably more likely to use recipes as a source of inspiration and ideas than as a set of instructions. I have tried to include both the instructions and the reasons behind them so that you can adapt and modify the recipe. I hope you will use it as a jumping-off point for recipes to suit your own tastes.

PART ONE

TOOLS

1 PENCIL AND PAPER

The most important tools in my kit are pencil and paper. Good designs can get most other work done free. I think of design as applying permaculture principles to the old business axiom of working smarter, not harder. Design is not just for aesthetic satisfaction. Good design can make an enormous, astounding difference to your workload, and to the irksomeness of the work.

Design is the difference between getting your manure deposited where you need it, or spending a couple of hours every week or so on the thrilling task of shovelling manure. It is the difference between controlling pests by sitting on the verandah with a beer watching the dragonflies do it, or setting yourself the never-ending task of hunting very small creatures.

At the same time, design is an art form. There is a very satisfying elegance in finding the perfect arrangement: the arrangement that is balanced and integrated, every part necessary to the whole. I think it is part of being human – the tool-making animal – to delight in this kind of cleverness. After all, a tool is not just a metal thing, but anything that is consciously designed for a purpose. Design comes so naturally to humans that it feels like play.

On the other hand, there is a very *unsatisfying* frustration in finding this arrangement only *after* you have paths laid and plants planted, when creation of it will involve demolition. When I started my garden I wasn't so conscious of design. I have a seedling avocado tree right where it is least wanted, but it is doing so well I don't have the heart to cut it down. Several beds are too small, but enlarging them would mean moving every path in the system.

The best designs happen on paper first. It is much more fun, and easier, to muck around with ideas, changing and moving things, on paper than in the ground. You would never contemplate building or remodelling a kitchen without first drawing it up to scale on paper. Yet many people do exactly this in their garden, and then wonder why it is not a pleasure to work in!

SOME DESIGN PRINCIPLES

TIME-AND-MOTION EFFICIENCY

Kitchen designers pay a great deal of attention to time-and-motion efficiency: a short direct path from fridge to bench, sink to crockery-storage cupboards, stove to serving area. Garden designers need to think the same way. Many of the tasks in the garden involve *moving* something: compost, mulch, manure, seedlings, produce . . . Taken individually each task might be quite minor, but collectively they add up to a lot of not very inspiring work.

In the small space of your garden you can easily travel several kilometres, usually carrying something – and in a garden the 'something' is usually bulky, awkward and heavy. Designs that place things right where they will be used, or at the very least as close as possible, will save an enormous amount of time and energy. Carrying is not an intrinsically enjoyable activity!

One of the tools permaculturists use to achieve this is **zone analysis**. Simply put, this means placing those things that need the most frequent access in the most accessible spots. Zone One is the closest zone, extending like the protrusions of an amoeba along your most used paths. Zone Five is the furthest zone, encompassing those areas that you most rarely visit. Seedlings, for example, need to be watered every day. You are much more likely to actually *do* this job if your propagating area is in Zone One, very handy and right on one of your most frequented trafficways. Potatoes, however, are dug up just once, so they can go in the middle of a bed at the far end of the garden.

MULTIPLE USES

In a limited space, with a limited budget and limited time, every element that serves multiple purposes pays for itself several times over. This idea requires a bit of lateral thinking – opening your mind to *all* the functions and attributes of something rather than single-mindedly focusing on one.

For example, a deciduous fruit tree doesn't just yield fruit. It also supplies shade in summer, mulch in autumn, nectar to feed bees and pest predators, a vantage point for birds, wind protection, and damaged fruit and insects to feed chooks. You can't really stop it producing all these extra yields. Depending on your design, they are either resources or waste products. In the right spot this tree can save you erecting shadecloth, raking, carting and spreading mulch, hand-feeding your bees, spraying pests, and feeding your chooks – five fewer jobs for you to do. In the wrong spot these same attributes can all *cost* you work: raking, pruning, collecting fallen fruit and spraying. Design and placement make a difference of nine tasks.

Similarly, a compost pile doesn't just yield fertiliser. It also generates heat, which can save you building glasshouses or cold frames to chivvy along early tomatoes. It burns out any grass or weeds under it, which can save you laboriously digging them out to clear a new bed. It breeds worms as it gets older and cooler, leaches a lot of nutrients into the area immediately around it, and can even be used to dispose of dead bodies!

If you are building a compost pile and at the same time clearing a new bed, building a hothouse, starting a worm farm, digging a grave and making fertiliser, you have cut your workload by four-fifths. If instead you are creating a barren patch, tying up space, burning heat-sensitive plants, decaying the timber of the box the compost is made in, making a heavy load a long way from where it is to be used and fertilising the weeds around it, you have massively *increased* your workload.

As a rule of thumb, a bit of designing should be able to bring at least three functions of any element into use. That's at least three resources for the price of one, and at least three waste products you don't have to deal with.

WORKING WITH NATURE

Natural forces are very strong. If you are working with them, they make powerful allies. If you are working against them, they make formidable adversaries. Powerful allies are handy. Formidable adversaries are things to avoid. It simply makes sense to work *with* nature rather than against it.

I am not suggesting that you abandon your garden to fend for itself. A garden is an artificial construct. Lettuces and sweet corn do not grow native – at least not the kinds that make a dinner party or an income. What I am suggesting is that you alter nature wherever possible by *enhancing* natural forces, not by fighting them. It is a bit like the theory of many martial arts. You *use* the force rather than try to block it.

Gravity is a powerful natural force that can make moving things either much easier, or much harder, depending on whether or not it is on your side. It is smarter to design your garden so that gravity is on your side than to try to overcome it. The impulse to diversity is another natural force that can be friend or enemy, depending upon whether you are determined to grow a uniform monoculture or not. If you are happy to observe, enhance and take advantage of the variety and interdependency between species and even within species, you are picking the winning team.

Trying to sterilise your soil so that there is no chance of a pathogen in it that might affect your crop is like a gnat attacking an elephant. The impulse of life to invade every unoccupied niche is a natural force that it is unwise to tangle with! It is simply much smarter to go with the flow and enhance this impulse, by encouraging so much soil life that there is negligible room left in the niche for pathogens.

Nature is enormous and natural forces are much too numerous, diverse and inchoate to enumerate. The tool needed is a mental attitude of curious observation – of *noticing* what natural forces are at work in your garden – and then a habit of looking first for ways of *harnessing* them, not for ways of overcoming them. This habit may well come hard at first. Our whole society has an implicit first assumption of a need to dominate nature that is so ingrained it is unconscious. But with practice you will find that it is much more fun to be on the winning side.

SYNERGY

Synergy means that the whole is more than the sum of the parts. It involves looking at the relationships *between* elements as well as at the elements themselves. When we choose furniture, we automatically look for synergy. Do the pieces clash or complement each other? Is there a natural flow from one to the next? Do the elements blend into a harmonious whole? Synergy is much easier to illustrate than to explain, and you will find many illustrations of it in the rest of this chapter.

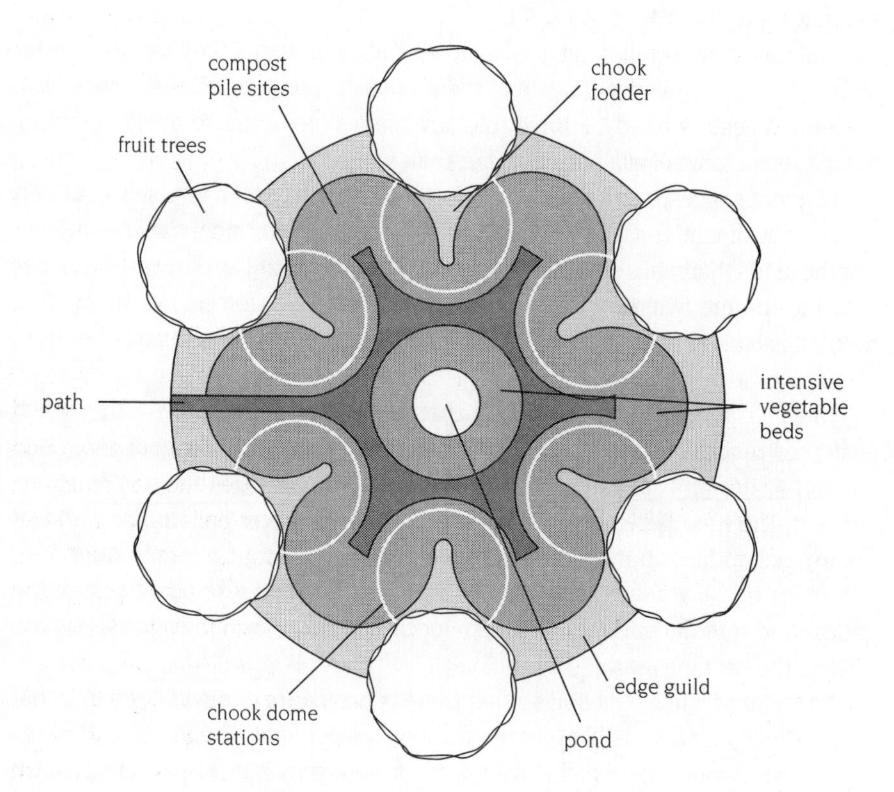

Figure 1 This design for a single mandala represents one unit or module of the design I use in my garden.

MY GARDEN DESIGN

Design is four-dimensional, in time as well as space, which makes it difficult to draw. As an example, however, I can introduce you to the garden design I use, at least in principle. My garden has evolved over a long time and has been the product of a lot of experiments. This design is now more representative of what I wish I had done than what I have actually done!

If your site allows it, you may be able simply to use this design, or some modification of it. Or you may be able to use some elements of it, or just use it to generate ideas. Your design will be unique, your own individual art piece, but mine may give you a useful starting point. If nothing else, it serves to illustrate the principles you should consider in designing a garden that will yield more kilojoules than it consumes.

Whether, or however, you use it, one of the chief pleasures of setting up a new garden is a clean slate to draw on, with no already established limitations to the perfect design and layout. If you have this opportunity, don't waste it!

Figure 1 represents a unit or module of the design – a single mandala. Several mandalas can be joined together in systems to provide for infinite expansion. I work a seven-mandala system.

INTENSIVE VEGETABLE BEDS

The areas in Figure 2 are intensive annual vegetable garden beds. They produce a continuous supply of a wide range of vegetables, with very little work besides planting and picking. I design them to need no digging; minimal weeding; no purchase, spreading or digging in of fertilisers; almost no pest control; and very little watering. It sounds almost too good to be true, but you can do all these jobs with a pencil and paper and not much else.

Digging is boring, backbreaking and counterproductive. It is the kind of work that makes more work. It destroys the habitat of all your underground allies, damages the soil structure, blocks water penetration and creates hardpans that hinder root development. I *never* dig the garden beds, not even initially to establish them. If you design the intensive beds so that they rarely need to be stepped on, and so that earthworms and chooks can get to them, you can entirely avoid the drudgery of digging and all the extra work it creates.

Figure 2 Intensive vegetable beds in a single mandala.

To achieve this, the beds need to be relatively *narrow*. They need to be planted with the most often picked vegetables along the path edge, and the things picked once only towards the inner edge, so that the beds rarely need to be stepped on. Chapter 10, 'Guild Planting', gives you more about this kind of planting. My intensive annual vegetable garden beds are 1.6 metres wide.

To design beds that are this narrow without devoting an inordinate amount of garden space to paths, the beds need to be a *convoluted shape*. My bed shape needs less than half the length of path that a rectangular bed of the same width would require. Less path length means less distance to travel carrying seedlings or produce. It also allows you to stand or kneel in one spot on the path and reach bed all around you, which is a minor but nice time-and-motion efficiency.

The bed shape is not just convoluted, though. It is convoluted to a particular size and shape – one designed to accommodate the shape and size of a 'chook tractor' (or chook dome). Chapter 6, 'Building a Chook Dome', is all about building and using a chook tractor, which is an immensely useful labour-saving device. It allows all the weeding, all the supply, spreading and digging-in of fertilisers, and a good deal of the pest control to be left to the chooks. It also allows the chooks to prepare areas for tilling by earthworms, and the spent and excess vegetables can be harvested as eggs with no digging-out or cartage.

If you can design your beds never to need digging and to attract earthworms, you can also minimise watering. Left undisturbed, the channels made by the worms and by the decomposing roots of spent plants will allow water to penetrate deeply, and the mulch will stop it evaporating again. You can reduce your watering to very little more than that needed by the seeds and seedlings. I breed worms in a worm farm so as to have large numbers to release into the garden regularly. Their food is what the chooks leave behind – manure and composting organic matter. A heavy mulch cover keeps the soil moist enough for them and allows them to surface to feed without being eaten, desiccated or sunburned. The worm farm also supplies high-protein chook food, and turns kitchen scraps into very high-value fertiliser and potting mix. Chapter 8 is about worm farming.

I keep my beds very intensively planted with rotating groups of companion plants at different stages of maturity. I design these groups, or 'guilds', to make a pattern of slow, medium pace and fast-growing plants so that you hardly ever see the mulch, let alone the soil, between the plants. The gaps between mature plants are filled by half-grown plants that will expand to occupy the space as soon as the mature plants come out.

This is called 'continuous polyculture', and is what Chapter 10 ('Guild Planting') is about. It means that there is a big variety at any one time, and it is reaching maturity continuously. It seems much more sensible to have half a kg of beans ready for picking each day than to have 20 kg ready at once. This principle holds true even at commercial scale. A producer who can supply a good variety of items with a reliable quantity of each, and supply them regularly, week in, week out, throughout their growing seasons, is much more valued than one who has a 'feast-or-famine' supply.

An intensive continuous polyculture also helps suppress weeds, control pests, minimise watering and conserve nutrients. It shades out the weeds, confuses the pests and makes them travel, and avoids wasting water and nutrients on weeds or erosion. This kind of circle of consequences, or jigsaw of pieces that each fit with several others, is what *synergy* is all about.

Provided it gets this level of fertilising, an intensive continuous polyculture is also by far the heaviest-yielding form of agriculture. One mandala will yield a complete supply of fresh vegetables for a family for a whole year. Seven mandalas will yield the equivalent in value of a professional job.

PATHS

A good path design is one that allows easy access for picking and planting, that allows you to move around without backtracking, and that has the shortest distance to walk and carry. The 'keyhole' shape in Figure 3 is by far the most time-and-motion-efficient path design. It does all the above, and it uses the minimum space – just 13.5 m^2 of pathway allows over 72 m^2 of garden bed to be reached.

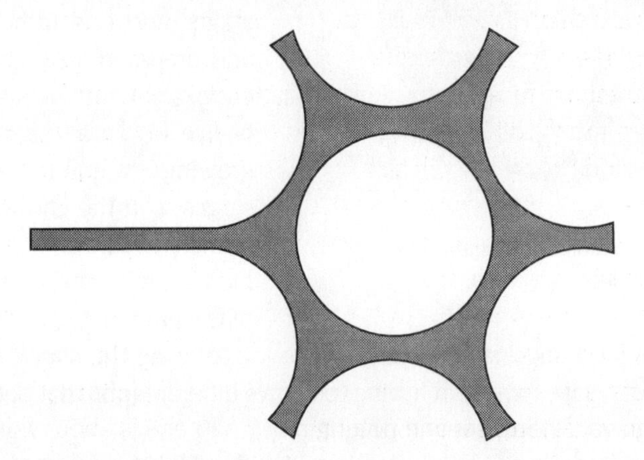

Figure 3 Paths in a single mandala.

An extra-good path design is one that also doubles for other purposes. I dig out the paths in my garden and fill them with sawdust to double as drains, because with my heavy clay soil, drainage is my biggest problem. The sawdust suppresses weeds, is pleasant to walk on, drains without becoming muddy or boggy, and is available free from the local sawmill. Moist sawdust also breeds an astonishing number of worms, which over time convert the sawdust into worm castings – a wonderful high-value fertiliser. Every so often I shovel the old sawdust – worms, worm castings and all – off a section of path and on to the adjacent bed, usually when the chooks are there to weed and spread it for me.

I then replenish the path with fresh sawdust. This path design does four jobs at once: provides access, provides drainage, breeds worms and converts sawdust into fertiliser. It is a great example of the design principle of multiple uses.

CHOOK DOME STATIONS

A 'chook dome' is a moveable chook pen or chook tractor housing about twelve chooks. It is built around the same principles as a dome tent and provides an airy, shady, weather-sheltered, roomy, escape-proof and predator-proof home for chooks. One person can move it easily in less than ten minutes. Chapter 6 ('Building a Chook Dome') includes a design for constructing one.

'Chook dome stations' (see Figure 4) are the places where the chook dome sits, moving one space every fortnight to the next adjacent station. It takes twelve weeks to complete a circuit of all six stations in a mandala. At any one time in these twelve weeks, five stations are growing vegetables at different stages and one is being cleared and prepared for planting by the chooks. For the subsequent twelve weeks all six stations are growing vegetables at different stages, and the chooks are either doing a circuit of Mandala Two or biding their time in another part of the garden.

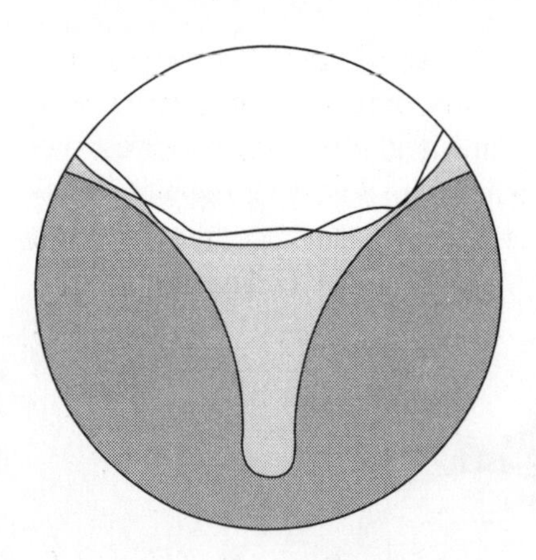

Figure 4 A chook dome station in a single mandala.

This design costs one extra ten-minute job: moving the chook dome every fortnight. But it saves me from having to do five different jobs that between them would take several hours every fortnight:

- It saves buying chook food and the small daily task of feeding it to the chooks. The chooks feed themselves.
- It saves the regular job of cleaning out the chook pen, carting the manure to the garden and digging it in. The chooks put their manure exactly where I want it in the first place and thoroughly mix it with mulch. The earthworms then dig it in for me.
- It saves the physically demanding job of pulling out weeds and grass and carrying them to the chook pen or compost pile. The chooks pull and scratch out the weeds and convert them into eggs, compost or mulch for me without my having to lift a finger.
- It saves me hunting insects, grubs, snails and slugs – a job I'm very badly adapted to do. The chooks hunt them for me. They're much better at it.

- It saves spreading mulch and trying to get the weed seeds and insect eggs and larvae out of it. The chooks spread it and search out and eat all the weed seeds and insect eggs and larvae in the process.

The chook dome also gives me an extra benefit: high yields of glorious, guilt-free eggs with yolks the colour of apricots. This is the design award for providing the chooks with an environment they like, enough to do so they don't become bored, and a varied, natural diet with lots of green food.

COMPOST PILE SITES

These are the parts of the intensive bed area that are not covered by the chook dome stations (see Figure 5). I clear and fertilise these areas once a year by building a compost pile on each of them.

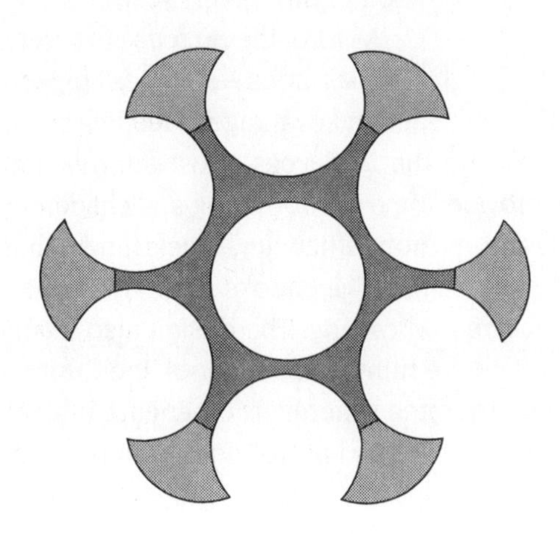

Figure 5 Compost pile sites in a single mandala.

When a chook dome is on the adjacent bed in spring or summer, I add an extra lot of mulch to it. As soon as the chooks are moved on, I rake out half the mulch mixed with manure and whatever else I have thrown to the chooks, and layer it with horse or cow manure and comfrey to make compost. Chapter 7 ('Compost') includes a fail-safe, easy compost recipe.

This design is very time-and-motion efficient. The chooks do half the work of making the compost, and made this way it usually needs only one turning. The finished product is used on the bed right next to it, which saves moving it from one end of the garden to the other. The design also incorporates multiple uses. Besides providing fertiliser, the compost clears, fertilises, and feeds the worms in the bed on which it is made. And it provides a cleared, fertilised area for long-season crops like onions and brussels sprouts that will not mature in the six months between chook dome rotations.

CHOOK FODDER AREAS

These areas (see Figure 6) cannot be reached easily from the path, so I design them to need reaching very rarely. They are reserved for perennial chook-fodder crops. Perennials only need to be reached for planting once, and chook-fodder crops don't need to be reached for harvesting. Some of them make good human food too, but that can be harvested by stepping on the bed just once, when everything else in it is finished bearing and just before the chooks go on it.

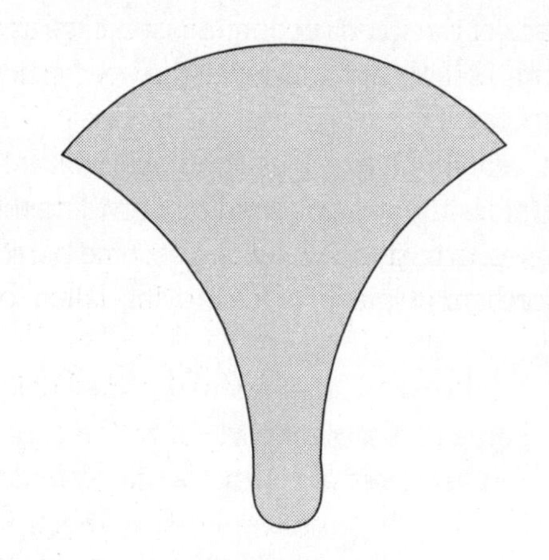

Figure 6 A chook fodder area in a single mandala.

The chook domes go over these areas, so the chooks feed themselves. These areas supply my chook-fodder staples, supplemented with vegetable residues, weeds, household scraps, insects, slugs, snails, worms, fallen fruit and some mulch and water weeds. In return the chooks give the perennials exactly what they require to bear well: manure, processed mulch, worm food and a good pruning every year.

Most of these crops are perennial legumes – such as pigeon peas, chick peas or lucerne – so they have the added advantage of feeding some nitrogen to the annual vegetable beds and the fruit trees. Most are medium height (around a metre tall), so they provide some windbreaking and shade.

This design incorporates time-and-motion efficiency. The things that require the least access are the least accessible. The chooks can harvest their share themselves with no human picking and carting. The design also incorporates multiple uses. The fodder crops are human food, chook food, nitrogen fixers and windbreaks. And it incorporates synergy: the benefits it gives to and derives from the other design elements add up to more than the sum of the parts.

POND

One year my garden was overrun with grasshoppers. Even 'Home Brew' – the grasshopper-hunting specialist of the chooks – couldn't make a dint in the population. As an experiment I built a tiny pond in the middle of the garden.

I have never had problems with grasshoppers since. Frogs and lizards moved into the garden. A greater variety of birds took up more permanent residence, and wasps and dragonflies hovered around. When they ran out of grasshoppers, they started in on other pests.

The pond is planted with edible water plants and has a very respectable yield in food. It also helps create a microclimate with air moisture and reflected light, and is a very pleasant place for contemplative sitting. Chapter 12, 'Humans and Other Pests', includes a design for a very cheap, easily built pond.

FRUIT TREES

Good design for fruit trees (Figure 7) includes low-energy maintenance, easy and convenient harvesting, and a high yield of good-quality fruit. This means:

- first and foremost, protection from grass invasion and competition, at least as far out as the drip line (the edge of the leaf canopy);
- adequate water and water conservation – which means mulch, preferably minus bugs and weed seeds;
- regular fertilising with much the same nutrient providers the vegetables need: manure, ash, shellgrit, worm castings, compost, seaweed brew and herbs;
- pest control, including the basic orchard hygiene of destroying fallen or infected fruit to stop pests breeding;
- proximity at fruiting time – the best-quality fruit is tree-ripened, picked daily, and eaten or sold fresh; and
- occasional surveillance, just checking on them.

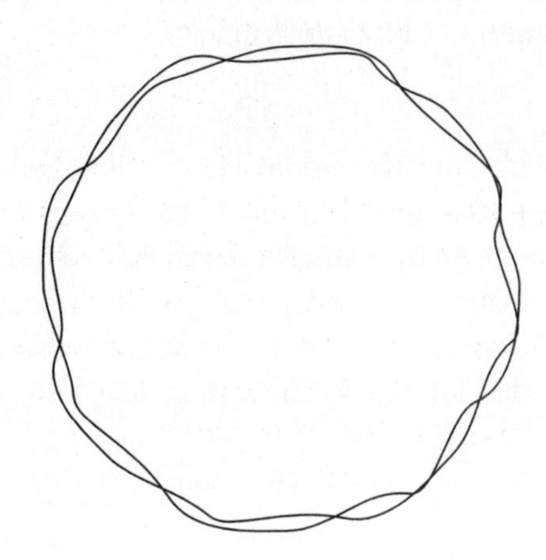

Figure 7 A fruit tree in a single mandala.

All these jobs can be made much easier – and many of them can be escaped altogether by delegating them to the chooks – if the fruit trees are planted *in* the garden. Tending the fruit trees becomes part and parcel of the garden routine, not an extra job, so they tend not to become neglected. It is much easier to provide mulch, water and surveillance to one garden/orchard than to two separate areas. Best of all, the geometry of circles means that very little extension of the garden perimeter is needed to fit the trees within it, which means very little extra work to protect them from grass invasion.

A bit of playing with a pencil and paper will give you garden space for at least the most demanding of your fruit trees. Extra-good design can make the process reciprocal – the trees benefit by being in the garden, and the garden benefits from having them. This happens if they are carefully arranged around the edge of the mandala in a *sequence* according to the time of year they bear fruit, so that the chook dome can be moved one space each time to be under a tree in fruit.

In my design the southern edge of the garden has evergreen trees and the northern edge deciduous trees, so that the latter throw some shade on the garden in summer but none in winter. The trees are placed so that their drip line does not extend over the intensive beds, which means that they are not in fierce competition with the vegetables. They share a root zone, though, with the chook-fodder crops, to gain the benefit of the extra nitrogen.

Since the tree in fruit is the one with the chook dome beneath it, picking fruit for eating and for the chooks can be done at the same time as collecting the eggs. Fertilising, weeding and cleaning up fallen fruit is delegated to the chooks.

The vegetable garden aids the fruit trees by keeping a stable population of pest predators fed and breeding, so the sudden influx of pests at the trees' fruiting time never gets a big head start. The chooks help feed the trees with their manure and scratched mulch, ash and shellgrit. The chook-fodder crops help the trees by fixing nitrogen in the soil for them. In return the trees help feed the chooks, both with spoiled or excess fruit, and with the insects they attract. They help the vegetables by providing shade in summer, a windbreak, nectar to attract predatory insects and a vantage point for predatory birds.

It requires a bit of finicky designing to select and arrange the trees so that they bear fruit one after another, but the payoff is virtually effort-free fruit. Chapter 11, 'Fruit Trees', will help you with this bit of designing.

EDGE GUILD

The edge guild is an arrangement of plants, mostly perennial herbs, that prevent grass, weed and pest invasion from the edges. Specific companions for each kind of fruit tree are concentrated around them. All the plants in this guild have other uses – as culinary or medicinal herbs, micronutrient accumulators, mulch, edible or decorative flowers, compost activators, and food for predatory insects. Chapter 13, 'Green Gatecrashers', includes a design for an edge guild.

SCALE

My standard chook dome design has a circumference of 12 metres, and the garden beds are scaled to fit this. This means that each circle in this design has an area of a bit over 11 m^2 and a diameter of 3.8 metres. One mandala has a diameter of 15 metres between the trunks of the trees, or 20 metres to their outside drip lines, and contains just over 72 m^2 of intensive vegetable garden beds.

At this scale, one mandala will fit neatly into an average suburban backyard with plenty of room left for the clothes line and the swings. Once established, the garden should take no more than four to five hours a week to maintain. This workload can easily be covered in a very pleasant routine. Half an hour each evening wandering, pottering, planting, picking and winding down from the day will take care of half of it. A couple of hours in the garden instead of the gym on the weekend – gathering mulch, making and turning compost, potting out seedlings and moving the chooks – takes care of the rest.

For a family of four, this scale will provide all the herbs, all the eggs, all the fresh vegetables and a good proportion of the fruit, with the odd surplus for preserving or giving away. Gardening at this scale will provide your family with a really healthy gourmet diet even if both your money and your time are tightly budgeted. It will provide a true sense of security: whatever else happens you will always eat, and eat well. It will provide an area of creativity in a sometimes treadmill existence, and an area of serenity in a sometimes madcap world.

This basic module is infinitely expandable. A two-mandala system, requiring about eight to ten hours a week, should provide all your herbs, eggs, fresh vegetables and fruit, and a fair surplus for preserving, gifts or trade. You can stock your shelves with tomato relish and chilli beans, and just about bypass the supermarket. A seven-mandala system, requiring twenty-five to thirty hours a week to maintain and just over one-tenth of a hectare or a quarter of an acre, should provide a good living in money and kind.

I cannot think of any reason to build a larger chook dome, as it would begin to get too heavy and unwieldy to be moved easily. The standard size fits twelve chooks, which is an ideal flock size, and larger beds would result in problems reaching the middle of them. One chook dome will serve two mandalas, giving each bed two weeks twice a year. If you are working on a larger scale, it is easiest just to add domes. I have four chook domes in my garden.

If you are gardening a pocket-handkerchief area, however, you may want to experiment with a smaller chook tractor and a system to go with it. One friend, Valerie, uses three beautiful fluffy white Chinese Silky hens in a miniature dome to garden for herself and her small daughter in the tiny courtyard of an inner-city terrace house (see Figure 8 on page 19). The Silkies cope with being cuddled several times a day and still produce a pair of eggs for breakfast every morning!

Alternatively, and especially if you have an unsympathetic local council or a rampant neighbourhood dog pack, you may wish to base your design around worm farming and sheet composting rather than chooks. Chapter 7, 'Compost', and Chapter 8, 'Worm Farming', will be especially relevant here.

WHY CIRCLES?

The chook dome design came first. My earliest moveable chook pen consisted of four star pickets, a length of chicken wire, and a pile of rocks to weigh the bottom down. It took two people half a day to move it, and meanwhile the chooks played havoc in the garden. Carpet snakes, eagles and foxes took their toll on the chooks, and every few days, when the kids left the makeshift gate adrift, I threatened to take an even bigger toll!

Nevertheless, for all its failings, the job done by the chooks in clearing and fertilising was so impressive that the hunt began for the perfect chook tractor design. It had to be large enough for a dozen chooks to be comfortable and happy in it. It had to be able to be moved easily and quickly by a single person.

It had to provide shade and wet-weather protection. And it had to be as predator-proof as possible – which is not easy with carpet snakes, eagles, foxes, feral cats and goannas to contend with.

The design that resulted, over a few years, was a circular dome shape, built using many of the same principles as a dome tent. I am now on Mark V. I think I have all the design bugs sorted out, and have found this tool so useful that it is reason enough for having circular beds even without all the other incentives.

But there *are* other incentives, and even if you don't use the chook dome tool, it is worth considering a circle-based pattern for your garden:

- Circles are the geometric shape that gives the maximum internal area for least circumference. This means minimum edge to protect from grass and weed invasion.
- Circles with keyholes give the least path length for the maximum bed area. Every time you carry a box of seedlings or a load of mulch, you will appreciate only having to carry it half the distance! From a single point on the path you can reach about 9 m^2 of bed. Being able to plonk yourself and your box of seedlings down in one spot and work from there not only means less energy expended, but also facilitates that quiet meditative state that is one of the prime joys of gardening.
- Circles end up where they started. In any rotation, moving in a circle means no carting anything back to the beginning to start again. You don't even have to remember where the 'beginning' is – one thing flows into another everlastingly.
- Circles have none of those tricky corners that are difficult to water with a sprinkler and where nothing will fit because neither the leaf crown nor the roots of plants grow in triangular or square shapes.
- And circles create a softer design, one that seems to foster calm and centred energy, and lends itself to flowing patterns of colour, shape and smell.

The word 'garden' almost automatically invokes, for most people, an image of rectangular beds and a row or block-shaped planting format. I suspect this comes from simply envisaging a miniature of a giant mechanised farm, which is not very creative designing! But even broadacre farmers do contour ploughing these days. Whether or not you include chooks in your design, it is worth considering a pattern based on curves.

The number of ways that different combinations of these design elements can be used is literally infinite. In addition each gardener and each site will call for some elements that are unique. Valerie's garden and Stephanie's garden are two examples. Figure 8, Valerie's garden, is for an area 4.5 m × 4.5 m in a temperate climate (e.g. Melbourne, Canberra, Adelaide or Hobart). It uses a miniature chook dome to house three hens (the Chinese Silkies). Figure 9, Stephanie's garden (see page 29), is for an area 6 m × 6 m in Sydney or a similar climate. It incorporates a large worm farm and does not use chooks at all.

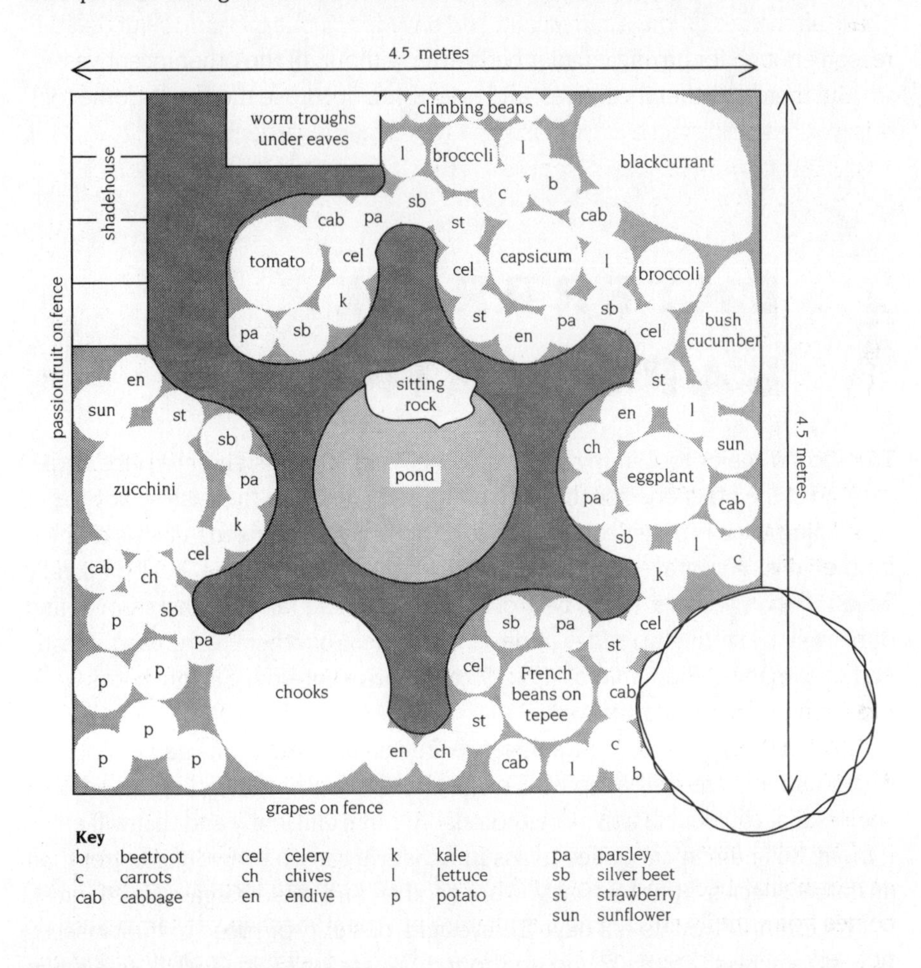

Figure 8 Design for Valerie's garden.

2 ENTERPRISE BARGAINING

The second major tool in my kit, after pencil and paper, is an enterprise agreement with the other species that inhabit my garden. Often the easiest way to get something done is to get someone else to do it! If the 'someone else' is doing it for their own advantage, that's even better. If the 'someone else' is also actually *better at it* than you are, that's best of all. I get a whole range of tasks done, and done well, by setting up win–win deals with a host of other creatures, domestic and wild, many of them microscopic. A cooperative enterprise is much less work, more fun and more productive.

Jobs that call for creative intelligence are just about the only garden jobs for which humans are well adapted. For almost every other task there is another species that can do it faster, more thoroughly, more efficiently and that will enjoy it more. It is human arrogance to assume that we can do everything better than any other species. Stick to what you are good at, and strike bargains for the rest.

For example, you do not have the eyesight, dexterity or speed to hunt insects. Why chase grasshoppers round and round the garden? Even with a spray-gun, humans make hard work of it. Call in a frog. He's an expert at the job, and his rates are very, very cheap: a pond full of waterweed with a trellis over it to deter frog-hunting birds. A deal in which you provide the pond, shelter from predators and a garden full of prey, and frogs provide a significant part of your insect control, is a win–win deal.

Why dig? For a start your backbone is not at all well adapted for it, and you have a brain that gets bored with digging so quickly that it is a positive handicap! Call in a team of earthworms. They will shift tonnes of earth, and work for a few barrowloads of mulch. Not only that, but they will do it much more thoroughly, delicately and non-destructively than you ever could.

Enterprise bargaining is the most efficient way to get a whole range of tasks done, from soil production and fertilising to pest control. However, it only works if you realise that your co-workers are unionised to an extent that makes waterside workers look like softies. The garden workers I am talking about have a 'one out, all out' agreement that is almost rock solid. You cannot do this bargaining by halves.

MAKING SOIL

Soil is the beginning point in any garden, and technology cannot create soil any more than it can create life. Soil is made *biologically*, by plants and animals. Deep-rooted plants find fractures in the subsoil, mine them for mineral elements, and fracture them a little bit more for the next generation. They cycle these minerals into the topsoil, where the other elements needed by plants and animals to make the chemical compounds we call soil are more available.

Soil life, particularly microlife, creates acids that dissolve mineral ions out of rock particles. Plants and animals also take gaseous elements out of the air, and soluble elements out of water, and use them to make chemical compounds in the form of solids. These solids accumulate in uncultivated soil at an average rate of around 2 *to* 4 *tonnes per hectare* per year. Provided it is not being lost at a rate faster than it is being made, the soil level increases.

Any method of farming or gardening (including organic methods) that does not include some deep-rooted plants and as much soil life as will fit is neglecting the process of soil production. *There is no technological substitute*. You may get good crop yields for a while simply by using up this 2 to 4 tonnes per hectare per year that has been made by natural processes. But sooner or later the store will run out, and without established populations of soil-producing plants and animals, it will take a very long time to accumulate again.

SOIL CONSERVATION

Unless the mineral elements are locked up fairly tightly in stable molecules, rain or watering will dissolve them and leach them away, and exposure to air will oxidise them and turn them back into gases. Even if they *are* locked up, cultivation or burning will allow them to escape, and of course exporting out produce is exporting out elements.

The best form of soil preservation is to employ plants, animals and micro-organisms to convert the elements they 'capture' from the air or mine from rock, and the ones you provide in the form of imported organic matter, to large, stable, insoluble molecules. These kinds of molecules are called *humus*. Big molecules, particularly the giant molecules of humus, are extremely stable.

The average age of the molecules of humus in soil is over 1000 years.

Humus itself is so stable that it has very little to do with feeding plants (although it has a lot to do with soil structure). Its main function in plant nutrition is that these enormous molecules have a very large surface area with lots of negative-ion exchange sites. This means that they can attract and 'capture' positively charged ions – ammonium (containing nitrogen), potassium, calcium, magnesium, iron, copper, zinc and manganese – just like magnets do. They can then store the ions, preventing them from escaping into the air or waterways. Although bacteria have a hard job breaking up the core of a molecule of humus, they can separate off these charged particles, thereby making them available to plants. Organic matter also captures metal ions by 'chelation' – a chemical process in which the organic molecule wraps itself around the metal ion, preventing it from oxidising.

Soil organic matter, besides preserving soil chemically by converting it into big stable molecules, also preserves it physically by 'gluing' particles together to form aggregates, or crumbs. Earthworms, fungi and microbes are all extremely important in producing slimy, sticky glues that hold soil particles together to resist wind or water erosion, and hold them apart to allow water and air penetration.

FEEDING SOIL TO PLANTS

Plants can only absorb fairly simple molecules. But simple molecules do not just hang around in the soil. By their very nature they are unstable, very easily either dissolved in water and washed away, converted into gases and lost into the air, or latched onto by bigger molecules.

There are two basic ways of making a constant stream of nutrients in the form of simple molecules available to feed plants. You can pour them on as soluble salts – which is what artificial fertilisers and a good many organic fertilisers are. But this method has a few inherent problems, besides the obvious one of cost!

These artificial fertilisers are a bit like fairy floss. They contain the major plant nutrients, but almost no trace elements – the plant equivalent of vitamins. Your plants will not exactly starve on them, but neither will they be getting a balanced diet. They will have very little natural resistance to pests and diseases, and produce food with a much lower nutrient value.

Because these salts are dissolved in water, plants have no choice about absorbing them. They cannot simply stop taking them up when they have had enough. Plants need water to replace that lost by transpiration through their leaves, and the only water around is salty. The result is a bit like a person drinking salty water to assuage thirst: it just makes them more thirsty. The plants develop too high a concentration of salts in their tissues, with no way of getting enough pure water to dilute them.

Humans do not have the dexterity to apply these soluble salts delicately to just the root zone of crop plants. Because these molecules are unstable, very little is stored in any form that plants can continue to use. So you need to apply a lot, and to reapply it often. It is a bit like trying to fill up a drinking straw by pouring water into it from a bucket, without a funnel. A large proportion is wasted: lost to water to end up in our rivers, lakes and oceans, where it causes major ecological problems, or to air where it becomes a significant contributor to the greenhouse effect. Moreover, in these kinds of concentrations, the salts kill off a lot of the micro-organisms that are building and storing soil for you.

The alternative method is to rely on your store of big, complex, stable molecules and breed a population of soil microlife to 'digest' these and feed a stream of major nutrients *and* trace elements to your plants. These micro-organisms perform much the same kind of function that gut or rumen bacteria do in animals. They pre-digest food, converting it to the simple molecules plants can absorb.

One of the most important of these kinds of micro-organisms is a family of fungi called *mycorrhizae*. Almost all plants, wild and cultivated, are known to have associations with their own 'special friends' in this family. Green-leaved plants do the photosynthesis for the partnership, providing the sugars. The mycorrhizae do both the underground foraging and the underground defence. They feed minerals and nutrients to plant roots in soluble form, and they provide a protective sheath on the roots and a supply of antibiotics.

This latter method of feeding plants is much more economical in the long run. It is the difference between taking on the job of supplying plant nutrients yourself, *and* the job of cleaning up after your ineptitude, or getting something much more competent to do it for you!

SOIL AERATION

Plants need not only mineral nutrients but also gaseous ones. Some they absorb from the air through their leaves. But land plants also need root exposure to air. Soil aeration is vitally important.

Humans can aerate soil by cultivation. However, being very large animals they can only do it in a very gross way. Cultivation 'unglues' soil particles, destroying the crumb structure of soil. Since the crumb structure is exactly what allows air to penetrate soil, this is a bit like one temporary step forward and two steps back. Unglued particles settle down into a much tighter formation, creating a hardpan that excludes air (and water) penetration. They are also much more vulnerable to erosion by wind and water.

Each cultivation brings to the surface a new set of ancient humus molecules, where they are oxidised and lost to the air – a bit like rusting. These valuable nutrient storage sites are lost. Soil life, adapted to underground existence, is exposed and killed, slowing down and eventually stopping the processes of soil production and digestion.

Other organisms, particularly earthworms, can aerate soil much more efficiently and much less destructively. Without inverting the soil, they create myriad channels and steadily improve the crumb structure. Air can get down without at the same time bringing humus and soil life up. The worms will do the job all day and night; they don't require the crops to be cleared off first; they need no petrol, oil or parts; there are no trips to the chiropractor; and, best of all, your task is reduced to having another cup of tea while they get on with it.

PEST CONTROL

A single microbat will gobble up 600 insects an hour, all night while you are asleep. One session with a spray-gun full of poison – organic or chemical – will deprive her of food and send her on her way. A ladybird will happily search out and munch on aphids while you are having breakfast in bed. Any method you try to get rid of aphids is more than likely to kill her too. A wren will snatch cabbage moths out of the air, giving you an incredible acrobatic display at the same time. There are any number of species that are awe-inspiring in their hunting skills.

In conventional agriculture, 'pest control' is a euphemism for pest extermination. Attempting to exterminate any creature for which there is a niche is a foredoomed fight against one of the most powerful natural forces there is – the impulse of life to occupy every unfilled niche. It is much smarter, and safer, to work *with* natural forces by enhancing them, filling every available niche to capacity with wild or domestic creatures, so that the 'pests' face stiff competition.

In *any* natural system there is no such thing as a pest. Populations of various species are balanced quite automatically. A plenitude of any creature is a feast for some or several predatory creatures. The word 'pest' just means a lack of breeding stock in the species that predate that creature, probably caused by earlier unsuccessful attempts to exterminate the prey.

No ecologically successful species will completely decimate its food source. Any that did so became extinct for lack of food many millions of years ago! So long as every available garden niche is filled, and you do not interfere with the process by fruitless attempts to empty them, the 'pests' will always leave plenty of food for you, and the predators will always leave plenty of pests, enough to ensure a continuing source of food. Any enterprise bargain with pest predators has to include the deal that they will keep your pest populations under control (*not* exterminate them), so long as you do not threaten them or their food source.

Take it. It's a good deal.

ENTER PRIZE GARDENING

My moveable chook pens, or chook tractors, are my favourite example of an elegant and economic win–win deal. What is work for humans – weeding, bug-catching, fertilising and digging – is play for chooks. And conversely, some of the jobs chooks find impossible to do for themselves – provide protection from predators and rain – are quite possible for humans.

Let me give you a picture. Sugar Cane the rooster and his eleven-strong harem have just been moved to a new bed. In the centre the pigeon peas are just starting to drop seed. The ground is littered with fallen mulberries from the bordering tree. Only the outside leaves of the harvested cauliflowers and cabbages remain, but they are starting to resprout and are infested with slugs, snails and cabbage-moth caterpillars. There is a row of spent dwarf-pea plants, with a few remaining late peas and aphids. Around the edge are some old silver beet and parsley, and a few broccoli going to seed. Throughout the lot are fat hen, chickweed, radishes, Chinese cabbage, amaranth, mustard and cress, sprouted from seed scattered just before everything else started to reach maturity.

There is a complete balanced diet for chooks in there – greens, grains, legumes, fruit, insects and worms – all for no cost in money and almost no extra effort to produce. Most of it is what would normally be considered waste, weeds or pests. The chooks can feed it to themselves, in the process getting some exercise and avoiding becoming bored and neurotic, while tilling and weeding the garden for me at no charge!

They start by scratching up and turning over all the mulch looking for worms as an entree. Every few days I will throw them an armload of mulch, a bucket of house scraps, and any odd slugs, caterpillars, weeds, spoiled fruit or spent veggies I happen to collect in my rounds, and at the same time I collect their eggs. Instead of being cross when I come across a snail or a grub or a dense patch of chickweed, I can look forward to the chooks' appreciation of these delicacies, which are instantly redefined from pest to resource.

Lawn clippings and tree prunings also go in. Each trip to town to do shopping yields several boxes of spoiled fruit and vegetables from the greengrocer, old bread and crumbs from the baker, and scraps from the fishmonger. The shopkeepers are glad to get rid of them, and the chooks demolish them before they have a chance to get smelly. What little they don't eat they bury in the process of scratching through the grass clippings.

If we have been to the beach recently, I might add a few handfuls of shellgrit and some cuttlefish. If we haven't, I might decide that a trip to the beach to collect these is an essential part of my work schedule for the week! I dump in the ash from the wood stove and the barbecue. The chooks enjoy dust-bathing in it, and spread and scratch it into the whole area, adding potash to the soil. And they leave their manure, which is both a fertiliser and a gentle way to adjust soil pH.

All of these activities cost me very little extra energy. Collecting cuttlefish at the beach and waste from the shopping centre are the kind of tasks that chooks cannot do at all easily for themselves, but that I can do so easily that they hardly count as work. The ash has to be emptied somewhere, and it might as well be in the chook pen. The mulberries dropped on their own, and I would otherwise have had to pick them up to prevent fruit flies breeding in them. The cabbage and cauliflower leaves are a by-product, and cost me no extra effort at all to produce, and infesting them with grubs was even easier!

After a fortnight, the chooks will have completely cleared the vegetable bed area, and radically pruned the pigeon-pea plants. The ground will be covered with several cm of well-scratched, seed-free, manured mulch, mixed with ash, shellgrit, citrus skins and other household scraps that the chooks don't eat. It is time to move the chooks on to the next bed, under the early peach tree, after first picking and throwing down any fruit-fly-infested fruit. Just the proximity of the chooks will help deter the fruit fly, and the cycle can begin again.

The bed just vacated needs no extra work to be ready for replanting. The worm population is strong enough, and the worms smart enough, that the chooks will have made no perceptible difference to the number of them. The warm, moist, mulched, manured environment with lots of organic matter is just what they like. Within a day, if I pick up the mulch I will find thousands of worms, busy finishing off the job of tilling, fertilising and aerating the soil. The natural predators of any bugs will have had every chance to breed up and eat their fill before the chooks finished off their prey. Since they are faster and more mobile, they will have moved on to search for bugs elsewhere in the garden.

I have a weed, seed and bug-free bed, tilled, fertilised, mulched, pH-adjusted and ready for planting, and a couple of dozen beautiful golden-yolked eggs, all for very little effort on my part. My chook tractors take all of ten minutes to move – certainly a lot easier than digging, weeding, spreading fertiliser and spraying.

A*nd* the chooks reckon they got the better end of the deal!

WITHOUT CHOOKS

In the farming district where I live, killing or even harassing 'stock' is a capital offence for dogs, and chooks are included in the definition of 'stock'. However, in city areas it is harder to protect animals from the local dog population. I remember when we were kids in suburban Brisbane and kept guinea pigs for pets. My father's guinea pig cage designs evolved into replicas of Fort Knox, but still the marauding neighbourhood dogs managed to massacre them every few months.

I'm not sure that it is *possible* to build a moveable or even permanently sited chook run that is secure against the Rottweilers and bull-terriers that are becoming popular breeds in our protection-conscious cities. If your local council does not police its dog laws, you may have to do your enterprise bargaining with less vulnerable species than chooks.

Even then, your local council may not be on your side. In some areas it is illegal to keep chooks. It cannot be out of concern over cruelty; after all, it is legal to keep them in tiny battery cages, with half their beaks cut off and subjected to sleep deprivation. It is also hard to believe that it is out of concern over noise when it is legal to build airport runways that keep half a city awake. It does not seem logical for health and environment reasons to prefer to dispose of food scraps in giant landfills that will remain noxious for generations. All in all, it is hard to think of any reason at all, but your local council may have blackballed chook union labour.

In these (and no doubt other) circumstances you will have to think of other creatures to do deals with. Chooks are such wonderfully skilled garden labourers that your wages bill is likely to be higher, but with good designing the enterprise can still be highly profitable.

CLEARING

After chooks, my second choice for clearing new ground of grass and weeds is the thermophilic bacteria of a well-built compost pile. These bacteria are my first choice even in some areas of a chook dome garden. They can create enough heat to kill grass and weeds (roots, seeds, bulbs and all), but without oxidising them to lose nutrients to the air. They are a slightly more expensive labour force than chooks for clearing work, in that you get less area cleared for an equivalent amount of effort on your part, but they have the advantage of multiple uses. Without chooks you will be relying extra-heavily on compost for initial fertiliser and for bedding your worms, so you might as well be clearing your garden beds while you are making the compost.

To clear Stephanie's 36 m^2 of shaly rock, concrete rubble, couch grass and other weeds required nine compost piles – a pile each Saturday for two months. As soon as each pile was turned, the square metre it vacated was mulched and planted. Each pile was turned three times, and so cleared 4 m^2. By the time Stephanie built a new pile and turned, mulched and planted out all the older ones, most of her Saturday was gone. But this heavy investment in time and labour to set up the enterprise was repaid in ownership of a very low-maintenance garden (see Figure 9 on page 29).

About half of the compost was returned to the beds as she went along, some in potting mix and some just around each new seedling as it was planted out. The other half went into establishment of a 4 m^2 worm farm.

FERTILISING AND SOIL BUILDING

My second choice for processing organic matter into soil is red manure worms. They would probably have been my first choice if I had ever been able to design a moveable worm farm. Their only handicaps compared to chooks is that their food must all be brought to them – they cannot easily be moved around the garden to deal with it in situ – and the product in the form of castings must be carried out to the garden. Of course, earthworms free-range in abundance in the garden too. But they are not concentrated enough in any one spot to make short work of a bucket of rotting vegetables – not before it has had time to become noxious and start inviting protests from the neighbours.

Worms eat about their own body weight per day and, in the right conditions, each one will breed twenty new worms every month. Stephanie's worm farm started with 1000 red manure worms in a big pile of compost – about a kilo of worms to munch their way through her kilo of household scraps every day. Within a month they had multiplied to a level where her next-door neighbour was invited to throw his garbage over the fence every day too. Within another month two more neighbours were recruited. Within six months she needed the local fruit shop and preschool to keep up the supply, and the worms were producing as much fertiliser as she could use.

She has never bothered with compost again. All her garden wastes, weeds, herbs, shellgrit and seaweed are processed through her worm farm. The kind of wastes that are available in real abundance in the inner city are much more suitable for feeding worms than for feeding compost bacteria.

MULCH CLEANING

Without chooks, my choice for processing mulch to remove seeds and bugs are wild and feral birds – wrens, sparrows, starlings, finches, mynas, robins, fantails, thrushes and tomtits. The main terms of an enterprise bargain with these species is water available for drinking and bathing, perches, and security from predators, particularly cats. Flowers for nectar (many birds are also nectar-eaters) and shrubs and trees for cover and nesting are extra incentives.

Stephanie has an old concrete slab under a large tree, where the local garden service dumps a trailerload of lawn clippings and mulched tree and shrub prunings every week. It has its own birdbath, and the concrete block wall beside it has rolled wire on top to deter the neighbourhood cats. Stephanie spreads the pile out, scatters a handful of breadcrumbs and some worms over it, and lets the local birds do the rest.

THE BARGAIN

'Feed the worms and pick the dinner' is Stephanie's afternoon gardening routine. 'Propagate seeds and plant out seedlings' is her Saturday gardening routine. Each seedling gets a good double handful of worms and worm castings and half a bucket of mulch. That 36 m^2 totally feeds Stephanie's small but wholly vegetarian family, and has gained her a reputation for the best dinner parties in Sydney!

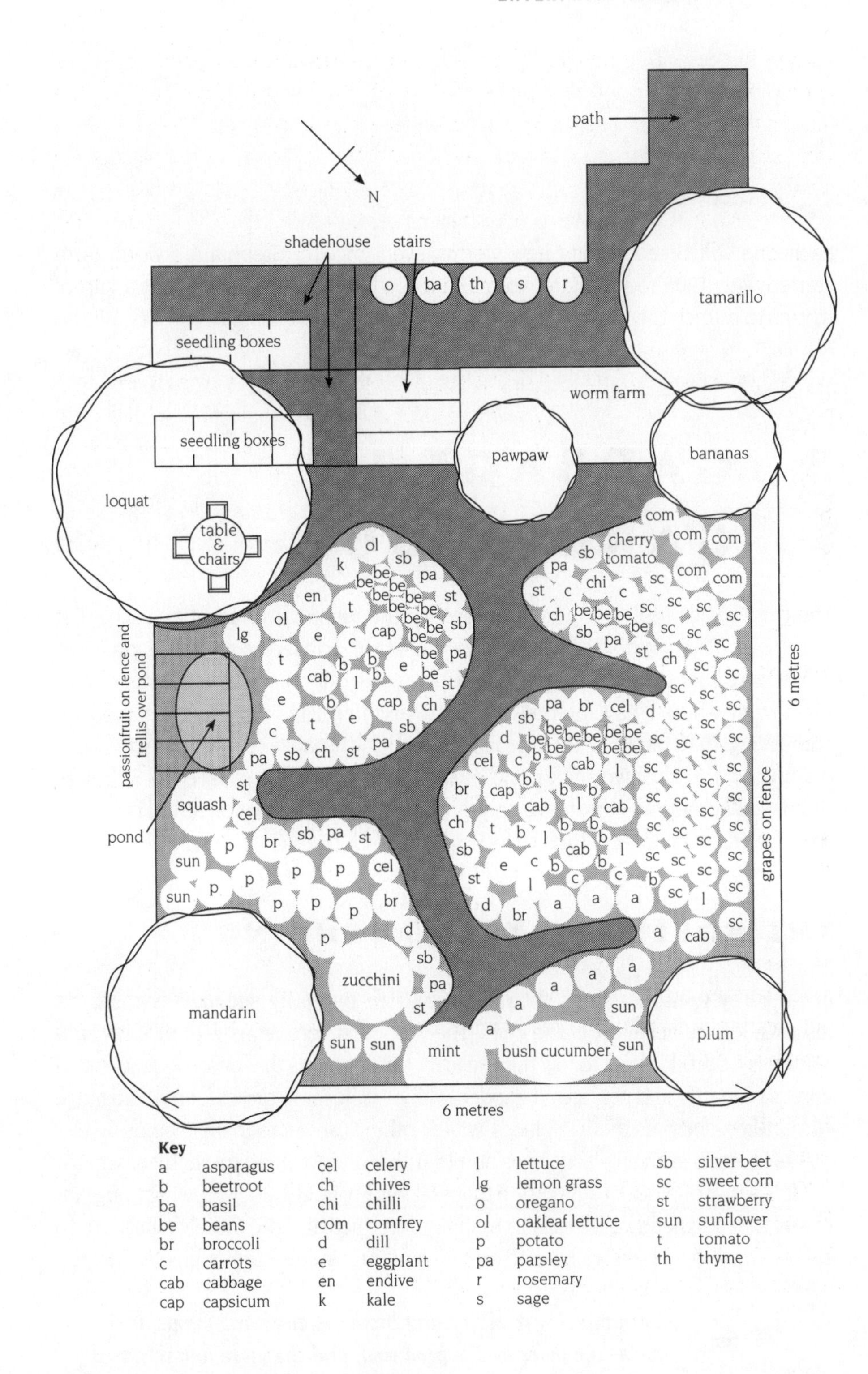

Figure 9 Design for Stephanie's garden.

3 GARBAGE IN GARDEN OUT

The third major tool in my kit is an eye for the resource value of *everything* that once lived. Organic matter helps prevent erosion, conserves moisture, provides a buffer against extremes of temperature, and is one of the main forms of currency with which I pay my co-workers. Everything that once lived is food for something that inhabits the garden – either the chooks, the compost micro-organisms, the earthworms or one of the thousands of other species. Through them, and sometimes through a sequence of them, it can be converted back into food for crop plants, and thus to food for me.

THE NOBLE ART OF SCAVENGING

In natural systems there is no such thing as waste. *Everything* is food. Everything is a resource for the next part of the cycle. The root of the problems with modern agriculture is that it does not follow this cyclic model. It forgets that dead bodies, rotting vegetable matter and poo are all good, healthy, wholesome tucker for a whole range of creatures, and puts them in places where nothing can get to them. It binds up elements in forms such as plastic bags and DDT that are not good tucker for anything.

It is a rule of modern agriculture that soil fertility is *depleted* by growing things on it, and that soil needs additions to maintain productivity. The more we take out to eat, the more fertilisers we have to add. In a natural system the opposite is true.

In a natural system, fertility increases the more plants are grown, the more food is produced, and the more animals are supported on a given patch of soil.

There is no such thing as soil that has been exhausted by growing too much or by supporting too many animals, even though no bags of chemical or even organic fertiliser are added to the system. There is absolutely no reason why humans cannot be animals supported by a system with steadily increasing fertility – without any additions at all. The key is understanding that there is *no such thing as waste* – or at least there shouldn't be any such thing. Nothing should ever be produced that is not a resource for the next link in the chain. Remember the law of conservation of matter. There are a finite number of atoms of nitrogen, phosphorus, potassium and so on. But there is no limit to the number of times these same atoms can be used. The faster we can get them cycling, the more times we can have a turn at using them – in asparagus mornay one time and apple pie the next!

Fertility is not a function of the number of nutrient elements. That number is finite. Fertility is a function of the distribution of these elements, and the amount of time they spend locked up in inaccessible forms. The faster elements cycle through a system, the more fertile it is. The key to depletion of fertility is the shunting-off of elements into pockets where they cannot be got at and where they cycle very slowly or not at all.

Scavenging is the art of looking for things that should be cycling but have been displaced, shunted off into a pocket somewhere. Cities and towns are notoriously full of these kinds of things. Scavenging is relocating resources to where they belong – where they are not waste, but food. The catch-22 is that relocating things usually involves using petrol to transport them, and burning petrol puts a whole lot of carbon dioxide into one of those pockets where it just sits because there aren't enough trees left to cycle it. The truly artistic scavenger will manage to do most if not all relocating *without going out of his or her way* to do it. Going out of your way is, in any case, too time-consuming to be worth it.

A purely decorative garden requires a great deal less relocation of resources than a food-producing one. Since very little is normally removed from it, the cycle of elements is much more nearly closed. A harvestable garden, however, routinely loses large quantities of material, usually from the fruits, seeds or growing tips where nutrients are most concentrated. This kind of garden is part of the much larger cycle that *you* inhabit, and needs you to relocate a lot more material from the *other* parts of the cycle you inhabit.

In my garden I use the chooks as first-stage sorters. Almost everything I bring in I just throw to them to pick over, mix and spread. Each chook pen receives about a trailerload of mulch in some form during the fortnight it sits on a bed, usually at the rate of a sugarbagful a day. Some of this I later rake into a pile and layer with other ingredients to make compost. Most is sheet-composted where it lies, the top 15 cm or so functioning as a mulch layer and the lower 15 cm as food for earthworms and micro-organisms.

With or without chooks, you will be looking for a similar quantity of material: about half a cubic metre per week for every 10 m^2 of garden. This may initially seem like an enormous quantity, but all of these materials are waste. They are available somewhere in just about unlimited quantities, and someone is currently spending effort to get rid of them. Collection may be as simple as letting that 'someone' know that your place is available as a disposal site.

One of the most useful tools of all is a big bag that goes everywhere with you – on wheels like those trolleys our grandmothers used if you travel mostly by foot or public transport, or in the boot if you travel mostly by car. Just carrying it will help you cultivate the habit of noticing anything that might be worth relocating. If you design your system, and the species you do your enterprise bargaining with, around the wastes most easily available, and make collection and relocation part of your normal daily routine, it can be a painless task.

Collection of organic matter is the second-largest item on the job description for the humans involved in a garden enterprise, second only to design. If you do enough of these two, you need do literally very, very little else. Since scavenging is such a major task, it is worth being very clever in designing ways to perform it very efficiently.

MULCH SOURCES

It usually takes me about an hour to collect a full trailerload of mulch. If it takes you much longer than this, you should audit your collection system and find handier or more concentrated sources. I have a large garden, with four chook tractors, so mulch collection occupies several hours of my week. Even so, it is highly economical in return for energy. I have seven main sources.

THE HOUSE

I keep a chook bucket with a lid in the kitchen and just about everything of natural origin goes into it, regardless of whether the chooks actually like to eat it or not. Tea bags, coffee grounds, dead insects, citrus skins, hair, fallen leaves, meat scraps and bones, cooking oil, dripping, egg shells (crushed in the hand first so that the chooks don't confuse them with whole eggs) and so on. I let sour milk sit on the window ledge in the sun for a day first so that it turns into curds, which the chooks love. I exclude paper and cloth because I worry about the chemical treatments and dye that might be in them.

This bucket is emptied straight onto the ground in a chook pen every day when I do my garden rounds. What the chooks don't eat they bury in the process of scratching in the mulch, and it becomes food for earthworms and micro-organisms. This process saves all the bother of worrying about what should go in or out of the compost, and of making compost with small quantities of household waste. If you have neighbours without gardens you could volunteer to dispose of their household waste too.

If you use worms rather than chooks as your primary domestic workers, you will simply have a worm bucket instead of a chook bucket. One friend has a spare blender jug with a lid that lives on her kitchen bench. Any household waste of organic origin goes into it. When it is full she simply pours in a cup of water, hits the blend button, and tips it into her worm farm at the back door.

THE SHOPPING CENTRE

Shops and restaurants throw out an enormous amount of compostable material. For some, disposing of it is a major headache. The local organic greengrocer jumped at the deal in which I supplied a couple of large plastic bins, and collected them full of unsaleable fruit and vegetables every week. Bakeries, butchers, fishmongers and restaurants are all likely sources. You may even be able to get your local school to keep a separate bin for half-eaten sandwiches, apple cores and banana skins. Chooks, compost microbes and worms are all good processors for this kind of material.

WATERWEEDS

One of my laziest sources, and the most fun (in summer at least), is collection of waterweeds from creeks, dams and ponds. This requires no mechanical energy, and is a good excuse for a dip in the hottest part of the day. My favourite weed is azolla, a tiny reddish floweret that grows prolifically in any still or slow-moving water, but I also harvest watercress, water hyacinth and anything else I find growing rampantly.

I discovered azolla by accident. As part of my habit of adding a bit of all sorts of things to compost, I made one compost pile with several buckets of this then unidentified weed – largely to get it out of my favourite swimming hole! The pile was steaming hot within hours, and ready to use in less than a fortnight, which made me suspect that the mystery plant was very nitrogen-rich. Then I saw a picture of it (in a pamphlet about problem waterweeds) which gave me a name. And then I discovered, in a novel, that azolla is used as a rice paddy fertiliser because it (like legumes) is symbiotic with nitrogen-fixing bacteria.

I am now cultivating azolla in my dam as a source of rich, easily accessible mulch and fertiliser. I suspect that, hectare for hectare, it will turn out to have a higher yield in available nitrogen, and in bulk, than any land plant.

Water plants are noxious weeds in many watercourses. They often go rampant because they are overfertilised with water-soluble nutrient salts in the run-off from other people's gardens and farms. So by harvesting it, you are getting the benefit of other people's expenditure on fertilisers, converted into a form that is actually much more valuable than the form for which they paid real money. It is like picking up wet twenty-dollar notes! At the same time, you are helping to get these aquatic systems back into an ecological balance before the plants deprive everything else of oxygen.

I throw waterweeds to my chooks, but they also make excellent compost ingredients and worm food.

THE BEACH

This is work and pleasure combined in a big way. Every few months I include a weekend camping at the beach in my work schedule. Of course the swimming, beachcombing, walking, reading and sitting around a campfire are just the price I have to pay! Seaweed is an extremely rich source of a range of micronutrients that are very hard to get from land plants, or even from freshwater weeds. The beach is also a good source of readily available calcium, in the form of shellgrit and cuttlefish. The shellgrit and cuttlefish can simply be thrown to the chooks, although I prefer to ration it by adding a couple of handfuls to their bucket every day. Worms also appreciate extra calcium, so you can process the shellgrit and cuttlefish through your worm farm. The seaweed I regard as too valuable to use this way. I make a fermented liquid fertiliser from it, which I use in compost and as a medicinal tonic for struggling plants. Chapter 7, 'Compost', includes the recipe for this.

CHAFFCUTTER

My fifth major source of mulch is trimmings from anything that needs trimming, put through an old-fashioned hand-operated chaffcutter: bladey grass, lantana, fruit tree prunings, wattle, stinging nettles . . . I found the chaffcutter at an auction many years ago, and it is a wonderfully efficient tool, cutting everything up into inch-long pieces with no undue exertion. It has already lasted almost forever, and seems likely to last forevermore. It uses no fossil fuel, and it creates no pollution and no noise.

Unfortunately chaffcutters are a bit difficult to come up with these days, and I find mechanical mulchers expensive to maintain and unpleasant to use. However, if you have access to plenty of this kind of material, it may be worth making a mechanical mulcher your one piece of machinery.

If you are using chooks, this material can simply be thrown into their pen by the armload. If you are not using chooks, it is best processed through a compost pile or used as surface mulch.

HERBS

My sixth major mulch source is herbs and other plants I grow partly for their value as mulch, mostly around the edge of the garden. Lemon grass, sugarcane leaf, comfrey, yarrow and horsetail are the major plants providing bulk mulch and lots of carbon, but I cultivate and harvest a large range of other herbs to provide other nutrients.

One of the main benefits of cultivating herbs is their value as micronutrient accumulators. These are elements that are essential for proper plant nutrition, but that are only needed in minute amounts – a bit like the role of vitamins in human nutrition. Some herbs accumulate very large amounts of micronutrients, even in soil that is quite deficient. Using these herbs in mulch and compost spreads the micronutrients around the garden, making them available to vegetables that may not be quite so proficient at mining them for themselves.

Below are some of the main herbs I cultivate for mulch and the nutrients they accumulate. Adding a bit of all of them prevents deficiency diseases ever showing up. If a deficiency does show up, however, these herbs provide a much gentler, safer, cheaper and easier way of correcting it than adding soluble fertilisers.

HERB	MICRONUTRIENTS ACCUMULATED
borage	silica, phosphorus
chamomile	calcium, potassium, phosphorus
comfrey	silica, nitrogen, magnesium, calcium, potassium, iron
fennel	sodium, sulphur, potassium
horsetail	silica, magnesium, calcium, iron, cobalt
nasturtiums	sodium, fluorine, sulphur, magnesium, calcium, potassium, phosphorus, iron
nettles	sodium, sulphur, nitrogen, calcium, potassium, iron, copper
primrose	magnesium
spurges	boron
vetches	nitrogen, potassium, phosphorus, copper, cobalt
yarrow	nitrogen, potassium, phosphorus, copper

All these herbs are so hardy that they grow semi-wild and can hold their own against competition. Planted around the edge of the garden they prevent grass and weed invasion and need almost no attention. I plant the more moisture-tolerant ones – comfrey, nettles and nasturtiums – along the bottom edge of the garden to trap any nutrients leached down before they escape down the drain.

Most of these plants can simply be clipped and added to the chook bucket. The chooks will select which to eat and which to let lie as mulch. Some are medicinal or very rich in particular vitamins, and the chooks can dose themselves as necessary. The spurges, however, are quite strongly caustic, so I reserve them to use in compost, and handle them carefully. Comfrey is also better reserved for compost: it contains an alkaloid called pyrrolizidine which could be unhealthy for the chooks to eat in too large a quantity, and it is so prolific that large quantities is what we are talking about! It is also such a good compost activator that it seems a pity to use it for anything else.

Alternatively, any or all of the herbs can be added to the perennial seaweed brew (see Chapter 7, 'Compost') to make a very micronutrient-rich tea that is good for wetting down compost piles or as a tonic for specific plants.

MOWING

My last source of mulch is a five-horsepower self-propelled mower with catcher and about a quarter of an acre of community playing field with a fair variety of meadow weeds and clover in the grass. This last source is the most energy-intensive, and involves use of a petrol-driven machine, but the kids (and adults) like to play cricket and volleyball, and the wallabies love the mown area, so at least it has multiple purposes.

If you are working a large, commercial-sized garden and relying on mowing for most of your mulch, then this size mower is probably not big enough. It will take too much time and work the mower too hard. At the other end of the scale, if you are growing only your own fresh food and have alternative sources of mulch, you may be able to skip mowing altogether.

Another potential source is opportunistic use of other people's work and already burned petrol in roadside slashing, park mowing, electricity line clearing and lawn mowing. In urban areas, your local lawn-mowing service may well be delighted to keep you supplied with clippings and save themselves a trip to the dump at the same time. It is well to keep in mind though that many of these sources may have been exposed to chemical toxins, and you should weigh the benefits of no extra petrol and little extra work against the risk of killing off your non-human partners in the garden.

NON-MULCH SOURCES

There are three major categories of organic material besides seaweed, comfrey and spurge that are not suitable for mulch and sheet composting because they are either too valuable, too smelly or too greedy.

ANIMAL MANURE

I reserve sheep, cow, horse and pigeon manure to layer with chook-processed mulch to make compost. Although you can make good compost using only plant ingredients, the micro-organisms that do the making seem to relish animal manure. Animal manure adds enzymes and gut and rumen bacteria that are not available from plant materials. It is a rich source of nitrogen and potassium, and makes the composting process much more reliable.

A good, concentrated, easily collected source of chemically clean animal manure, somewhere not too far off your normal routes, is worth hunting down. Any herbivorous animal will do, although I like to vary it as much as possible.

I also use dried cow pats to make propagating mixture. Sieved compost can be substituted, but cow pats are definitely preferable, and unfortunately no other animal manure is really suitable.

GRAVE ROBBING

Though it may seem a little gruesome, roadkills decompose in a compost pile very quickly and with no smell, and are a valuable source of free blood and bone. While it is illegal to pick up native animals that have been skittled, in rural areas roadkills are so prolific that just the feral animals, such as rabbits, will probably be more than enough for any garden. I travel to town with a coal shovel and a bag in the boot.

SAWDUST

Because of its high cellulose content, sawdust takes a very long time to break down in a compost pile or in mulch. Its carbon to nitrogen ratio is so high that it must be combined with a relatively large quantity of very nitrogen-rich material to be palatable to compost micro-organisms. If you add it to compost or mulch, the organisms will try very hard to digest it, but they will scavenge every scrap of available nitrogen from the area to do so. This will starve your crop plants of nitrogen until the process is complete.

Yet sawdust is an organic material, and our local sawmill 'wastes' such enormous quantities of it that I felt duty bound to find an economical way to convert it. My initial strategy was to soak it with urine (which is a good way to recycle human urine), then use it to build a special compost pile that was allowed to sit for a year or so before being used. This is still an effective way of dealing with sawdust (and urine), so that their nutrients can be brought into the cycle.

But there is a much more energy-efficient way. Sawdust makes good path material. It makes good drain filler. And if it is kept wet by being used as a path and drain, earthworms love it. It still takes six months to a year to break down to an extent where it can safely be added to mulch or compost, but in the meantime it is working, not just sitting.

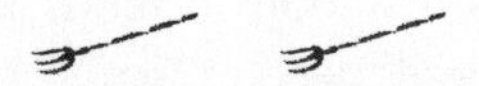

There are a number of other non-food things that are likely to be available free for the looking, and relocating them will at least mean reuse, if not recycling. Polystyrene boxes and river sand are useful for propagating. Two-litre plastic milk containers are good for seedlings. A tractor tyre and a sheet of vinyl or old swimming pool liner are handy for a pond. Old lawn-mower grass-catchers make excellent laying boxes, and you can never have too much baling twine.

Scavenging is also a very good way of obtaining propagating material, particularly for herbs and perennials. Whenever I go visiting I take with me not only my bag but also a box of potting mix and a pair of secateurs. Most people are happy for you to take cuttings, and this allows visiting to be part of your work schedule too! Combining work and pleasure is not just for big-business executives.

4 EXECUTIVE MANAGEMENT

LUNATIC GARDENING

The fourth major tool in the kit is a lunar planting calendar. This is a calendar that sets out planting days and times according to the phase of the moon and its relationship to constellations. Now I am an extreme sceptic. I first tried lunar planting for reasons that had nothing to do with plant health or vitality. But I am now convinced that, in some way that science does not yet fully understand, it works! In brief:

- The first week of the waxing moon, as it goes from dark to half-full, includes the times for planting crops from which the leaf is the most important yield.
- The week before the full moon includes the times for planting fruiting crops.
- The week following the full moon includes the times for root crops and perennials.
- The last week before the dark of the moon is the best time for weeding.

For each kind of crop there is a period of between one and four days each lunar month that is best for planting. These are the days when the moon is in a 'fertile' astrological sign.

The lunar planting calendar has three functions. In order of importance for my purposes:

1. It is a time-management tool; an externally imposed schedule that reduces the complete anarchic time flexibility to a manageable level.
2. It is an organisational tool. It allows a bewildering list of jobs with comparable priority to be reduced to short daily lists that you can tick off. Nothing is neglected.
3. It actually *does* increase the germination rate and vitality of plants.

Time management is still the biggest challenge I have in being a successful commercial organic grower. Though not quite as vital for non-commercial gardeners, time management is at least as important as a site plan in making the whole enterprise pleasurable. It is a deceptively simple problem – one you would have trouble believing is as intractable as it is.

When you work as an employee, there are always some very, very highly paid people organising your time for you: deciding what your tasks are, how long they should take, what is the cheapest way to do them, what your hours of work should be and how much flexibility can be allowed. They are executives, and they are rare enough to be paid very highly. When you work for yourself, you have to be your own executive. This task in itself takes time, and you have to budget your time to allow for it.

If you are self-employed running a shop or service business, the expectations of your customers and clients, to a large extent, organise your time. The shop has to be open certain hours, the appointments with clients have to be met. If you are self-employed producing things that have an immediate unit value when the work is done, it is easy for you and everyone around you to count and *see* the consequences of taking the morning off or working late.

But agriculture, along with some professions like writing novels, art and composing music, is the worst of all possible worlds for time management. There is no externally imposed schedule of any kind, and the results of your work are difficult to count hour by hour, as they will not be worth money until some indeterminate time in the future. It is hard enough to make your work time sacrosanct to yourself, let alone to your family, friends and everyone else who has a claim on your time.

The lunar planting calendar is a nice time-management tool – an external framework to schedule your work around. It creates deadlines that are visible, to yourself and to everyone around you. I found I could still be flexible in my working time, but it meant I was not always *available* for whatever urgent task needed doing and couldn't be done by someone else because they had to go to work that day. The days didn't slip past without any awareness of where they were going.

The lunar planting calendar is also an organisational tool. It reduces a dishearteningly long list of jobs to short daily lists, with specific days for planting, harvesting, weeding and contemplating, so that everything gets its turn. It allows you to divide the seeds up into three boxes – one for leafies, one for fruitings and one for roots and perennials. You only have to get out one box at a time, and only on a limited number of days. No category is accidentally neglected.

It also allows you to reduce the overwhelming goal of 'building a garden' to a series of manageable goals, like 'making sure there is enough bed space ready for the lettuces by Thursday', and 'getting some propagating mix ready for the cuttings before next weekend'. Goals of this kind are much less daunting. You get to experience much more often that rewarding sense of satisfaction in a task completed.

By the time I started using a lunar calendar, I was already in the habit of keeping a fairly detailed garden diary. It wasn't long before I noticed that, despite my initial scepticism, the seeds planted at the right time did have consistently better strike rates and healthier growth than those planted even a day or two earlier or later. I also began to notice how often my own moods and direction of focus and energy seemed to follow a cycle in time with the moon. If I picked tasks that fitted with the cycle, I had productive and enjoyable days. If I didn't, Murphy's Law worked overtime.

There are several plausible theories to explain why lunar planting should work, the most likely having to do with tidal forces on soil, plant and animal-borne water. There is also a measurable correlation between astrological phases and sunspot activity, which affects electromagnetic radiation, which in turn affects plant growth.

However, even if it only achieved a solution to those very thorny problems of organisation and time management, that would be well and truly enough. The lunar planting calendar, whether by coincidence or cosmic design, is a wonderfully *comfortable* schedule for gardeners. It is almost like a dream boss – one that rewards you when you meet a deadline, knows there will be a next time when you don't, hangs silently on the wall and looks decorative!

DEAR DIARY

My final major tool is information. I am a full-moon person – a doer. Cultivation of a capacity for quiet observation has been one of the hardest lessons I have had to learn. Yet quiet observation is the key to any system that involves a cooperative relationship with a site and its indigenous inhabitants.

The trick is to see more than just what you are consciously looking for, to see the unexpected and the unexplained. It is like collecting the pieces of a jigsaw puzzle before you start trying to put it together. With too many pieces missing, the pattern refuses to show itself. With enough pieces, it will simply fall into place.

For me the best times of day for this kind of observation are early morning and late afternoon. These are the times when the busy, planning, scheming part of my mind is quietest, and often I see things that I wonder at never having noticed before. What sort of wasp is that? What is it up to? That patch of potatoes has recovered from the damage caused by an early frost, while all the rest are just struggling along. What is different? I wonder if that line of smallish plants is an old track, where the soil is compacted. I noticed stinkweed coming up along that line, and also along the road.

There are two tools I use to keep these collected pieces of the jigsaw on the table – a *garden diary*, and *names*.

My first garden diary was a cheap, unlined, kids' exercise book. Since then I've tried large sketchbooks, ring-binders, ruled-up formats, and beautiful, expensive, hardcover notebooks. I always go back to the exercise book. Expensive paper makes me feel as if I have to have something important to write in it. Large sketchbooks are cumbersome to handle resting on my knees, and prompt for each page to contain an integrated story. Ruled-up formats, even those I design for myself, restrict me to what I *expect* to see. The only improvement I have ended up with on my original diary is using one of those pens that has four colours in one, so that I can easily differentiate between plans and notes.

My diary is a very messy but delightful melange of sketches, notes, clippings, seed packets, plans, observations and ideas. No-one else can make any sense of it, but in a fire it is one of the first things I would grab! Whatever form you use, it is important to keep a diary from Day One, and it is important to choose a format that will allow you to collect all sorts of scraps of information, few of which will initially seem to fit into any pattern at all.

The second tool is naming. I name everything – chooks, compost piles, garden beds, wind patterns . . . I give my own invented name to any weeds I don't recognise, and even to some that I do! I name vegetable varieties bred from my own saved seed, and give individual names to many of the creatures that live in and visit the garden. Sometimes I spend an inordinate amount of time mulling over the right name, which is extraordinary for someone as ruthless with time as I am. There is something about the process of discovering the perfect name that pushes you that one step further into close observation, into looking for the essential features, into pulling together an intuitive knowledge of a thing's true nature. I suspect that it is what is meant by the Wicca philosophy that knowledge of a thing's true name gives one power over it.

I doubt whether I would have noticed that the Hillary beans (named after Sir Edmund) do better on higher ground had I not been searching for a name for them. I have a variety of strawberry I call 'The Holy Grail'. It was named after I noticed that it seemed to do much better when there was some borage around it. Like the knights of the Round Table, it seemed to need 'borage for courage'.

Names are also mnemonic. They prompt you to *remember* what it was you noticed about something. It is difficult to forget to look for the highest spot when planting Hillary beans, or to companion-plant with borage when planting Holy Grail strawberries. I have a pair of chooks named Bonnie and Clyde because when they are together, they seriously upset the established social order of any pen. On the rare occasions when I reorganise the chooks, I remember to keep Bonnie and Clyde in separate pens!

The first compost pile I made with lots of azolla I named 'The Fire Engine', partly because of the red colour of the then unidentified new ingredient, and partly because it heated up so quickly. This name kept the notion that the new ingredient might be very nitrogen-rich alive in my mind. It reminded me to be curious about whether very nitrogen-hungry vegetables like silver beet would do particularly well on it, and to be careful about using it with plants that do not like too much nitrogen. Names keep the pieces of the jigsaw mobile, so that when enough accumulate, they simply fall into place.

Naming may seem facetious, but it is actually very serious garden work. Time is probably more productively spent in naming a troublesome weed than it is in pulling it out! While you are naming it, you are gathering the observations that you need to exercise your creative intelligence. While you are straining your back on it, you are merely doing a job that something else can do better, and can probably be contracted to do for you if you use your intelligence. In fact, as a general rule of thumb, the more facetious *any* garden work feels, the more productive it probably is.

PART TWO

STARTING OUT

5 SITE AND LAYOUT

CHOOSING A SITE

The first thing to do if you are starting a new garden is to select a site. There are only five criteria to use in selecting a site, and soil *isn't* one of them. It is important to know what your soil is like, and what is already growing wild will give you a good indication of that. If you are starting off with good soil that is an extra bonus. But virgin soil is almost never good enough, and soil quality is very correctable. Proximity, water availability, slope, drainage and aspect are much more difficult and expensive to correct than soil. Good soil is very seductive, but it is important to resist the temptation and not sacrifice any other site considerations for it. Soil can be built, but distance, rainfall and gravity are given, and there is not much you can do about them!

PROXIMITY

The first and most important criterion in site selection is proximity. If at all possible, build your garden as close as you can to your house. Even if it takes only ten minutes to get from where your boots are to the garden, by the time you come home for lunch you will have spent *nearly five hours a week* just travelling. If you come home for morning and afternoon smoko too, that's over nine hours a week. In even five hours a week you could build an extra thirty compost piles a year and still be ahead on time. Over the lifetime of the garden you could correct almost every other site problem fifty times over!

Secondly, there is nothing worse than having to decide what you want for dinner, and for breakfast tomorrow, and for cut lunches tomorrow, before you knock off work. In the middle of making coleslaw, a perfect cabbage ten minutes' travel away is not nearly as attractive as a very mediocre one right here. Pasta with fresh herbs is a quick, easy meal for those nights when you come in late and tired and hungry. But if the fresh herbs are not right there, you will settle for baked beans on toast, and wonder why you bother to have a garden.

Thirdly, a great deal of my most productive and pleasant work is done sitting in the garden with a cup of tea very early in the morning, or taking a cold beer down after my shower of an evening. Many insects, birds and reptiles are active at night or in the early morning and late evening, and this is the most fruitful time for observation of just what they are up to. Those little snippets of time spent quietly planning, observing and ruminating, when you are in the garden but not actually working in it, are exactly what turns toil into play. They are extremely productive, and they are very difficult to organise with your garden anywhere but within spitting distance.

In addition, carpet snakes, cats and foxes are likely to be less of a problem close to human habitation. They are all night hunters – but if your chooks are close enough for you to hear them kick up a stink, you can save yourself coming down in the morning to a scene of carnage.

And finally, gardens produce a lot more than just the food you harvest, and the more of these benefits you reap, the more value you get for the same work. The scent of flowers in the evening air, the hover of a butterfly, the patterns of colours, shades, shapes and movements, and the sounds of frogs and birds need to be around your home to be fully appreciated. Food-producing gardens, even commercial-scale ones, can be stunningly beautiful. They can add value, and a great deal of amenity, to your home. A food-producing garden, even a heavily mulched one, is also an effective firebreak and a much safer way to landscape and beautify your home than native trees and shrubs.

If you can do your home landscaping and decoration at the same time as gourmet food production, why make two tasks out of one?

WATER

I use several strategies to reduce water consumption, the main one being a constant and heavy mulch cover. Overwatering wastes a precious resource, and leads to leaching of nutrients and eutrophication of waterways – which means your favourite swimming spots end up clogged with waterweeds and blue-green algae. A*nd* your plants become dependent and won't let you go away on holiday for a week.

Living in an area with an annual rainfall of 150 cm (60 inches), I am not as conscientious about water conservation as I should be. In a seven-mandala system, I use about 1000 litres a day in peak periods, when the weather is very hot and dry and I have newly planted seedlings or fruits like tomatoes just ripening. Using the lunar calendar, it is surprising how often rain comes just in time for planting. Nevertheless, since we get several months, in spring, with very little rain, I bank on needing a water storage capacity of at least 50 000 litres for my commercial-sized garden.

Lack of access to adequate water is just about the only reason good enough to locate your garden other than right next to your house, and even then, perhaps you should look at moving your house!

TERRAIN

The ideal site is a gentle slope with good drainage and a north-easterly aspect. Oh to be so lucky!

Too much slope and poor drainage are both correctable. Terrace gardening has advantages, but terraces are a lot of work to build and materials can be hard to get or expensive, especially if you are working on a larger scale. Without terraces, gravity means that all your work ends up at the bottom of the hill. A flat or bowl-shaped site with poor drainage is going to be equally difficult and expensive to correct, and it is equally fundamental that it be corrected. Very few vegetables and fruits, especially those that we are familiar with, will tolerate waterlogging to any degree at all.

If you live on the side of a steep hill with a bog below it, and there is a nice, gentle, north-easterly slope ten minutes' walk away, you have a difficult decision! If you only have a choice between a slope and a bog, choose the slope. Old railway sleepers are probably the most economical terracing material you are likely to be able to get hold of. If you are stuck with a bog, perhaps you should be thinking about aquaculture rather than gardening.

ASPECT

Aspect is not correctable – no amount of money or work will change where the sun rises – but I suspect that in Australian climates, especially the northern half, too much is made of it. Some of the best gardens I have ever seen are tucked away in little valleys or city backyards and get direct sun for only a few hours a day. Perhaps we have just followed a European tradition of seeking maximum sunlight, or perhaps the hole in the ozone layer has made a difference, but my garden tells me it wants more shade much more often than it tells me it wants more sun.

The Australian climate is very different to the European one, where most of our gardening lore originated. Our summer days are shorter, but the sunlight is much more intense. We get over double the annual solar radiation of Britain and most of Europe. Even on the east coast, our light intensity is only matched by the Sahara desert, the Arizona desert and some areas of very high altitude. We have pretty near the highest light levels of any arable region in the world.

If you have a north-easterly aspect, use it. It will allow you a bigger range of winter crops. But if you haven't, I wouldn't worry about it too much. For most of the year your problem is much more likely to be too much sun than too little.

ACCESS

Access is only important if you are working on a larger scale, but then it is very important. To make a living, you will need to harvest something like thirty boxes of produce a week, and carrying thirty boxes of produce any distance is time-consuming and no fun. At this scale you will also be bringing in about three trailerloads of mulch, manure and waterweeds per week.

Gravity is a free resource. The ideal arrangement is vehicle access to the top and the bottom of the site. Loads are much lighter when gravity is harnessed to help carry them.

Really the choice boils down to the closest spot to your house that has acceptable slope, drainage, water availability and, if you are working on a commercial scale, access. If you have a choice of two, then take the one that faces north-east. Only if you have a choice of several sites that meet all these criteria does soil become a factor.

UNDERSTANDING YOUR SITE

Soil is not an important criterion in choosing your site because it is so very amenable to change. It is useful to understand your virgin soil, but even that is not terribly important. The cure is nearly always similar whatever the diagnosis. An accurate diagnosis of your site's microclimates is much more important than an understanding of its soil. Climate is nearly as amenable to change as soil and it can be changed in a much wider variety of directions.

SOIL

The plants growing wild on your site have settled there because it provides conditions that they like. They can tell you, without the need for expensive soil tests, what those conditions are. Ironically, however, the question is mostly academic. The cure for heavy clay soil is to add organic matter to break up the clay and improve drainage. The cure for sandy, dry soil is to add organic matter to retain water. The cure for acid soil is to add organic matter, particularly bird manure, to bring the pH up and make more nutrients available. The cure for alkaline soil is to add organic matter to buffer it. The cure for hardpan is to add organic matter to feed earthworms.

Compost, mulch, animal manure and worm castings are the great cure-alls. You can build a garden on a concrete car park if you add enough of them. It is usually easier and safer just to add enough of them to correct *any* deficiency than to worry about which particular deficiency you might have. Just as it is better to feed a person a good, balanced, varied diet than to eat junk food and then worry about which vitamin pills to take, it is better to feed plants plenty of humus than to grow them in skeletal soil and worry about which supplements they need.

Nevertheless, interpreting the weeds on your site can give you a very good indication of your soil type, and of the kind of soil problems and adjustments you might need to deal with. It is extremely valuable to notice and interpret your weeds *before* you remove them. Once you have a garden on your site, it will be all but impossible to remember what weeds were there initially. If you do strike a problem that you suspect has to do with soil type, you will not have the information you need to diagnose and solve it unless you recorded what was there before the garden. Get out your diary and map the weeds growing on your site. Take notes and sketches for later identification of any you do not recognise. You will thank yourself in time.

WEED INDICATORS OF SOIL TYPE

Weeds which are good indicators of fertile soil include **chicory, chickweed, fat hen** and **groundsel.** Good soil may be indicated or created by **clover, lantana** and **blackberries**, but either way where they are is usually where most plants would like to be! **Kangaroo grass** indicates well-drained soil, and if the plant is thick and healthy the soil is probably fertile too. If you have a preponderance of these weeds on your site, thank your lucky stars. You will probably need to do very little initial soil-type adjustment. Your main task will be to maintain soil fertility and avoid depleting the nutrients or damaging the soil structure.

Dock, mullein, sorrel, plantain, bracken, wild strawberry, stinging nettles, bladey grass and **milk thistles** all like acid soil. Dock, plantain and milk thistle, as well as **chicory** and **dandelions**, are also indicators of clay soil. Bladey grass thrives on very heavy acid soil that has been repeatedly burned, and this soil will probably require a great deal of organic matter, chook manure and calcium added. If you have a preponderance of these weeds, it may be useful to add a small amount of dolomite or ordinary lime to break up the clay and bring up the pH of your soil.

Normally I steer clear of any bought soil adjustments, including lime or dolomite. The micro-organisms that inhabit your site have also chosen it because it provides conditions that they like. Changing those conditions suddenly and radically will land you with sterile soil. All your microscopic workers will stage a walkout, which will instantly escalate to a general strike, with the worms, lizards, frogs and birds going out in sympathy.

Chook manure added gradually by the chooks themselves will raise pH just as effectively, but in a biologically active way, adding micro-organisms adapted to a more alkaline environment at the same time. However, having said all that, a little judicious meddling in the initial stages can mean the difference between discouragement and a first crop that is morale-boosting enough to keep you going, particularly in the case of very heavy, acid, clay soil. A double handful of agricultural lime or dolomite per bed is plenty.

Use dolomite if you suspect a magnesium deficiency as well as acidity. Otherwise use lime – it's cheaper. Sprinkle it over the surface and allow the chooks to scratch it in. They will use it to de-louse themselves at the same time. Magnesium deficiency is most common on bladey grass soils – soils that have been repeatedly burned. Clay soils are usually rich in magnesium, but burning kills off the micro-organisms that hold magnesium in an available form and increases the potash, which in turn decreases the availability of magnesium.

If you are unblessed with *very* acid soil, you may have to repeat this treatment occasionally. You can use a pH test kit to find out. They are quite cheap and easy to use. Or, more reliably, you can use your crop plants and weeds as indicators.

As ongoing treatment, you have a perfect excuse for frequent trips to the beach! Cuttlefish and shellgrit fed to the chooks are useful for any soil type, but particularly for heavy acid soils. Comfrey, horsetail, buckwheat and nasturtiums also help boost the calcium levels. Err on the side of heavily populating your chook domes to increase the amount of chook manure.

Kikuyu likes fertile soil, but can cope with a great deal more waterlogging than most vegetables or fruit. **Dock, sorrel, nettles** and **plantain** also like wet conditions. They tell you that your paths, like mine, will probably need to be dug out to double as drains to prevent waterlogging. I dig the paths a short section at a time around a chook dome, throwing the excavated soil, weeds and all, to the chooks to break up and spread, and keeping the drains sloping gently towards the bottom of the garden.

Each time I go to town I bring home a bag of sawdust from the local mill, filling the excavation back up to ground level with it. The sawdust allows water to drain freely, suppresses weeds, provides a nice surface to walk on, and is relished by worms. Once a year or so when the paths begin to turn into worm castings and weeds, I shovel the old sawdust off a section of path and into the adjacent chook dome, renewing it with fresh sawdust. This drainage technique works very well, and is much cheaper and easier than agricultural pipe or mole drains or rubble drains.

Tussock grass and **stinkweed** can cope with very compacted soil, which will take a lot of earthworm activity to be really suitable for gardening. Add worms and ensure that the levels of organic matter are kept high to feed them. Maintain a good layer of mulch over your beds to keep them moist and provide the worms with cover when they surface to feed. Make sure you include some deep-rooted ground breakers like horseradishes in each initial planting.

Wattles and **legumes** sometimes grow in fertile soil, but since they create their own nitrogen they can also cope with very nitrogen-deficient soil – soil that is quite starving for organic matter.

Eucalypts present a special problem because they are so strongly allopathic. Eucalypts try very hard to prevent anything else growing except more eucalypts. Get as big a distance as possible between your garden site and any gum trees.

CLIMATE

A huge part of the success or failure of garden crops is getting the climatic conditions right. The common perception is that climate is immutable – you are stuck with whatever light and heat, rain and humidity, wind, frost and snow your part of the world is susceptible to, and all you can do is choose crops that will stand up the extremes. However, I'm not at all sure this is true.

Climate varies enormously, even within very local areas. If you go for a walk around your garden site at different times of the day and in different seasons, you will notice a great deal of variation in how comfortable you feel, even within a few paces. Sit in one spot in the early morning and your jumper will be off several hours before it would be somewhere else. On a hot, windy afternoon there will be places you can only last an hour or so before heading in for a cool drink, and others where you can keep working comfortably till sunset. On a frosty night you might paddle out to the shadehouse in your slippers but you would want boots and two pairs of socks to visit the bottom corner.

We have no compunction at all about fiddling with climate for the comfort and amenity of humans, creating places that are warmer or cooler, shadier or sunnier, that catch the breeze or are protected from the wind. Good designs even manage to do so without an uneconomical expenditure of energy, by using elegantly simple strategies like heat sinks (such as a nearby brick wall) and breezeways. Garden crops have their climatic comfort zones too, and appreciate the same concern. Individual crops vary, just as different people do – but not by as much as you might think.

LIGHT

All plants need light. But, as with most things in life, just because something is good doesn't mean that more of it is better! The most important thing plants use light for is, of course, photosynthesis. This is a chemical process that uses the chlorophyll (green pigment) in leaves to turn carbon dioxide, water and light into carbohydrates, oxygen and heat.

Plants use more intense light for this than for anything else for which they use light. But even the biggest users, like sugarcane, still use only half the light hitting them between 10 a.m. and 4 p.m. in Australia. They simply cannot cram enough chlorophyll into their leaves to use more.

More light is less than useless. Once saturation point is reached, photosynthesis *decreases* at higher light intensities. Your silver beet leaves grow slower than they would with *less* light hitting them. Our climate is often too hot for plants to reach even this saturation point. Photosynthesis declines rapidly at too high a temperature, and more light usually means more heat. Unless you can cool them down, your plants cannot use even *half* the light they get on a summer's day.

Plants use light for two other purposes. The first is to determine their body shape. Too little light can make them go 'leggy' – tall and spindly and pale – while too much can make them squat and thick and malformed. But in Australian light intensities, too much is much more likely to be a problem than too little. It is very difficult to get deep enough shade to cause plants to go leggy outside a shade-house or building.

The second use for light is photoperiodism. Plants determine what season it is, and whether it is time to fruit or seed or whatever, not so much by the air temperature as by the length of the day, or more accurately the night. There is rarely any shortage of light for this purpose, however. This is partly because photoperiodism only needs very low intensities to be effective, and partly because the kind of light plants use for it is at the far red end of the spectrum. This kind of light is bounced around much more than other parts of the spectrum, and so is available for use more than once.

The hole in the ozone layer also has profound implications for agricultural theory. Plants can be damaged by 'sunburn' even more than humans. Ultraviolet light is fatal to micro-organisms and especially deadly to earthworms. Worms die of sunburn before they die of desiccation. Exposure for a matter of seconds is fatal. Ultraviolet light is an invisible killer. Most of Australia is now exposed to it, and it is recent enough that the full implications for agriculture aren't yet appreciated.

European gardeners and gardening books will advise you to look for the sunniest spot for your garden, to space your plants so that every part of them receives full sun, to plant in rows to allow sunlight to penetrate, and to orient your rows to the sun. But we have heaps and heaps of light – too much light – and definitely way too much ultraviolet light, for optimum plant growth.

Don't be afraid of shade.

Australian crops need a hat and long sleeves where their European counterparts don't – just like Australian people do. And since micro-organisms and earthworms are doing our digging and fertilising, it is vital to shade the soil all the time, and to avoid digging it over and sterilising it by exposure to UV. Europeans might be able to get away with digging. We can't.

Look for patterns of light and shade on your garden site. Notice and record in your diary where the sun rises and sets, and the length of shadows cast by any permanent features, in different seasons. Try to select and design for a compromise between enough northern light in winter when the intensities (especially of ultraviolet) are lower, and enough shade in summer. If you have a choice, the best garden site will be well shaded to the west, moderately shaded to the east, but open except for deciduous trees from the north-east around to the north-west. Tall buildings or large evergreen trees will be mainly on the western and southern sides.

Even if you have no choice as to site, it is useful to map the light availability in different parts of your garden over different seasons. The spot that gets the sun earliest and latest in the day in spring is where you will plant your first eggplants and capsicums of the season. The shadiest spot in midsummer is where your lettuces will thrive.

We can also afford to ignore a great deal of classic European gardening advice. Provided there are enough water and nutrients we can space plants much closer together, because spacing to allow light penetration is unnecessary. We can dispense with row formations altogether. Equal spacing in every direction limits the available light, but enables better use to be made of water and nutrients. And we don't need to sacrifice other criteria like proximity or access to get the sunniest garden spot.

TEMPERATURE

Photosynthesis is a chemical reaction and, like all chemical reactions, it can only happen within a particular temperature range. Plants cannot shiver, run on the spot, move into the shade or go indoors for a cold beer. They have very limited means of controlling their temperature. Their main means is *transpiration* – the plant equivalent of sweating.

If the temperature they are exposed to is too hot, or the water not available enough to cool down by sweating, all they can do about it is stop photosynthesising. This means that they stop producing carbohydrates, so stop growing. Normally plants put about 70 to 80 per cent of the carbohydrates they produce into new growth – leaves, roots, shoots, flowers, fruit and tubers. The other 20 to 30 per cent goes in *respiration*. This is another chemical reaction – one in which plants 'burn' part of the carbohydrates they produce to provide energy for everything else.

In the daytime there is light for photosynthesis and, provided it is not *too* hot, more carbohydrates are produced than are burned. At night, when there is no light, photosynthesis stops. But if it is warm enough, respiration doesn't stop. When the nights are as hot as the days, plants can be burning overnight all the carbohydrates they can save up in the day, and there are none left for new growth. In extreme situations they can even go backwards, with plenty of light, carbon dioxide and nutrients, just because the temperature is wrong!

For most plants, the optimum temperature for photosynthesis is around 25°C. For some heat-loving plants (like melons) the optimum can be as high as 35°C. But this is the *leaf* temperature. A dark leaf, like for example a silver beet leaf, in full sun, can be as much as 10°C hotter than the surrounding air. Most of our crop plants are adapted to places where the ambient temperature is too *low* for efficient photosynthesis most of the time, so they have dark-coloured leaves. (Plants adapted to very hot climates often have silvery-green leaves in order to stay cooler.)

In addition, plants themselves produce extra heat in the chemical reactions of photosynthesis and respiration. The more they are growing, the more heat they are releasing. So the optimum *air* temperature for most of our crop plants, when they are in full sun, is between 15°C and 25°C.

In this part of the world the temperature is rarely too low for photosynthesis even in the dead of winter. Our daytime winter temperatures are as warm as most of Europe in the middle of summer. What limits the crops we can grow in winter is not that the days are too cool, but that they are too short (and, of course, frost at night). For most of the summer it is way too hot: plants cannot use the over-abundant light and they stop growing.

The ideal night-time temperature is as low as possible without freezing (which causes damage to plant tissue). Anything above frost temperature is fine. High night-time temperatures are for plants a bit like a very noisy party next door every night. They get no rest and start to lose weight.

Adjusting the microclimate of your garden site to provide cooler temperatures in summer will dramatically increase the growth rate of your plants. With our very intense light, you can afford to sacrifice some to obtain cooler temperatures. You can afford trees, trellised vines and tall shrubs around and even within your garden, shading it from every aspect except north. You can even afford some north-westerly shade if it means protecting your garden from hot north-westerly winds. If you have a heat sink, like a building or a solid wall, on the eastern side of your garden site you should take particular care to shade it. Otherwise it will get the full belt of the afternoon sun, and re-radiate all that heat back to your garden overnight (see Figure 10).

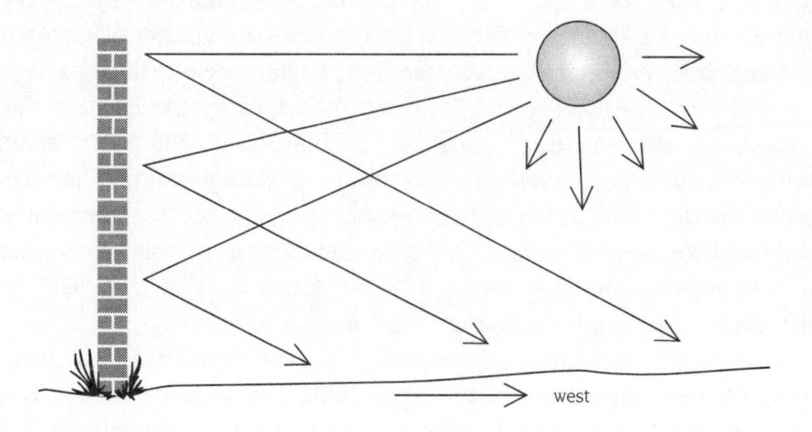

Figure 10 An unshaded west-facing wall will dramatically increase day *and* night temperatures.

The other main source of heat at night is that stored in the earth. Soil with lots of organic matter heats up much less. A nice thick blanket of *dry* mulch will block the sun from heating up the earth too much in the daytime. Light-coloured mulch is best of all. This will also keep what heat *has* been absorbed from escaping back into the air around the leaves of your crop plants at night.

Wet mulch is about as much use for this purpose as a wet blanket is at keeping heat in or out! So if at all possible, do your watering in the early morning so that the mulch layer dries out by evening. This will also cool the air by evaporation and provide your plants with enough water when they need it most to cool themselves.

WIND

If your garden and your clothes line are situated side by side, one of them is in the wrong spot!

Clothes hanging on the line dry best in hot, windy weather. Plants dry worst in hot, windy weather. Any wind will increase the water consumption of your garden enormously. Watering will be a much more arduous task, and you will only be able to go on holiday in the rain! If you do manage to get away, you may well find that the water authorities have inundated your favourite bit of bush to provide for all those thirsty gardens. A north-westerly wind can even increase consumption to the point where your plants cannot suck up water fast enough to keep up with losses and will wilt or die, even in well-watered soil.

Some wind is good. It stirs up the air so that there is always a fresh supply of carbon dioxide. But strong winds, especially hot ones, are so dehydrating that plants close their stomata (the minute holes in their leaves) to conserve water and cannot take in carbon dioxide anyway.

If your garden site is not already very well protected from everything but gentle cool breezes, include a windbreak in your design. This can be a fence, trellis, structure or band of trees and shrubs. Wind is one of nature's most formidable forces, and trying to stop it dead will make all the force you can muster look ludicrous. Solid windbreaks straight across the path of the wind will either be demolished or create an eddy pattern in their lee that makes the effects of the wind even worse. If you are working *with* nature rather than against it, your windbreak will be designed to channel about 60 per cent of the wind around and over your garden and let the other 40 per cent filter gently through. Lattice, palings, sheoaks, wattles, callistemon, pigeon peas and even lantana make good windbreaks.

FROST

Imagine pouring a giant pot of treacle on your garden site. This is exactly how frost behaves. Any plants under a cover of structures or other plants will initially be protected. The treacle will slowly roll downhill, pooling up against obstacles then slowly making its way around them. It is so viscous that even quite permeable obstacles like low bushes are enough to protect the plants in their lee. But those plants that didn't cop it initially because they were under cover will be engulfed if they are on the uphill side. Any substantial wall, fence, building or row of plants will bank up a big deep pool behind it. A gap at the lowest point, however, will allow the treacle to drain away.

If the uphill sector of your garden site is to the north-west, you are lucky. The windbreak that arcs around this side can double as a frost deflector, channelling the treacle around either side of your garden. The downhill, south-east sector will be much more open to allow any frost that occurs in your garden to drain away.

Whatever your garden aspect, if your part of the world is susceptible to frost, sit for a minute with your diary and imagine your site deluged with treacle rain. Can you deflect it from flowing in from uphill? Can you prevent it pooling by allowing it to drain away freely? Are there parts of your site that are more prone than others?

LEAD

City gardeners often worry about contamination of their soil, air and rainwater with the lead from car exhaust fumes. Lead-free petrol is making a difference, but the lead levels in our smog are still high enough to be a concern. Even if you live in the inner city, however, the fact remains that gardening is probably your best chance of keeping down the level of heavy metals in your food.

The romantic image of the source of supermarket vegetables is, unfortunately, not very accurate. That pristine family farmlet with clean soil, air and water is so rare now that it is too valuable as real estate to use for growing supermarket vegetables. Instead, your vegies most likely come from a farm situated right beside a highway for ease of transport. Just about every operation on the farm is highly mechanised, and the fuel used is likely to contain lead. The farm depends on artificial fertilisers, which contain high levels of many heavy metals, and the crops are sprayed regularly with poisons to kill pests and weeds. Then your vegetables will spend several days on a highway before they get to you, travelling on average several thousand km.

If your garden soil contains high levels of organic matter, this will block the uptake of heavy metals. The air in your backyard may not be quite as clean as the air at that farm, but it will not be as far behind as you might imagine. At least you don't drive vehicles *on* your garden. If you avoided the contamination of artificial fertilisers, insecticides, fungicides, herbicides, soil fumigants and post-harvest treatments, you could probably garden beside the Sydney Harbour Bridge and *still* be lower overall in heavy metal concentrations. So go ahead and make that garden!

DECIDING ON A SCALE

Digging a garden bed and adding fertiliser (or ploughing a farm) is like paying rent. You get quick, easy results, but you have to do it over and over again, with no permanent advantage gained each time. My design, like all permaculture-based designs, is like building a house as opposed to paying rent. It takes a heavy initial investment, but that investment is in capital growth. It is never lost and, with maintenance, will appreciate.

I have never been money-rich, so I look for capital investments in the form of labour. It takes sixteen weeks to establish a system, and in this time the workload will be easily double that of an already established system. As with any small business, it is a fatal mistake to go in undercapitalised.

Timing is important. If you are using chooks, they will have to be moved every fortnight, or else they will run out of food, and you will have to put money and time into feeding them rather than letting them feed themselves. During this time they will need mulch, or else the bared ground will crust over, the worms will migrate out and weeds will invade. Then you will have to weed as well as mulch, and the mulch will have seeds in it, so you will have to weed again. While you are busy doing all this to catch up, you are not mulching the next pen, and the problem compounds. The moral is to tackle only as much as you feel very confident about keeping up with. It is easy to add mandalas, like modules, later.

It is important to assess carefully the amount of time you actually have available. A single mandala system will take about eight to ten hours a week to establish, but can then be maintained in four to five hours a week. If you work or play at something else full-time, then this scale is probably enough. It can be built without major stress if you can make it your major spare-time project for four or five months. Then it will provide you with a beautiful, easily maintained haven, a healthy gourmet diet and some sensational dinner parties! You will probably not grow enough to bottle your own tomato sauce or dry your own beans, but then you probably don't have time for this anyway.

If you are working a single mandala system, your chook dome will complete a circuit, giving each bed a fortnight, in twelve weeks. It will need somewhere else to go for the next three months till it is time to begin another circuit. In the centre of a circle of banana, pawpaw and/or tamarillo trees at the bottom of the garden is a good location in tropical and subtropical regions. In temperate areas, a cane or bramble-fruits patch is a good alternative.

Add some native trees and shrubs, some hardy rampant vines like chokos, pumpkins and cherry tomatoes in the corners and around the edges and a small patch of meadow-weed lawn, and you have a complete backyard ecosystem.

If you have a slightly larger area than a suburban backyard to work with, and enough time to make the garden a serious part-time project for several months, you can probably tackle a double or triple mandala system. Unless you have a very big family, a great deal of extra time is going to be taken up processing or otherwise disposing of the excess produce. But at this scale, if you add a goat or cow, you can aim at something very like self-sufficiency in fresh and processed food.

Establishing a seven-mandala system that will earn you a living will take sixteen weeks of full-time hard work with no other commitments and, if you have children, a supportive partner. I have a very persistent habit of biting off more than I can chew. Trying to establish a seven-mandala system ten minutes away from home (I neglected the proximity rule) with a spouse who was occupied full-time, two kids and a half-built bathroom was, in retrospect, definitely *not* a good idea!

If you paid yourself wages, this would represent about $8000 investment – not an exorbitant price for a going small business, but still not an amount to be sneezed at. After establishment, it should take no more than twenty-five to thirty hours a week to maintain *if* there were no short cuts taken in establishing it. If there were, this can blow out to a ridiculously excessive workload.

The gap between a two-mandala system (the produce from which can be consumed by a single hungry household with a little help from friends) and a seven-mandala system (which justifies a full-scale marketing operation) is a tricky one. Marketing $100 a week's worth of produce can take more time and energy than marketing $400 worth. If you are planning to work on this scale, make sure you look carefully at the time and labour economics of your marketing operation first.

LAYING OUT

It is important to lay out the entire area you might eventually want to garden before you start, even if you are planning to start small with the option of extending later. Any area that is not big enough, or the wrong shape for your design, will cost you extra work you don't need.

Finding that you have *almost*, but not quite, enough area for a dome on one edge, and also a tricky, narrow little area on the other edge, can very easily be corrected before you start, by just moving the whole system a few feet. If you only discover these problems after you have established the rest of your garden, you will be stuck with either weeding, pest control, fertilising and tilling those areas by hand forever, or trying to move an established system. Believe it or not, moving the entire system is easier in the long run.

If you are using a dome-based design, then each circle has a diameter of 3.8 metres, so a radius of 1.9 metres (it is best to call it 2 metres to allow a little extra). A bed slightly bigger than a chook dome is not a problem. One slightly smaller is a major problem. A complete mandala has a diameter of 15 metres, so a radius of 7.5 metres.

Here are some instructions for laying out your garden easily and simply (see Figure 11):

1 Take a piece of string 7.5 metres long. Tie one end to a stake and tie a loop in the other.
2 Dong a second stake into the middle of the area you propose to garden, put your loop over it, and trace a circle around it using the first stake like a pencil. Move your centre stake until this circle is positioned where you want it, then use a garden hose, sticks, rocks – anything – to mark it.
3 Repeat this process to mark out a second mandala and a third, and so on, until you have marked out all you can ever visualise. These large circles should just touch each other. The ideal shape for a seven-mandala system is in a giant circle, 45 metres across, but terrain is not usually so accommodating! My garden is a triangular shape.
4 Allow some space right at the entranceway to your garden for a propagating area.
5 Now shorten your bit of string to 2 metres.
6 Trace a circle around the centre stake of the mandala you propose to start with, and mark the edge of it. This will be the position for your first chook dome.

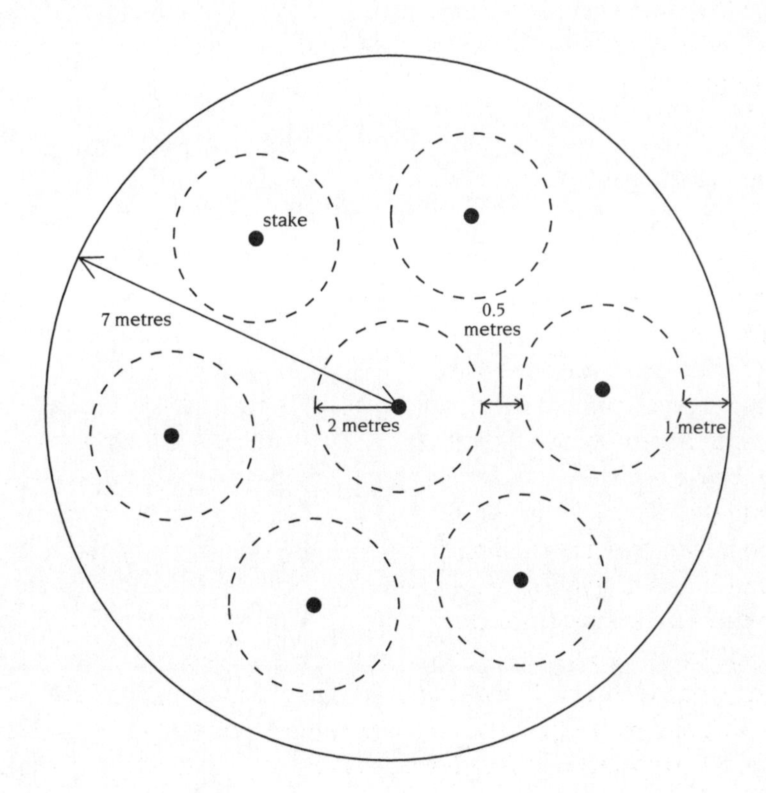

Figure 11 Layout for a single mandala.

7 Measure 4.5 metres out from this centre stake in any direction. This will be the centre of the next position for the dome. If you trace a circle around it, there should be a half-metre path between the two circles.

8 Keep going until you have marked out all seven circles. You should have a metre-wide border left around the inside edge of your big circle.

You are now ready to build your first chook dome.

6 BUILDING A CHOOK DOME

Chooks are fascinating to watch. They have a very sophisticated social structure and the biggest stress you can impose on them is to disrupt it. They should never be kept in flocks of more than about twenty in *any* kind of enclosure. Up to this number, they can all recognise and remember each other and their respective rankings in the pecking order. A new group of less than twenty will fight, sometimes quite viciously, for a day or two until they get their order sorted out. After this they will settle down and fight very rarely and never viciously.

In a group of more than about twenty, they cannot recognise and remember each other, and every encounter will involve a new battle to establish a social structure. Commercial 'free range' egg farming is in some ways even more cruel than battery farming, as groups of thousands of chooks maim each other in a neverending battle. Farmers de-beak and de-spur them to prevent outright killing, but this doesn't make the chooks any happier or less stressed.

Chooks were originally native to the Malaysian rainforests. They are a *forest* species. They lived in small flocks of one rooster and his harem, feeding on insects, grubs, worms, fallen fruit and leaves scratched for in the litter of a forest floor. Their instinct is to roost as high as they can in a tree, safe from at least the ground-prowling predators, with the chook highest in the pecking order commanding the highest perch.

The dome is a design for a chook tractor that has a number of advantages over standard designs. It houses about a dozen chooks – an ideal flock size. It provides them with plenty of fresh air, sunlight, shade, wet-weather shelter and protection from their predators. With an area of 11.35 m^2, it has plenty of room for them to move about, scratch, flap and generally behave like chooks. Because of the round shape, those ranking lowest in the pecking order are much less easily cornered and harassed by the camp bullies. The chook dome is 2 metres high, with the roost in the loft, so the chooks can follow their instinct to roost high. It is also escape-proof, which is important since free-ranging chooks can create an unbelievable amount of devastation in a garden in a very short time.

By far the most valuable feature of the chook dome, however, is that it is so easily moveable. A chook tractor that is an ordeal to move will simply provide a constant temptation to defer the job till another day. No garden task, especially a routine one, should be an ordeal! This design can be moved by one person in less than ten minutes, even across rough ground or gutters or over plants. You will tend to do it, even in your best clothes, in the ten minutes you have to spare before your bus goes.

A chook tractor in the garden is a very elegant solution to the problems of weeding, fertilising, tilling and controlling pests. These are all jobs that are laborious, difficult, time-consuming and boring for humans, and that, for all our effort, we are not adapted to do very well. No human has the patience, or the eyesight, to search out every single aphid or weed seed. No human would spend hours laboriously turning over and mixing mulch, manure, ash, soil and compost. No human would dig up every root, nut or runner of grass and keep moving it around to prevent it re-rooting.

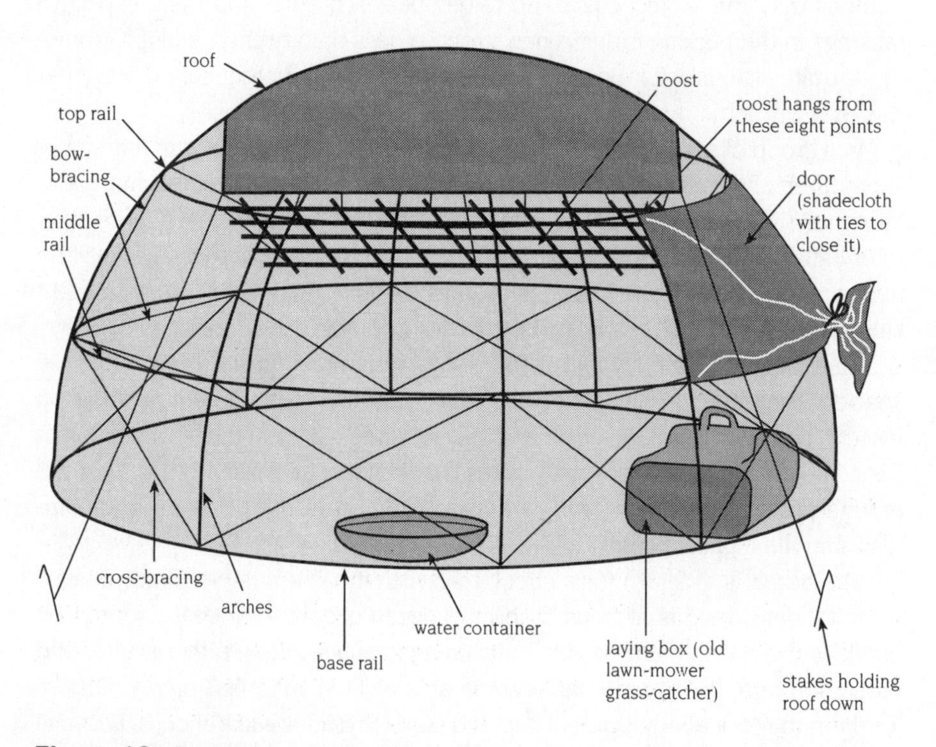

Figure 12 Design for a chook dome.

Yet chooks will very happily do all these jobs, all day every day, week in week out, and thank you for the opportunity by turning weeds and pests into golden-yolked eggs. For the cost of building a dome and spending ten minutes a fortnight moving it, you can get twelve garden beds built and completely maintained for you.

Figure 12 illustrates my chook dome design. The task of building the dome can be done alone, but it is one of those jobs that goes more than twice as fast with two. Try to rope in a helper for a few hours!

YOU WILL NEED:

- Nine lengths of 20 mm class 12 PVC pipe, each 6 metres long
- Blue PVC glue
- One 20 mm PVC joiner
- Tie-wire
- Twenty-two metres of 1.5 metre wide bird wire, chicken wire or net
- Baling twine or some other strong, UV-resistant twine
- Two metres of shadecloth
- Bamboo or light pine slats
- One old lawn-mower grass-catcher or similar for a laying box
- One cheap 2.4 metre square woven plastic tarp
- Four tent pegs
- One water container

FRAME

HORIZONTAL RAILS

First, join two 6 metre lengths of pipe, gluing them together with the blue glue, to make a circle with a 12-metre circumference. This will be your base rail. Cut 1.4 metres off the end of another length of pipe (not the end with the socket), and join the remaining 4.6 metres to a 6 metre length. This makes a circle with a 10.6 metre circumference. This will be your middle rail. Using the joiner, join the remaining 1.4 metre length to another 6 metre length to make a circle with a 7.4 metre circumference. This will be your top rail. See Figure 13.

ARCHES

Divide the base rail into eight equal lengths and mark it. The marks should be at 1.5 metre intervals. Using a very small drill bit, drill a hole horizontally through the pipe at each mark. Drill a similar hole in each end and in the middle of four 6 metre lengths. Pushing tie-wire through these holes, join these four lengths to the *inside* of the base rail, arching them over and crossing them in the middle. Thread tie-wire through at the crossover to join them all together in the middle of the arch.

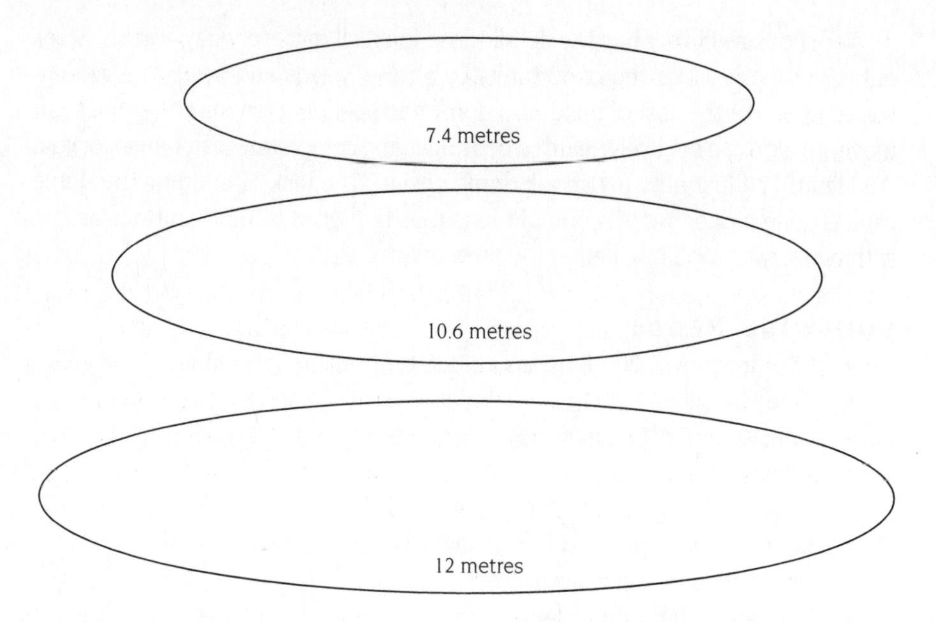

Figure 13 The horizontal rails of a chook dome frame.

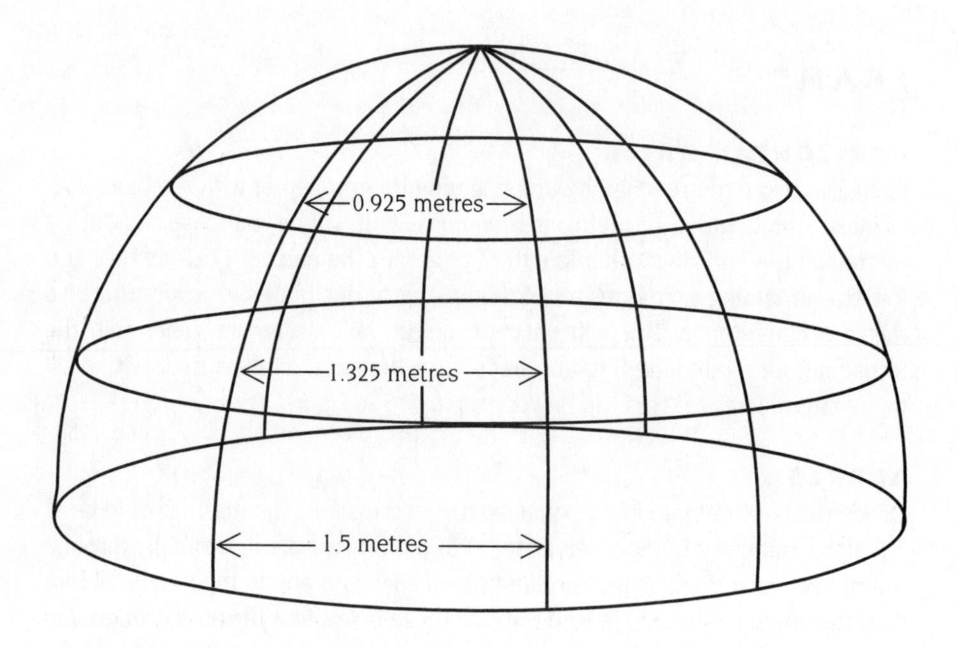

Figure 14 The arches of a chook dome frame.

Mark the middle rail at 1.325 metre intervals. Drill a hole at each mark. Measure 75 cm up each leg from the base rail and drill a hole. Put the middle rail *inside* the dome, and join it to each leg using tie-wire through the holes. Mark the top rail at 0.925 metre intervals, and follow the same procedure to join it. See Figure 14.

BRACING

Using baling twine, cross-brace each of the eight squares around the base. Measure the diagonals to make sure they are the same and adjust the tension on the bracing until it is all square and tight. Again using the baling twine, brace each arc of the middle rail between the arches like a horizontal bow. Also brace each arc of the arches between the middle and top rails like a vertical bow. See Figure 15 for an illustration of bracing. This completes the frame, and you will be amazed at how strong and rigid it is!

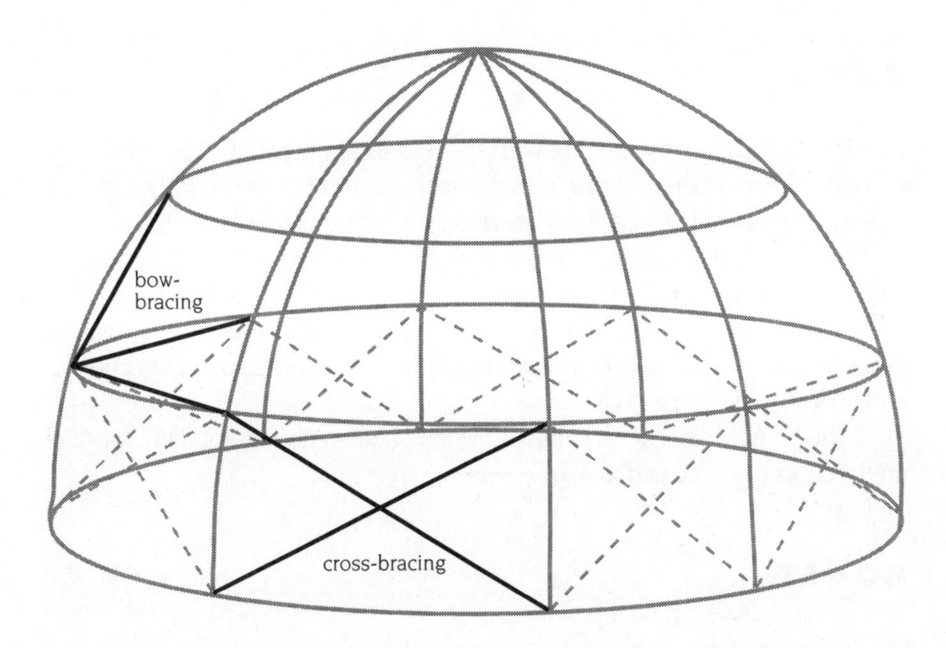

Figure 15 Cross and arc bracing of a chook dome frame.

Note for Shorter People If you are not very tall, there is one modification you might want to make to this basic design. Measure how high a rail you can easily step over. If it is lower than 75 cm, you will need to lower the centre rail. This will also mean increasing its circumference.

COVERING

The next job is to cover the whole thing, and how you do this depends on what your main chook predators are. My biggest problem is carpet snakes, so I cover the whole thing in bird wire, joining it together at every hole so there is no gap more than 1 cm wide. If you have no carpet snakes, chicken wire is adequate. If wild (or neighbouring domestic) dogs are your main problem, it may be worth using heavier wire around the bottom part and a light wire or net over the top to compensate for the extra weight. If you can get hold of some fairly heavy-duty fishing net cheaply, this would be ideal.

Whatever material you use, cover the whole frame with it except for one segment between the middle and top rails, which will be your door. If predators that dig (foxes or wild dogs) are a particularly bad problem, extend the covering 30 cm *below* the bottom rail to make a fringe around the bottom. Cut darts in the fringe to allow it to sit on top of the ground around the pen. With the pen in place, you can cover this fringe with soil to foil digging predators.

DOOR

The door takes up one sector between the middle and top rails. This allows you to have the door open to throw in mulch without the chooks instantly escaping. A person can enter fairly easily by stepping over the middle rail.

Because carpet snakes are my main predator, I have opted for a door that can be closed with no gaps. It is like a square tunnel 85 cm long, sewn in shadecloth, with ties to close it. To enter or to throw in mulch, I undo the tie and push the tunnel in so that it is like a chute into the dome. To close it, I pull the chute out and tie it closed.

If you do not have carpet snakes to worry about, a door framed in pipe, covered with wire and hinged may be easier.

ROOST

The theory behind my roost design is that although cats and foxes can jump *at an angle* just about as high as a chook can flap, they find it more difficult to do a vertical leap. Carpet snakes find it difficult to rear higher than about a metre or to climb the inside of an arc. My roost (see Figure 16) is a lashed grid of bamboo suspended from the frame just below the level of the top rail. The grid has 15 cm gaps – too small for a cat or fox to get through – and is only about 30 cm smaller in diameter than the top rail.

This means that even if they gained access to the dome, a cat or fox would have to do a near vertical leap and a carpet snake would have to either rear or climb the inside of the dome to reach the roost. So far no chooks have been murdered in their bed on this roost!

Bamboo is a perfect material for the roost as it is very light and strong, but if you don't have access to bamboo, light pine will do. Dowelling is stronger, but chooks actually prefer to roost on a 50 mm wide slat. The grid should be suspended from the eight points where the arches cross the top rail so that it hangs about 50 mm lower than the top rail. Even my geriatrics can manage to flap this high, although they approach it like someone attempting to summon up the courage to dive off the high board!

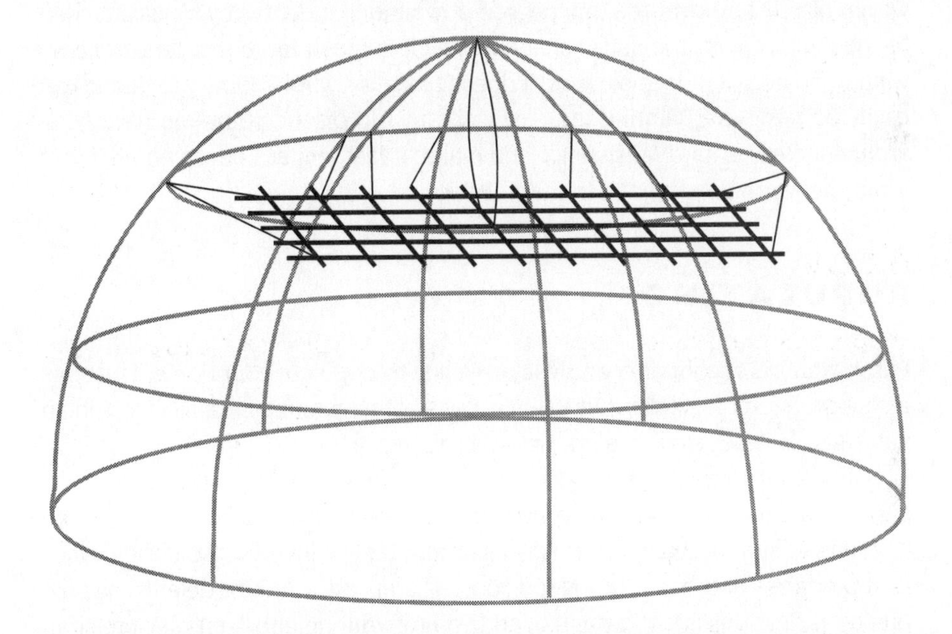

Figure 16 Roost design for a chook dome.

LAYING BOX

Old grass-catchers from lawn-mowers make wonderful laying boxes. They are just the right size, they are ventilated, and the handle on top means that you can reach in and lift them out to collect the eggs. I find that all the chooks like laying in the same box, so one per pen is enough. Keep an eye out at the dump or ask at lawn-mower repair shops.

If your chooks start to develop the habit of eating their own eggs, there is most likely some dietary reason. But if you cannot think of any, and it seems plain bad manners is the only reason, putting your laying box up on the roost will discourage them.

ROOF

My early chook dome designs featured a sewn-in roof made of tent nylon that covered the top half of the dome instead of wire. It was very light, but in a big wind behaved just like a giant umbrella, lifting the whole dome and kinking the frame.

Now I cover the whole dome with wire, and use a cheap 2.4 metre square woven plastic tarp over the top, pegged down independently, by ropes attached to the four corners. The flatter shape means it is much more resistant to heavy winds, and even if it does blow off, it doesn't take the whole dome with it and can easily be retrieved. Painting the tarp with any old plastic paint you have lying around increases its UV resistance and makes it last longer. I haven't tried it, but it may be worth painting the frame while you're at it.

POPULATING

Put in your water container and you are ready to populate your dome. I just use a shallow bucket for water, but if you go away often you may like to invest in an automatic waterer, available from produce stores.

I find that between ten and fourteen chooks, depending on size, are very happy in a dome. I include one rooster in each pen because I like to rear my own chickens – I believe that no form of life is completely fulfilled without the chance to reproduce – and because a good rooster is an extra line of defence against predators. But this is not essential, and you (or your neighbours) may prefer an alarm clock that allows you to adjust the time of your wake-up call! Unless they have been raised together from chicks, two roosters will fight literally to the death. They will also set each other off crowing *very* early in the morning.

Point-of-lay hens (hens that are ready to lay) are obviously the best to start with, as you can immediately start getting eggs from them as well. If your budget does not stretch to point-of-layers, however, geriatrics will do fine to establish the system. If you are lucky, some of them will go clucky and you can begin to breed up some good layers. Geriatrics from backyard flocks are often quite easy to come up with for free if you let it be known you are after them. If you start with chickens you will have to wait several months before they become vigorous enough scratchers to establish garden beds.

The best source for stock is a good backyard breeder, especially one who shows his or her birds. Most of these people breed as a hobby and have limited space. They keep only the best of each generation, and buying the second best from them is not as expensive as you might imagine, especially if they will be going to a good home. They keep their flocks healthy, and usually have space for them to scratch. Be careful not to buy birds that have been de-beaked or de-spurred, or that might be carriers of diseases.

Chooks learn to scratch from their mothers. It is not an inborn knowledge. If you get chooks like retired battery hens that have never had access to an area to scratch in, they will have to be taught how to do it. They will probably also have no social skills and will end up on the bottom of the pecking order if you mix them in with experienced chooks. Unless you fancy trying to show them how to scratch yourself, it is best to include *one* who knows how, and only one, as more will gang up and severely harass your poor retardees.

If you have to mix two established flocks, introduce them to each other just on dark as they are about to roost for the night. Make sure that they are roughly equal in fighting strength and keep an eye on them for a day or two until they get their social ranking sorted out. If you have to introduce new chooks to a flock, try to introduce three or four at a time. A single new hen introduced to an established flock will be picked on relentlessly, and occasionally even killed, in the first few days.

USING YOUR DOME

Place your dome on its position in your garden layout. If the ground is uneven, you may need to stake it down with tent pegs. Put the roof on and stake it down separately. Introduce a dozen or so chooks to it.

Throw the chooks all your household compostables, any compostables scavenged from the shopping centre, any wood ash, shellgrit or cuttlefish you have available, plus an armload of mulch every day or two. What they don't eat they will turn into compost.

When you are establishing a new bed, you will probably also have to provide some supplementary feed for the chooks. The grass and weeds in the dome are not a high-protein enough diet for them (although they will give a good vitamin A content and lovely orange colour to your eggs). If I have to buy feed, I use mixed grain or sprouted wheat. I feed them half a handful per chook twice a day, scattering it around the pen. They will scratch vigorously searching for the food. Do not use mash as it needs to be fed to them in a container, not scattered. By the second rotation over established beds, no bought feed will be necessary. You will be growing all the food needed.

Within a fortnight the area will be cleared of grass and weeds and covered with a thick layer of organic matter.

To move the pen, simply pull up the stakes that hold the tarp down, get inside the pen, and lift it by the roost a couple of inches off the ground. Walk with it to the next site in its rotation, put it down and restake the tarp. The chooks should move along with you. If you move them just before feeding time, any escapees can be lured back in with food.

Water the old site well. By the next day, if you lift up the mulch, you will find a thriving population of worms feeding on the litter. This bed is now ready for planting out.

7 COMPOST

Compost-making is very labour-intensive, so I try to avoid it. Chooks and earthworms are responsible for most of my compost-making. Nevertheless there are times when making compost is worth the effort.

WHY MAKE COMPOST?

1 To clear and fertilise areas where you aren't using a chook dome, or that you want to keep out of the chook dome rotation to allow for long-season crops. Well-made compost gets so hot that it 'burns' everything under it, clearing even couch or kikuyu grass. Native soil life can retreat down under the surface hot zone and survive. Enough nutrients leach down into the soil under a compost pile to feed them. The area *under* a compost pile is a very fertile, cleared planting bed – too good to waste by just putting another compost pile on it!

2 To give an initial quick boost to the population of soil micro-organisms when you are first establishing. Using compost to plant out, at least the first time, seeds your garden beds with starter cultures of micro-organisms.

3 To feed earthworms – under the compost pile site itself, in the beds where compost is used to plant out, and in worm farms. One of my big uses for compost is to feed a worm farm: to get worm castings to use in seedling-raising and potting mixes, and worms to put back out into the garden and to feed to the chooks.

4 To use, along with the worm castings, in making seedling-raising and potting mixes. Combined with river sand, compost makes a seedling-raising mix that has the right texture, water-retaining and drainage qualities, and that is nutrient-rich enough to give seedlings and cuttings a good start in life.

5 To top up the nutrient levels in the garden when you are planting a heavy feeder following another heavy feeder. I try to use rotations that avoid this, but if, for example, I want to interplant some lettuces in a bed that has just had corn, I give each seedling a double handful of compost when planting it out.
6 To incorporate organic matter that is not suitable for feeding to chooks. Seaweed is too valuable a source of trace elements just to add to the chook mulch. The chooks don't eat it, and it is such a rich source of nutrients that are essential but needed only in minute amounts that it needs to be thoroughly diluted and carefully rationed! Roadkills are an excellent source of blood and bone, but I'm too squeamish to feed them to chooks. I also like using large quantities of comfrey, which has alkaloids in it that might be dangerous to the chooks in too large a quantity. All these ingredients, though, go very well in compost, and provide a bit of extra variety in nutrients.

I make six compost piles per mandala per year, most of them in the spring and summer when they mature faster. In a seven-mandala system, this adds up to almost two a week throughout these seasons. After the initial establishment phase, however, they can be made by the 'Easy Method', which cuts the labour drastically. In a one-mandala system, you only need to make compost once every couple of months. The chooks and the worms will be making the rest for you, twenty-four hours a day, every day. If you are worm farming on a large scale, you will need to make compost only to initially establish your garden.

There is a bewildering array of theories on compost-making, and plenty of material on the science of compost. These are a useful basis for designing your own experiments, but can be quite mystifying initially. Over the years, by trial and error, I have developed a formula that uses readily available ingredients, produces large quantities without an uneconomical workload, and is ready for use within three weeks. It is like a no-fail bread recipe: it works every time!

JUST ENOUGH SCIENCE TO GET YOU BY

Compost is a *living* culture, like yoghurt or sourdough. It is a colony of micro-organisms that convert organic matter into humic acid, locking up the nutrients in very large molecules that are not readily water-soluble. This means that they don't get leached out of your soil as soluble fertilisers do, and the nutrients are not 'force-fed' to plants as they take in water. Plants can absorb and digest these nutrients with their feeder roots, taking just what they need for healthy growth.

Making compost is a process of *cultivating these particular micro-organisms*. Think of it as keeping a pet, or rather, a large pile full of pets, all eating, drinking, breeding and dying. Like all pets, they need caring for. These specific micro-organisms need water, air, lots of carbon-rich food, not too much nitrogen-rich food, micronutrients, an acid environment and heat.

- The water comes from wetting down each layer of the pile when making and turning.
- The air comes from not compressing the pile, using some ingredients that are bulky and have air pockets, putting holes in the pile, turning it and not wetting it so much that it drowns.
- The carbon-rich food comes from plants, particularly dryish or woody plant material like hay or raked leaves or lantana put through a mulcher.
- The nitrogen comes from green plant material (especially lawn clippings, comfrey, azolla or legumes) and from animal manure.
- The micronutrients come from mixing in as big a variety of materials as possible, including seaweed brew, waterweeds, herbs and weeds.
- The acid environment happens of its own accord provided you do *not* add lime, dolomite or wood ash to the pile. If you have wood ash, mix it with your mature compost, or better yet, just give it to the chooks to scratch around as they dust-bathe in it.
- The heat is generated by the compost micro-organisms themselves. Your role is to help them *conserve* it. Heat conservation comes from having the minimum surface area, and the geometrical shape that does this best is a sphere. (Remember your high school geometry?) Gravity is a bit of a problem for spherical compost piles, but a hemisphere or dome is close enough.

RECIPE NO. 1: MAKING COMPOST FROM SCRATCH

INGREDIENTS

- One trailerload of fresh green mulch *or* half a trailerload of waterweed *or* several bins of vegetable and fruit wastes, *or* a combination of all three
- One trailerload of dry or woody mulch or hay
- Three to five bags of manure
- Seaweed brew (optional)

NOTES ON INGREDIENTS

Green mulch The weedier the better, although just lawn clippings will do if they are fresh and green. The perfect material to mow is about 10 to 20 cm tall green grass with lots of soft-stemmed meadow weeds like wild cotton, wild strawberries, clover, dandelions, dock and nettles. Make yourself the curator of a local playing field or vacant lot.

Waterweeds One of the quickest, least labour-intensive ways of getting large quantities of compost material is harvesting waterweeds from creeks and pools. Watercress, azolla, water thyme, pondweed, water hyacinth and duckweed are some of the weeds that grow rampantly in watercourses, ponds and dams, especially those that are being polluted with the run-off from other people's soluble fertiliser use. They are relatively easy to collect, and are rich in nutrients. If you have easy access to a very concentrated source of varied waterweed, you can substitute them for all or some of the green mulch required, and be doing your bit for cleaning up the waterways at the same time. Azolla is particularly valuable, as it forms a symbiotic relationship with a kind of bacteria that fixes nitrogen from the air. Azolla is the reddish flowerets you see floating in dense mats in many weirs, dams and slow-moving streams. In Vietnam it is cultivated in rice paddies to add to fertility and increase yield. If you have easy access to a rich source of azolla you can use it to substitute for both the manure *and* the green mulch requirements.

Vegetable and fruit wastes You cannot make good compost with just household vegetable wastes. You simply cannot accumulate enough all at once. But if there is not enough mowing to be done and there are no nutrient-polluted waterways in your vicinity, then you probably live in the inner city. Somewhere within easy travelling distance there is bound to be a fruit and vegie shop, restaurant, institution or simply enough neighbours to get several bins full of food scraps at once. Making compost with these scraps is, however, the least labour-efficient way of processing this kind of material. If this is your source, use it to make compost only when you absolutely have to. It is much better used to feed your chooks or your worms.

Hay The perfect material to mow for this is thick, old, ungrazed kikuyu. This is not critical, however, and you can substitute a number of materials: raked leaves (if you have a very concentrated source), woody weeds (like lantana), kangaroo or bladey grass (chopped), or as a last resort bought bales of spoiled hay from a chemical-free source. If you have a mulcher, almost any material that will go through it will do. This ingredient has two roles: it is a source of carbon to feed the micro-organisms making the compost, and it creates air pockets in the pile for them to breathe. To be easily accessible as food, it needs to have a large surface area – which means it must be chopped into small pieces. But to trap air efficiently it needs to have air spaces between the pieces – which means largish pieces. Look for a compromise between the two.

Manure The easiest-to-obtain material in rural areas is about five bags of dried cow pats collected by hand, then mowed to a fine powder. To do this, spread the cow pats out on some short grass, preferably an area soon to become garden. Remove any rocks or other obstructions, and set the mower to the second-lowest height setting. With the grass-catcher on, mow over the pats. Your grass-catcher will fill with manure minced to the texture of shredded coconut.

This is so easy that a concentrated source of cow pats somewhere within easy range is worth hunting down. But you can substitute any herbivorous animal manure. You need similar quantities of goat or sheep manure, but horse manure is much 'hotter' – that is, nitrogen-rich – and you will need to use less (only about three bags). Racecourses or racing stables are good city sources.

The best urban source of manure I have found was during a holiday in Melbourne. A derelict house next door had been used as a roosting place for all the local pigeons, and there were enormous piles of droppings. That, combined with the proximity of St Kilda Beach with all its seaweed, made starting a garden irresistible, even on holiday!

If you don't have access to manure, you can substitute a plant material that is very high in nitrogen. Chopped comfrey, azolla or any legume will work, but even a small amount of animal manure is better than none.

Seaweed brew Although seaweed is not absolutely essential, who would want to avoid the task of spending a day or two at the beach? I wander back to camp from beach walks dragging strands of kelp behind me like Linus and his blanket. Seaweed is too valuable and rich in micronutrients to put straight into compost. I fill a large bin with it, cover it with water, and let it sit for at least a couple of weeks. Then I use bucketfuls of the liquid to wet down the compost. I top up the bin with water, and let it brew again for the next compost pile. One bin of seaweed will, unfortunately, serve at least a dozen compost piles used like this. Perhaps I should think of a less efficient way of using it! I keep a bin of seaweed on the brew all the time, simply refreshing it with each trip to the beach. Occasionally I add some other ingredients to it, particularly herbs.

METHOD

You can use either of the following methods to build your compost pile.

The Lasagne Method Lay a base of dry material about 1 to 1.5 m across and 15 cm high on the designated site. Cover it with a layer about 3 cm thick of manure, and 'fluff' this into the dry mulch. Wet the pile down until quite damp, but not until water starts to run out the bottom. Cover with about 10 cm of green mulch, then a layer of waterweed if you have it. If you have seaweed brew, throw a bucketful over. Repeat these steps until you run out of ingredients, finishing off with a layer of dry material. See Figure 17 for an illustration of a compost pile built using this method.

The Bolognaise Method Lay the base. Put the other materials in batches in a trailer. Mix and wet them well, and turn them out onto the base with a pitchfork.

Whichever method you use, the idea is to have the maximum internal area for the minimum surface area, so try to keep the sides of the pile rising as vertically as possible. Aim to end up with a dome shape, not a pyramid or cone. Keep sprinkling the pile until it is as wet as possible without water running through and out.

Don't stand on or tamp down your pile; keep it as light and airy as possible. When you have finished, from the top but without standing on the pile shove a crowbar or stake into the middle of it two or three times to create air holes. If the weather is hot and dry, it might pay either to sprinkle your pile with water every day or two, or to cover it with old hessian bags. D*on't* cover it with plastic – your pets need to breathe.

In a matter of hours your pile should start generating heat. Within twenty-four hours, it should be too hot to put your hand in the middle comfortably. It should be turned the first time five to seven days after building, by which time it should be filled with greyish-white tendrils. This is the fungus that starts off the composting process. The spot where the pile was will be clear of grass and weeds and well fertilised. Steal an armload of mulch from the nearest chook dome for it, and the spot is ready to plant out.

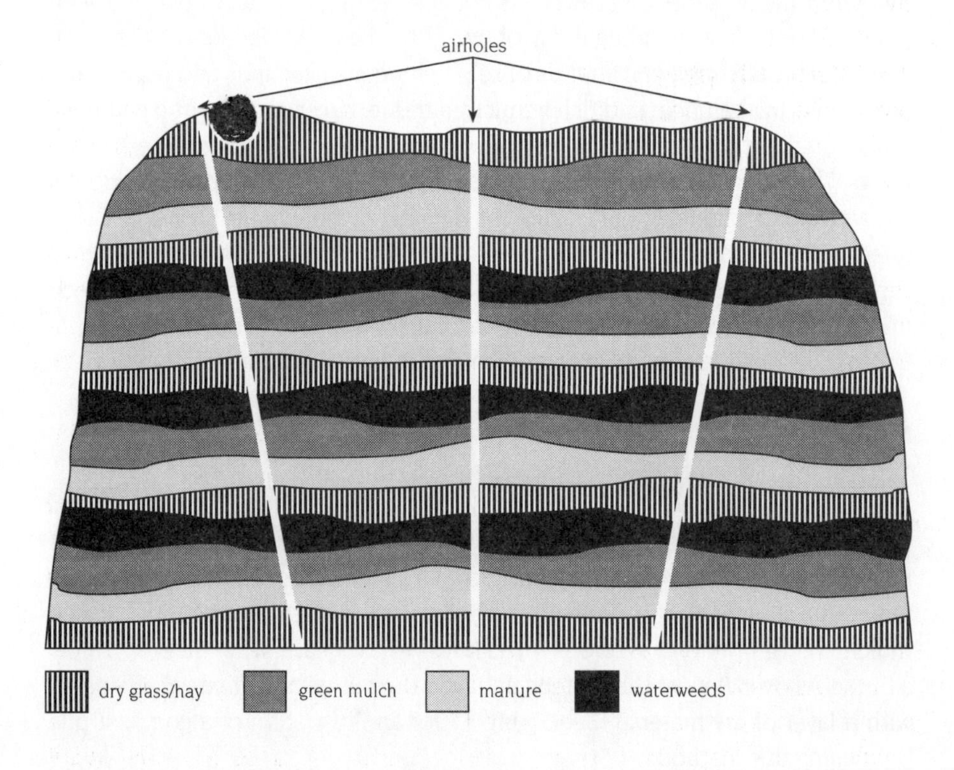

Figure 17 Design for a layered compost pile.

The pile should be turned the second time at ten to twelve days, by which time the greyish-white should be giving way to a humus-like brown. By this time the fungus has been overtaken by a kind of bacteria, called thermophilic bacteria, that especially like the hot conditions. This second site also needs only some mulch to be ready for planting.

By the third turning, at fifteen to seventeen days, the pile should be almost all brown and beginning to develop a characteristic crumbly texture.

A pitchfork is a good implement for turning. Break up any clods, incorporate as much air as possible, sprinkle with water as necessary to keep it as wet as a sponge, and move the outside to the inside as much as you can. By about the twenty-first day the pile should be cooling down and beginning to be invaded by larger creatures like earthworms and beetles. It is now ready to use.

Accumulation of all the ingredients for a compost pile should take you no more than four hours, including travelling time. If it takes more you will have to audit your system, finding more concentrated and/or handier sources. Building and turning should take no more than an hour each, making a total of four hours. The grand total equals eight hours per ready-to-use pile. This is a heavy investment of time, but at least in the establishment phase it is justifiable.

TROUBLESHOOTING

If your pile fails to generate heat within twenty-four hours, pull it apart and build it again. If it hasn't started heating up by then it never will, and although it will gradually rot down, it will take a very long time and a lot of nutrients will be lost to the air in the process.

Failure to heat up means that the necessary micro-organisms have scorned the living arrangements and/or diet you have provided and failed to take up residence. Why? Ask yourself these questions:

- Is the pile too wet or has it matted down so much that there is not enough air in it?
- Are there too many bulky ingredients, and the weather has been hot and dry, so the pile has dried out and there is not enough water?
- Is the pile too small, so it has too much surface area in relation to its internal area and is shedding heat too fast?
- Are there too few nitrogen-rich ingredients, so the microbes are being offered a diet that is like dry bread without any butter?
- Are the layers too thick, so the microbes are being offered a diet of carbon or nitrogen in different places, but not both at once? Neither the bread nor the butter is very enticing on its own.

Turning the pile to incorporate more air and mix it up, sprinkling it with water if necessary, and adding some more green mulch and/or manure to boost the nitrogen levels are the most likely cures. But if none of these seems to be the problem, there are two other possibilities. There is an outside chance that lack of a starter culture of bacteria is the problem. This is unlikely, especially if you are using some animal manure. It has never happened to me yet, but if you suspect it, add a few shovelfuls of rich soil to the heap as you reconstruct it.

There is also a possibility that some ingredient was contaminated with an antibiotic or general biocide. Could your manure be coming from animals that have been treated with veterinary drugs? Could your plant ingredients have been recently sprayed?

If your pile is hot (even very hot) but smells of ammonia when you turn it, it means it is releasing nitrogen into the air. If all else looks fine, this probably just means an overabundance of nitrogen-rich ingredients. The micro-organisms can't use all this nitrogen, so they are shedding some to the air. This is not a serious problem except for the smell. It just means that you have wasted some effort collecting all those nitrogen-rich ingredients! Ignore it for now, but next time increase the ratio of dry grass or woody material so that they have something to combine the nitrogen with to save it.

If all else is not fine, particularly if you have mats of material that are retaining their original colour, it means that you are breeding anaerobic bacteria instead of aerobic ones. Anaerobic bacteria are used in some composting systems but I consider them very inferior as garden fertiliser manufacturers. If you are growing vegetables, your garden will need to be too well drained for them, so they will not survive to go on to make sheet compost for you. They need liming or they will make compost that is too acid even for themselves. They use a lot of nitrogen, which is the scarcest resource, and they create too many unpleasant smells. Not enough air is the most likely cause for their occupation of your heap. Turning it to incorporate more air and break up compaction is the most likely cure. Next time, increase the quantity of dry or woody material a little or supply it in bigger, bulkier pieces. Try to keep the pile looser.

If your heap is very dry when you turn it, it probably means that it has too much surface area and so is losing moisture and heat too rapidly. The larger your pile, the smaller the ratio of surface area to internal volume. So it may be that your pile is just too small. The most likely problem, however, is that the shape is wrong. Sprinkle it thoroughly with water and rebuild it, aiming for a dome shape. If it was a dome-ish shape originally, and large enough, you may have to resort to covering it with old hessian sacks to conserve heat and moisture. *Don't use plastic to cover it.*

RECIPE NO. 2: THE EASY WAY

This is the method I use for most of the compost I make.

INGREDIENTS

- One or two trailerloads of scratched, manured mulch from a chook dome
- One or two bags of other manure *or* a good armload of comfrey, *or* a combination of both*
- Seaweed brew if available

---

* If there was plenty of azolla or legumes or fruit or animal material or other nitrogen-rich ingredients added to the chook mulch, this ingredient can be reduced or even omitted.

METHOD

Increase the amount of mulch you throw to the chooks to about two or three trailerloads. Move them on a few days early and off a few days late, so they get an extra week or so to process it. Set aside a site for a compost pile on a garden bed next to the chook dome. As soon as the chooks are moved to their next position, rake out about half the mulch, leaving the rest spread over the bed.

Layer this with the other ingredients, wetting down each layer, as in the Lasagne Method. Turn the compost pile once at Day Seven. Investigate it at Day Fourteen, and if it seems to need it, turn it again. It should, however, require only the one turning since it has already been turned several times by the chooks. It will be ready to use by about Day Twenty. If you do not need to use it all immediately, check to see whether it is full of worms, and if not, add a handful from your worm farm. They will turn it into an even more concentrated fertiliser.

RECIPE NO. 3: THE EASIEST WAY

An ideal soil ecosystem is one big compost pile. This is what soil is like on the forest floor: a teeming mass of life busily making sure that not one iota of nutrients escapes from the system, and every life form trying its hardest to add extras from the air, water and subsoil.

But since there is no room for vegetables in a forest, you will not be starting your garden on this kind of soil! Most likely you will be starting with soil that is all but dead – an inert conglomeration of only the hardiest elements, and even those disappearing before your eyes. The object of compost-making is to start up on this kind of sterile soil the same process that happens on the forest floor of its own accord.

Once you have established a healthy population of soil biota, though, you can leave most of the compost-making entirely to them, only bothering to do it yourself for special purposes. This is called **sheet composting**, and basically means treating your entire garden like a giant compost pile in progress. You can add a relatively thin layer to any part and let the resident co-workers do the rest.

To sheet compost successfully you need first to ensure that there are enough soil organisms of sufficient variety to self-regulate: bacteria, fungi, worms, insects and vertebrates. You need to ensure that there is just enough moisture to maintain this population, and to keep your crop plants from wilting, but no more – not enough to drown them or to leach away nutrients. Equally importantly, you need to ensure that there is enough oxygen. The only way to keep both enough moisture and enough oxygen is to use a thick mulch cover. This maintains a constant moisture level and minimises watering. Saturating soil has exactly the same result as saturating a compost pile. It kills off all the aerobic life, creating a niche suitable only for anaerobic organisms. If the soil then dries out again, the anaerobic life will die too – a very quick way to create dead soil.

You need to make sure that there is a net gain, or at least a constant level of basic elements supplied for them to work with. This means keeping the soil covered with living things, particularly at least *some* deep-rooted perennials to mine subsoil minerals. Solar energy is the main source of energy for this work of soil production, and plants are the only things capable of capturing solar energy. Any time your soil spends unplanted is wasting solar energy that could have been capturing elements from the air to replace those constantly being lost to the air. Bare fallow periods are soil vandalism.

It also means cycling back the elements you remove, returning all 'wastes' to the soil. This principle is a bit difficult in practice. You will have trouble getting back the outside leaves of the cabbage you sell, let alone the sewage and the dead body of the person who eats it! In practice this means replacing equivalent value in elements, but the most economical source is still what is normally called 'waste'. The object is to mimic the kind of ratios in 'waste' you would find on a forest floor – lots of carbon-rich leaves, twigs and dead plant material, some green plant material and fruits, a small, well-scattered quantity of animal manures, and the odd dead body.

It also means avoiding, at all costs, doing *anything* that might kill off the underground life that is making compost for you. Before you do anything in the garden, you should consider whether you would do it to a compost pile. Would you spray fungicide (even organic fungicide) on your compost? Would you light a fire on it? Would you saturate it or allow it to dry right out? Would you pour concentrated salts on it or spread it out exposed to the sun and air?

Pesticides, burning, cultivation, overwatering and even soluble fertilisers are all grounds for divorce of the partnership. Unless you actually *like* making and turning compost piles, it is wise to respect the relationship!

8 WORM FARMING

Worms ain't worms. There are probably hundreds, maybe even thousands, of different kinds. I have identified at least four different types in my garden. Among them are imported red manure worms (*Lumbricus rubellus*), and several different species of native earthworms. The latter have a thriving, healthy population in the garden, and the only thing I do with them is worry if I don't find several in every forkful. They do not breed well in captivity, but seem to do fine free-ranging provided there is enough mulch, organic matter and moisture.

The main work these native worms do in the garden is tilling and aerating the soil. They burrow very deep, leaving channels through the soil that break up clods and allow air to enter and water to penetrate and drain away. In the process of eating at the surface and eliminating lower down, they introduce organic matter to the deeper levels and steadily increase the depth of topsoil.

Unlike mechanical tillers, earthworms do not damage the soil by inverting it, creating hardpans or breaking up the crumb structure. They never have mechanical breakdowns, they do not create noise or pollution, and they use garbage for fuel. There are enough of them do this work at a pace I couldn't match with even the biggest machine.

The red manure worms were initially introduced into my garden as a starter population of 1000 bought by mail order from a worm breeder. They are now very widespread. They seem to congregate wherever there is fairly raw organic matter. If I lift up the mulch where a chook dome has been, even a day or two after moving it, I will find literally thousands of these worms feeding on the mulch. Their main role is to digest decomposing organic matter, converting it quickly into a form plants can use as nutrients. Red manure worms breed very quickly in captivity, doubling their numbers every month or so. Besides the millions of them that free-range in the garden, I keep a tub of them as breeding stock. They provide starter populations for any new areas, high-protein chook food, and worm castings to use as high-value fertiliser.

Worms make wonderful pets. They don't need elaborate housing, they create no smells or noise, they harbour no vermin and they don't bite or sting. No-one will get upset about escapees, and they are easily protected from predators. They have a high dietary requirement for calcium so they need some lime or dolomite added to their food, but other than that they need only feeding.

Red manure worms are not too fussy about their diet and will eat anything that was once living. They particularly like rotting potatoes, pumpkin, green vegetables and low-acid fruit like pears or bananas. They also relish manure and compost and don't mind a bit of wet shredded paper or cardboard. They are not too keen on meat, or very acid fruit like citrus or pineapples, or onions or garlic, but will cope with them so long as they are mixed with other more desirable food.

Each worm will eat its own body weight per day. A thousand worms weigh about a kilo when they are full-grown, at about three months old. They will breed up to a million or more within a year, and be capable of munching their way through nearly a tonne of garbage every day. This same kind of garbage is also suitable as a compost ingredient or as chook food. However, compost bacteria like it mixed with at least an equal quantity of high-carbon food like hay, and processing it through chooks may not be acceptable in some neighbourhoods. If the waste that is most accessible to you is more suited to worm food than to chook or compost bacteria food, you should consider a large-scale, well-designed worm farm as your main fertiliser factory.

Since I live in a rural area where food wastes are not overabundant, and I use chooks as my primary processors, I farm worms only on a small scale. But Stephanie is an inner-city gardener. She has virtually unlimited access to food scraps but hay is hard to get. She farms worms on a large scale and dispenses with chooks and compost.

PATIO WORM FARMING

A pair of old concrete laundry tubs in a shady spot is a good home for a worm farm. Right next to your kitchen door will be the most convenient spot for feeding them, and near your propagating area will be the most convenient for using the product. If you have followed the proximity rule, these two locations will be very close together!

Leave the plug out and put a strainer in the hole so that any excess water can drain out. Fill the first tub with compost into which is mixed a scant handful of dolomite or agricultural lime and maybe half a bucketful of soil. Put a bucket under the plughole, and water this mix with a fine spray until it is quite saturated and starting to drip into your bucket.

Tip in your starter population and cover the surface with an old hessian sack, wet cardboard or something similar. There are lots of professional worm breeders around who will sell you a tub of 500 to 1000 worms to start with. They will fit in a container somewhere between the size of a margarine and an ice-cream tub, and can be sent through the mail. Check the yellow pages, keep an eye out for advertisements, or ask at your local garden supply store. Any close-fitting solid lid on your farm will suffocate your worms. But you may like to fit a fly-mesh or shadecloth-screened lid to keep fruit flies out.

For the first month you need do nothing except make sure the farm is kept quite moist but not awash. If your farm is exposed to rain, make sure the plug is left out or your worms will drown. The compost itself will feed the worms for quite a long time, but to get maximum breeding it is best to add some supplementary feed every few days, especially as the population starts to increase. Add a scant dessertspoonful of lime or dolomite to each kilo of food. I like to vary the feed, rotating between:

- A bucket half-filled with water and cow or horse manure, mixed to a slop and poured over the surface.
- A blender filled with household scraps, excluding citrus peels, blended to a slop and poured over the surface.
- Rotten potatoes, pumpkin or fruit, just placed on the surface.
- Half a bucketful of new compost, spread over the surface.

Because worms court by blundering into each other, and because the numbers increase by geometric progression, the population will seem to increase more and more rapidly. Within a few months the tub should be filled with a writhing mass of worms, and it is time to colonise the second tub.

Half-fill the second tub with the same mixture of compost, lime and soil. Put a strainer in the plughole, and water the mixture until saturated. Burrow down to the plughole in the first tub, and put the plug in. Now set a hose to *just* dribbling into the first tub until it is half-full, being very careful not to forget it and fill it right up. Leave the hessian on top to exclude light. The worms will all migrate into the top half to avoid drowning. Scoop them out and, reserving some to put into the garden, transfer them to the second tub. Let the plug out of the first tub and drain it into a bucket. What you are left with is a bucket full of very, very rich liquid fertiliser, and a tub half-full of worm castings.

Alternatively, you can expose your farm to some strong light for an hour or so. Most of the worms will move down to avoid the light. You can scoop out the top layer to use in the garden, and transfer the bottom layer, where most of the worms are, to the second tub.

From now on you should be able to repeat this process every month, transferring about a third of the worms out into the garden (or feeding them to the chooks) each time.

MULTIMILLION WORM FARMING

Multimillion worm farming is just patio worm farming on a larger scale. You may even wish to start with a patio farm to breed up your stock and establish your big farm when the family needs to move into larger digs. You can keep your patio farm for convenient disposal of household garbage.

Design will depend very much on your circumstances. The essential features are accommodation, drainage, dark, screening and food.

ACCOMMODATION

You will need a box, pit or pile of mature compost to accommodate your worms. It will be most convenient and breeding will be fastest if they are all in one home than if they are in multiple smaller homes. Stephanie had a concrete block retaining wall across the top of her garden. This became the back wall of her farm. A house demolition down the road yielded some 3 metre concrete pillars that were laid on their sides and stacked four high to make a front wall. The same demolition provided old bricks to build end walls. The result was a concrete-and-brick trough 3 metres long and just over 1 metre wide. This took several compost piles to fill, but the compost heat was needed to clear her garden beds anyhow.

DRAINAGE

Although worms need to be kept quite wet, they will drown if their home is flooded and emigrate if it contains stagnant water. Stephanie's worm farm is built straight onto the ground, with a piece of agricultural pipe running the length of it and out through an end wall. The pipe is covered with broken brick, from the same demolition, and leads into a patch of banana trees surrounded with comfrey. The bananas appreciate the extra moisture and fertiliser, and the comfrey is harvested to feed back to the worms. In dry weather the farm can be hosed down, in wet weather it can be left exposed, and the worms' food bins can be hosed out without fear of drowning them. The worms could escape by burrowing down, but they actually like crowded conditions, since blind dates by chance encounter are their usual pick-up technique!

DARK

Worms have light-sensing organs in their skin, and will avoid even artificial light if possible. They will go to great lengths to avoid sunlight, since exposure to ultraviolet will kill them. They cannot surface to feed if their food is sitting in the sun. Stephanie covers her worm farm with a layer of wet cardboard from old boxes, obtained from the same fruit shop as the bulk of her worm food. She simply tips the next day's food on top of the cardboard, and covers it with another layer. The worms munch their way through yesterday's wet cardboard to get to the food.

SCREENING

House flies do not normally breed in a worm farm. Fruit flies, however, can become a nuisance, and open farms can attract mice and both fruit-eating and worm-eating birds. Stephanie has two old aluminium-framed security screen doors on top of her farm. She opens one door to feed them each time, alternating between ends. When she wants to remove castings for use in the garden, she simply feeds them at one end for a few days. The majority of the worms move to that end, allowing her to remove castings without taking too many worms with them.

FOOD

Within a year 1000 worms will breed up enough to fill a worm farm the size of Stephanie's and be capable of turning a tonne of garbage a day into fertiliser. If a tonne seems like a ridiculous quantity, don't despair. You can always move some out to free-range in the garden, and they will self-regulate their population so long as there is a fairly consistent quantity of food supplied.

However, if you are worm farming at this scale and gardening without chooks or compost, your household garbage will not be enough to feed them, or supply your garden with fertiliser. Feeding the worms will be your major routine garden task. You should use your designing skills to make all garden tasks, but especially routine ones, as painless and as much fun as possible.

Think carefully about what bulk food sources might be accessible to you without much extra travelling or effort. Site your worm farm so that it is easily accessible and if possible so that gravity will help you feed them. Whatever your worm feed, add agricultural lime to it, at the rate of about a cupful per bin, sprinkled over the food. Stephanie has four sources:

1. Her own and her neighbours' household garbage. She has a small plastic rubbish bin that lives next to her front gate, where the neighbours are invited to empty any household waste of organic origin. The yield is about half a binful each day. The worm farm is on a lower level, at the bottom of a path leading from the front gate. It is a simple matter to trolley the bin down the path and empty it over the end into the farm. Gravity is conscripted to help.
2. The shop at the corner. Twice a week, on her way to work, Stephanie takes her wheelie bin with her for a walk, one block up to the bus stop in front of the corner fruit shop and snack bar. In the afternoon it takes her for a walk one block down the hill and down the path. It is usually about half-full of unsaleable fruit and vegetable wastes and half-eaten hamburgers with chips,

and includes some folded-down cardboard boxes on top. Over the end into the farm, a quick hose down to clean it out and wet the boxes, and the bin is ready for the next journey.

3 Her daughter's preschool. A bucketful of fruit and lunch scraps comes home with her every day, and a bucket of worm castings goes to the preschool garden every month or so. The kids feel quite proud to be doing their bit for the environment.

4 Her own garden. All the garden wastes, tree prunings, comfrey, herbs and spent vegetables are put through a small electric mulcher and fed to the worms.

Altogether these four sources require no extra travelling, very little time or effort, and no expense to obtain several hundred kilos of worm food. Feeding the worms is relegated to the second major routine gardening task: picking dinner takes longer.

PART THREE

PLANTING

9 RAISING SEEDLINGS

Just as an egg does not need feeding for the embryonic chick to grow and hatch, a seed does not need feeding to germinate. Seeds carry their own nutrient needs, enough to germinate and to put out the first leaves and roots. Seeds do not need to be planted in fertile soil.

However, just as an egg needs the perfect amount of warmth – too much and it will cook, too little and it will die – a seed needs the perfect level of moisture. Too much and it will rot, too little and it will either fail to germinate at all, or die straight away. Seeds need to be planted in a medium that is very well drained but able to hold just the right amount of moisture. At the same time, they need to be able to reach light as quickly after germinating as a chick needs to reach air after hatching. So they need to be covered with *just twice their own diameter*, no more, of a medium that is fine and soft enough for the tiny, fragile shoots to penetrate.

It is obvious from this that the perfect seed-raising medium is very different to ordinary garden soil. But seeds need only a very small amount of it. Ten lettuce seedlings will germinate and put out their first leaves in just 50 cubic cm – a small bowlful – of this kind of medium. Yet the conventional technique is to laboriously work a third of a cubic metre of garden soil to the degree of fineness required to raise seeds in – over 6000 times the amount actually needed! Not only is this in itself a colossal waste of energy, it also creates even more work further down the track. You set yourself up for a continuing program of extra soil replenishment, fertilising, weeding, watering and pest control.

Soil worked to a fine tilth (friability) is very vulnerable to oxidation. Many of the nutrients you have worked so hard to supply will disappear into the air. It is also very vulnerable to physical erosion. Watch the impact of a summer storm on a patch of soil worked to a seed-raising tilth. First the wind picks up dust and carries it away in tiny whirligigs. Then the first raindrops hit, leaving little craters and breaking the soil crumbs up into minute particles. Raindrops hit surprisingly hard! Pretty soon muddy puddles and rivulets form, washing soil away. If you go out and dig after the rain, you will be surprised at how shallowly the rain has penetrated, especially if you compare it to a plant-covered patch. There are no channels left by decomposing plant roots, and the lack of shade means that earthworms have not surfaced and left their channels. Those tiny particles broken up by the raindrops have washed into the air gaps between soil crumbs, creating little dams and blocking the water penetration.

Without a mulch layer, the surface water will evaporate almost immediately. The sun will sterilise the top few centimetres, killing much of the microlife that was making, preserving and digesting soil for you.

Soil worked to a seed-raising tilth is suitable for germinating not just crop plant seeds, but also weed seeds. Weeds invade the open areas between seedlings and choke them out, which means more work weeding. Seedlings exposed to full sun need daily (and in summer even twice daily) watering. Most of the water is not going to the seedlings but to the spaces and weeds between them – which is a waste of both water and the work of watering.

Your tiny seedlings just emerging are also at their most vulnerable. Slugs and snails can munch all day on a half-grown lettuce and only be fattening themselves up for the chooks with negligible damage to the lettuce. But they can make tiny seedlings completely disappear overnight. Mature plants, and even adolescents, are much better than infants at defending themselves. If your seedlings can be protected, there is a whole host of otherwise troublesome pests that can safely be ignored.

I solve all these problems by planting most things out into the garden as fairly advanced seedlings. This means:

- I can build just enough seed-raising medium to raise seeds in. I don't have to turn the entire garden into a seed bed.
- I can keep everything that needs daily attention concentrated in one small area. Most days the only work I do in the rest of the garden is picking. If I'm in a hurry, the only area I need to visit at all is the seed-raising area.
- I can leave the decomposing roots of spent plants, and the channels left by earthworms, undisturbed. When they are not destroyed by tilling, these channels allow rain to penetrate deeply and be stored in the soil. Combined with the shade and mulch, this bank of water stored in the soil reduces the need for watering. Most months, if there is even a sprinkle of rain, I will only need to water the seedlings in trays and pots and when they are first planted out.
- I can keep the garden soil pretty well covered, both above and below ground, with growing things most of the time. This keeps the soil shaded, alive, and bound by roots to avoid losing or damaging it.

- I can keep faith with my microscopic co-workers by leaving them undisturbed, so they can get on with fertilising the soil for me.
- I can choose only the strongest seedlings for planting out, so I don't waste garden space and work on plants that will never bear an edible or saleable crop.
- I can avoid overreacting to pests.
- I can construct guilds, or companion groupings, of dissimilar plants, placing each plant individually.

Planting out advanced seedlings is a major strategy of labour economy. Working your whole garden to a tilth fine enough for seed-raising is an enormous amount of unnecessary and destructive hard work. I plant very few things directly into the garden as seed. Most are raised in a propagation area and planted out as very advanced seedlings.

I also never, or at least very rarely, buy seedlings. I do all my own propagation, from seed or from cuttings. Seeds come in a much wider range of varieties than seedlings, so you have a much better chance of choosing or fluking a variety that is right for your situation. If you save your own seed, you can even create new varieties, tailor-made for your own garden. Seeds are very cheap compared to seedlings, even counting the time and resources it takes to raise them. Your own saved seed is even cheaper!

I very rarely even see seedlings that are tempting. Most are sold at a stage when they are already too big for the punnets they come in, and have already suffered some growth check by the time you get them. Their roots are all tangled together and cannot be separated without damage, and they have too much leaf to cope with the shock of a transplant with damaged roots. Those that survive will spend several weeks recovering, and some will never fully recover.

Bought seedlings can also harbour some insidious imports. They usually come in a fumigated seed-raising mix because there is a high risk of disease. If the fumigation is thorough your babies will be starting life with no bacterial friends. The chemicals that persist in the little bit of mix adhering to their roots can be enough to get them blackballed by your microscopic unionists. This will mean that they will also have to grow up without any bacterial friends. If the fumigation is not so thorough, you could be importing some very nasty, persistent and epidemic diseases. Propagation is also so easy that there is just no point in buying seedlings.

PROPAGATING SEEDS

I propagate most seeds in a shadehouse in shallow polystyrene boxes of home-made seed-raising mixture. This mixture has negligible nutrient value, but is the perfect *texture* for seed germination. A shadehouse can be any kind of structure, covered with shadecloth or shade-providing plants. A bench at working height saves your back. The shadehouse keeps the seed-raising boxes out of the direct sun and maintains the fairly constant moisture level that they need.

The seed-raising mixture I use is half medium-grade river sand, and half old dry cow pats mowed to a fine powder. Fine river sand or sharp builder's sand is not suitable. To make the mixture, spread the cow pats out on a patch of short grass and, with the mower set low and the grass-catcher on, mow over them, reducing them to the texture of shredded coconut. Mix 50/50 by volume with the sand. The sand gives drainage and prevents a crust forming on the surface. The mowed cow pats do the same job as peat moss in commercial potting mixes, absorbing and holding moisture. But they have two big advantages over peat moss – they are not mined from anywhere and they are free!

This mixture gets better and better with age. After you have potted seedlings on, you can plant another batch of seeds in the same mix, topping it up as necessary with extra sand and manure. Old cow pats are the only manure I have discovered that is really suitable. Fresh manure is too nitrogen-rich, and burns the seedlings. If you don't have access to cow pats, strained mature compost will do. And seed-propagating mixture is the one spot in the garden where worms are not welcome. Their castings make the mixture too puggy.

To plant the seeds, fill a shallow polystyrene box with holes in the bottom with the sand–manure mixture. Make sure it is level, or when you water it the seeds will be washed down into one corner. Water the mixture well and pat it down to a smooth surface. Scatter the seed finely, pat it down, and cover with a *thin* layer of mixture. Seeds should be covered to a depth no more than twice their own diameter, and with small seeds this is the most difficult part.

Water with a fine spray and label the box with the variety and the date. I use a triangle cut out of a plastic yoghurt or margarine container and a waterproof marking pen. Don't forget to note in your diary what varieties you planted and when. Otherwise you will have Buckley's chance of remembering, in several months when they mature, what they were. If I am using bought seed I usually staple the packet into my diary.

Keep the seed trays in a shady spot and don't let them dry out. With very fine seed in summer I lay a piece of an old sheet over the top of the box until the seedlings first appear. This helps them stay moist but still lets through enough light so the seedling knows which way is up!

If you have trouble with damping-off, use a tea of comfrey, horsetail, stinging nettle or chamomile, or a combination of these, instead of plain water, to germinate seeds. Damping-off is a fungus that causes newly germinated seedlings to rot off at the base, but it is usually only a problem if moisture levels are allowed to fluctuate too much.

I try always to plant seed on the right days by the lunar calendar. By trial and error I have found that it really does make a difference to the germination rate and to the strength and vigour of the plants.

RAISING SEEDLINGS

As soon as the seedlings begin to show their second pair of leaves (usually their first true leaves, the initial pair being part of the seed pod and shaped quite differently), I choose the strongest to transplant into pots full of a very nutrient-rich mixture. At this stage they are still very tiny – only 3 cm or so tall – and their root systems are still very undeveloped. Transplanting is easy and fast, and doesn't upset them at all. I keep the potted seedlings in a closely supervised, moderately sunny spot until they are about 15 cm tall, when I plant them out into their spot in the garden.

The pots I use are two-litre plastic milk containers with the top *and* the bottom cut out, leaving a squarish hollow cylinder about 15 cm tall and 10 cm across. They neatly divide a polystyrene box into twelve individual pots. Two-litre plastic soft drink bottles, with the top and bottom cut off, work fine too, although because they are round they don't divide the tray quite as neatly.

Seedling mixture is different to seed-raising mixture. At this stage the seedlings will have used up most of the nutrients stored in the seed, and they will need feeding, the more the better. But they still need a loose texture and very good drainage. The mix I use is one-third river sand, one-third worm castings, and one-third mature compost.

Fill a shallow polystyrene box with twelve cylinders and fill them with mixture. Make a good-sized hole in the centre of each pot with your finger. Water the seed tray well then carefully prick each seedling out and transfer it to a pot. 'Pricking out' is gardening jargon that just means lifting each seedling out without pulling on the stem or disturbing the others. A triangular piece cut out of the corner of a plastic container like a butter or an ice-cream container makes a good tool for pricking out. An ordinary kitchen fork also works quite well. Try to disturb the roots as little as possible in the process. Fill the hole back in so the seedling is planted at the same depth as it was before, lightly press the mixture in around it, and water it in.

Plan exactly how many of each kind of seedling you want to plant out, and pot out only about a third more than this, feeding the rest to the worm farm. It is important to be ruthless. There is no point spending time and energy raising seedlings that will never be planted out. But it is also important to allow some extras for non-survivors and so that you can again select only the strongest when it comes time to plant them out.

I try to do this job also on the correct lunar calendar date. This is not always possible, as it is more crucial not to let the seedlings get too big in the propagating tray. Otherwise they will be difficult to prick out without damaging the roots, and they will begin to run out of nutrients and starve. I do at least make sure that potting out is done on a fertile sign and, unless it is very cloudy, last thing of an afternoon. When seedlings suffer from transplanting, the main reason is that they lose moisture through their leaves at a rate faster than the disturbed roots can replace it. Transplanting last thing of an afternoon gives them the night to settle in.

You can save yourself carting later on if each tray contains a group of companions that will be planted out together. So I usually pot seedlings from several different seed trays into one seedling box. When it comes time to plant them out, I can carry one box to the bed and find all the companions I need together in it.

Some large seeds like corn and beans are such fast and reliable germinators that I can skip the first stage and plant them directly into seedling-raising pots. The trays of seedlings live on a bench in a spot that gets morning sun but no direct afternoon sun. They are more exposed than the seed trays, but still not in full direct sun. If you rig up an automatic watering system anywhere, this is the area to do it, as seedlings do not yet have extensive enough root systems to survive drying out.

PLANTING OUT

When the young plants are about 15 cm tall they are ready to plant out. A day or so before planting day, I move the boxes out into the garden and put them on or near the bed where they are to be planted. This gives them a chance to become acclimatised to the site.

Make a little burrow in the mulch and, using a small fork, dig a hole just big enough for the pot. Lift the seedling, pot and all, out of the tray and put it in the hole. This is when the reason for the bottomless pots becomes clear! They don't need to be up-ended to remove the seedling, and so there is almost no trauma in the transplant. When you are planting such advanced seedlings, this is important. Some never recover from a big shock at this stage. Others decide that they are mature enough already to make a run for reproduction, and prefer to bolt to seed rather than take any more risks. The pots can also double as a miniature fence around the new seedling, which gives it some protection against wind and pests while it settles in.

Slide the pot up so that only the bottom centimetre or so is in the ground. Pull the soil and mulch in around it and water well. Leave the pot in place as a fence for a few days.

PROPAGATING BY CUTTINGS

You can tell a fellow gardener from someone who is just showing polite interest by his or her passion for taking snips off almost anything that looks as if it might grow from a cutting! Many perennials, and most herbs, can be propagated by taking cuttings from a mature plant. Cuttings are clones, genetically identical to the parent plant, and in a similar environment will grow into a very similar plant. They are a very good way of obtaining plants that are well adapted to your local conditions. My lavender, grown from a cutting from a spectacularly healthy plant in a neighbour's garden, has done much better than the expensive bought seedling whose parents probably did wonderfully well in a very different locality.

Woody, soft-stem root and leaf cuttings are the most common kinds of cuttings, and some plants grow best, or will only grow, from a particular kind. However, cuttings take so little work that if you don't know what kind to take, take some of each and see which strikes! The same basic technique works for all of them. Use a sharp knife or secateurs, and trim off any parts that are damaged or bruised in the process. Bruised spots are vulnerable to fungus infections that will cause your cutting to rot before it is established enough to defend itself.

The cutting is most likely to send out new roots from the node where a leaf emerges from the stem, or from a leaf scar, where a leaf has grown and fallen off. Cut just below this node, so that it is the part that will be underground for the new plant. I don't know why, but cutting at a 45° angle seems to work best.

Loss of moisture by evaporation from leaves, before the new plant has roots to replace the moisture, is the single most likely reason for failure. To counter this, trim off most of the leaves from your cutting, and don't take too big a piece. In most cases a cutting around 7 cm is about right. Anything more than 10 cm is probably too long.

Try to get your cutting into a propagating mix as soon as possible. On roots and perennials planting days, I take a box of mix and my secateurs visiting with me! Whether it is planted or not, however, protect it from evaporation as immediately as you possibly can. At the very least, get your cuttings out of the sun and into a plastic bag very quickly. I slip my whole box into a plastic bag to transport it home.

Most cuttings can be stimulated to send out roots by dipping them in a rooting hormone. This is available in packets from any gardening centre, and the instructions are on the packet. But you can make your own for free, by steeping some cuttings from a willow in water for a few days, and dipping your cuttings in this solution. It is not really magic – willows are a rich source of hormones, and the merest whiff is enough to signal plants to send out new growth. I take a jar of this solution with me on cutting expeditions too.

Like seeds, cuttings don't need nutrients to strike. After all, without roots to feed, what use have they for food? But soil texture is critical. To persuade them to send out new roots, they need a mixture that is constantly moist, presents no challenge to newly emerging roots, and is very well drained. Seed-germinating mixture is ideal, and since they are not in any competition for light or nutrients, they can be placed very densely – just about wall-to-wall – in it. Don't poke your cutting into the mix, since this will bruise it. Use a pointed stick or a pen to make a hole, and plant it just deep enough to make it stand up.

Since cuttings are so vulnerable to drying out, I cover the whole box with a sheet of plastic supported by a frame fashioned out of old wire coat-hangers. I punch a few holes in the plastic to allow air exchange. The propagating tray lives in the shadehouse with the seed-germinating trays. Every week or so I inspect the tray, remove any cuttings that have clearly died, and prick out any that are showing signs of new growth. Death can be tricky to determine, since some cuttings just sit there for weeks looking all but dead, then surprise you by putting out a whole batch of new leaves at once.

The survivors are transplanted into pots full of a nutrient-rich seedling-raising mixture, with room to grow, and are moved out into the seedling-raising area where they get a bit more sun. Until their roots are well established, though, they are still very vulnerable to losing too much moisture through their leaves. Old plastic soft drink bottles make good mini-glasshouses. Cut them in half, punch a few holes in the bottom, and use both halves to cover cuttings in pots until they are well away.

Cuttings are planted out in exactly the same way as seedlings. Make a burrow in the mulch, dig a hole with a fork just big enough for the pot, put the plant in it, pull the soil and mulch in around it, and water.

Even if none of your cuttings take, cutting expeditions are a wonderful excuse for an in-depth guided tour of someone else's garden!

10 GUILD PLANTING

A guild is a group of individuals that associate for common benefit. The word comes from the name for coalitions of self-employed tradespeople in the days before trade unions. In permaculture, 'guild' is a jargon term that means a grouping of individual *different* kinds of plants.

Although it is jargon, 'guild planting' deserves a word of its own, because there is no existing word that quite covers the concepts it involves. Obviously it is different to the standard monocultures of farming, and gardening, where plants of the same kind are all grouped together, whether by the fieldful, or just by the metre-wide row. It goes further than just companion planting, as it combines the concepts of interplanting, catch-cropping and rotations as well. And it is not just a random assembly (although these kinds of accidental guilds often work very well!).

Ideally, a guild is a carefully constructed assembly of species that each contribute to the synergy of the whole, a bit like the way individual dabs of different colours add up to a painting.

Guild planting has lots of advantages:

1 **It gives maximum productivity.** You can only plant a certain number of, say, onions in a given area. If you try to plant more, they will starve each other and total yield will drop. But you can fit a whole planting of carrots in the same area at the same time. Onions have shallow surface roots whereas carrots have deep tap roots, so the two kinds of roots aren't competing. Carrots have feathery leaves and onions have straight tall leaves, so the two plants don't compete for light. Carrots fork and go all to leaf with little root if their diet is too rich. Onions are heavy feeders and take up all the extra nutrients. Onions deter carrot fly, and carrots deter onion fly. The association is of benefit to both crops, and it doubles your total yield.

2 **It makes pests work much harder for their supper.** Most pests are very species-specific. They only attack one kind of plant. Some recognise their dinner by the shape and colour of the leaves. A cauliflower silhouetted against bare ground is a prime target, whereas if it is set in among dill, celery, parsnips, turnips and beets, especially with a light overhang of leaves, it is very difficult for a cabbage moth to recognise. Some recognise their host by scent. Strong-smelling neighbours mask the scent and put these bloodhounds off the trail. Some go by a nibble and a taste, which can be a tiresome and risky procedure when the palatable is mixed up with the inedible. If nothing else, spreading similar plants around the garden makes their pests travel much further, and on the wing they are much more vulnerable to predators. It also means that you can afford to be philosophical about any disease or infestation that does occur. It is much less likely to spread, and even if you lose one tomato plant, you are unlikely to lose all of them – let alone your entire crop.

3 **Fast-growing plants can 'nursemaid' slower growers, and established plants can nursemaid seedlings.** Lettuces, cabbages and beets grow very quickly. Planted as fairly advanced seedlings, they will be in and out within six to eight weeks. If you plant them around your baby tomato plants, they will shade the soil and 'nursemaid' the tomato seedlings. By the time the tomatoes are big enough to provide their own shade and to need the space, the lettuces, cabbages and beets will be out. A new batch of seedlings can go in to replace them, nursemaided by the mature tomato plants. By the time *they* are needing the space, the tomatoes will have finished bearing and can come out. Besides providing very sheltered planting sites for babies, this makes maximum use of space and keeps the garden too full for weeds to gain a foothold.

4 **Allopathy** is now well recognised in scientific circles. Some plants release root exudates that harm specific other plants. Not so well recognised in scientific research, but part of companion planting lore for centuries, is the fact that the opposite is also true. Some plants grow better together than either of them do separately, for no reason that can be traced to such obvious factors as pest reduction or nutrient supply. Beetroot and lettuces are a prime example.

5 **Guild planting gives you a good variety**, for eating or for sale. Gluts are nearly as much of a problem as shortages, in the marketplace and the kitchen. If you absorbed the 'waste not, want not' ethic as well as I did, a surplus of cucumbers evokes groans as you realise that most of the week is going to be spent making pickles! Twenty lettuces ready at once is *not* gourmet gardening. Two lettuces, a cabbage, five beetroot, a kilo of beans, ten radishes, ten shallots, some broccoli, a kilo of tomatoes and some cucumbers would have fit in the same space. Which would you rather eat?

Figure 18 (see page 100) is an example of what I mean by a guild. This one starts with two weeks of chooks in late winter or early spring. As soon as the chooks are moved on the bed is planted as in the top circle (Guild One). The potatoes are planted as well-eyed seed potatoes at 40 cm spacing in a single undulating row. The shallots and baby carrots are planted as seed mixed together and sown directly in small 'patches'. The rest are all planted as well-advanced seedlings, individually placed.

The beans, lettuces and cabbages are the first to be harvested, six to eight weeks after planting. They are immediately replaced with well-advanced seedlings of tomatoes, capsicums and eggplants, with beets and shallot–carrot mix as interplants.

The original tomatoes, eggplants and capsicums are next to come out, fourteen to sixteen weeks after planting. As fast as they are removed, they are replaced with beans, cabbages and lettuces, again as well-advanced seedlings with interplants of beets and the shallot–carrot mix.

The potatoes and leeks come out next, at sixteen to twenty weeks. As soon as they are harvested, the area is scattered with mixed seed of radishes, daikon, mustard, cress, bok choy (Chinese cabbage) and chook fodder weeds.

The silver beet, parsley, celery and basil should bear right up until the chooks are moved on again at twenty-four weeks, when they can be harvested or left for the chooks to finish off. With early spring plantings, the broccoli should continue to yield side shoots right through. With later plantings it will start to bolt, and can be replaced with leaf lettuces. By week twenty, the guild should look like the bottom circle (Guild Two), and by week twenty-four it will be ready for the chooks again. Over six months this one bed will yield:

15 to 20 kg potatoes	8 lettuces
30 to 40 eggplants	20 to 25 bunches silver beet
19 leeks	30 to 40 beetroot
25 to 30 capsicums	20 to 25 bunches parsley, basil or coriander
12 to 15 kg beans	
20 to 25 kg tomatoes	40 to 60 shallots
5 cabbages	30 to 40 sticks of celery
5 to 8 kg broccoli	40 to 60 baby carrots

You will also get as many radishes and as much cress, mustard and Chinese cabbage as you can eat!

If your chooks are laying, the bed will also indirectly yield about seven dozen eggs with a very high vitamin A content, by providing a week or so's worth of high-quality feed for them. Compare this with the yield you would expect from the same area planted to a monoculture!

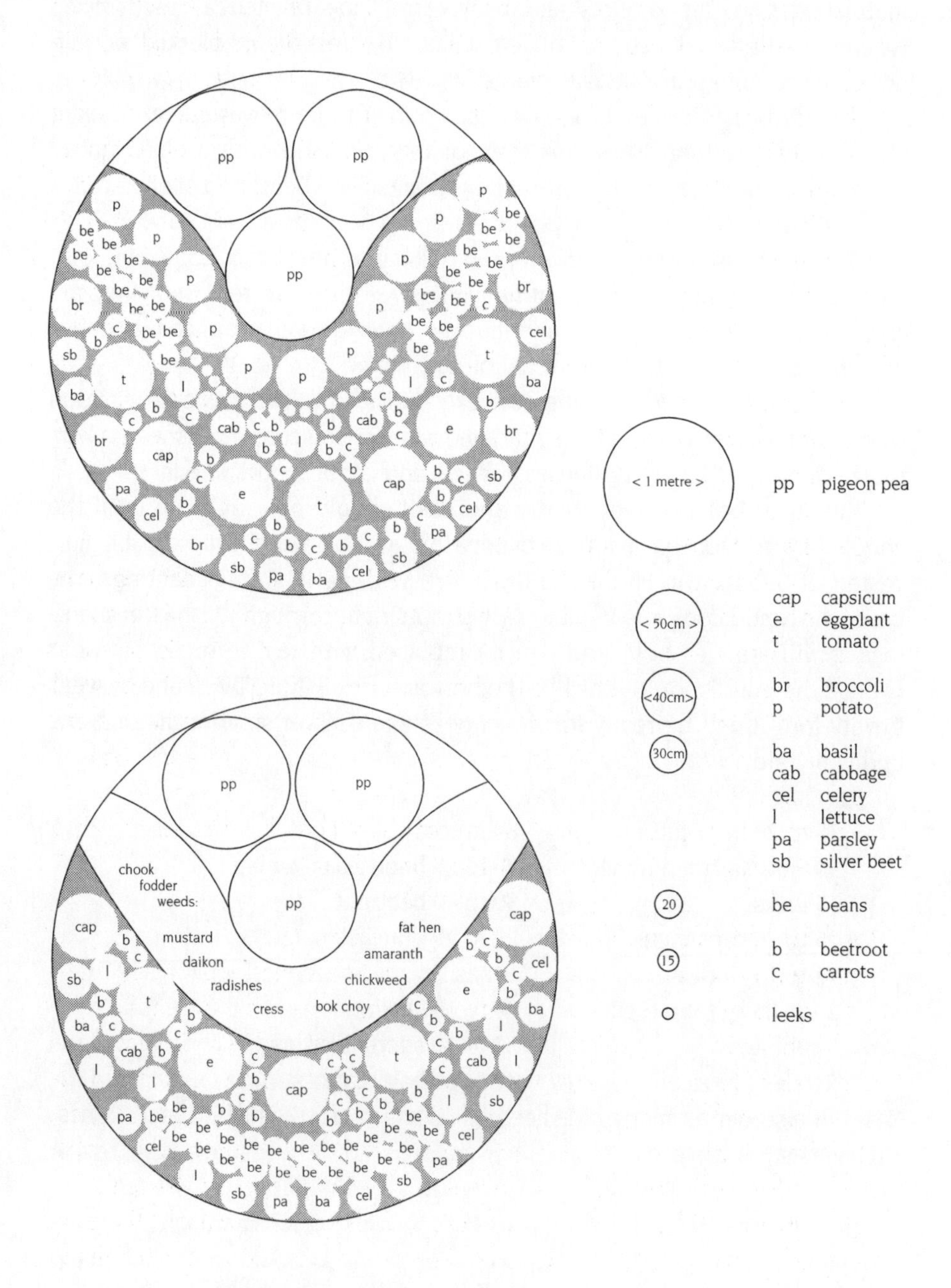

Figure 18 Design for Guilds One and Two.

PRINCIPLES OF GUILD DESIGN

TIMING

The rotation starts with chooks to clear and fertilise the bed and ends up, six months later, with all the human food harvested and a bed full of chook fodder. This requires careful design for timing so as to avoid leaving most of the bed idle while waiting for the last few harvestable plants to mature before moving in the chooks. I try to use a fairly exact six-month rotation, which allows every bed to be weeded and fertilised regularly twice a year. After six months of this kind of very heavy yielding, the store of soil nutrients is starting to get exhausted, and this is when problems start. I plan for everything I want to harvest to be out within six months, and no part of the bed to be idle for any of that time.

It is impossible to give exact instructions about the time to maturity of every crop plant, since even identical varieties will perform differently in different microclimates. Your own diary will evolve into your most reliable source of this kind of information. Nevertheless, just for starters, most seed suppliers include information on time to maturity on the packet, which can be used as a rough guide. Planting advanced seedlings gives you a margin for error.

AVOIDING BARE GROUND

Bare ground is avoided as much as it possibly can be. The aim is to achieve maximum living cover for the whole bed over the whole time of the rotation. In space, fast-maturing plants are interplanted with slow maturers to nursemaid them and keep the ground shaded until the slowcoaches need the space. In time, fast-maturing plants like lettuces and beans are succeeded by medium-pace plants like tomatoes and capsicums, and vice versa. Slow maturers like potatoes are paired with very fast maturers like radishes and cress, so that the bed is full to capacity for the whole six months. This maximises not only the harvestable yield, but also the 'capture' of solar energy and soil-building.

COMPANION PLANTING

Things are planted in companion groups. Tomatoes, lettuces, cabbages, beets, carrots and parsley are all good companions. Tomatoes and basil are good companions (in the ground *and* in the pot), as are eggplants and beans. Carrots and spring onions are particularly good companions. Beans and any member of the onion family are bad companions: legumes (beans and peas) are symbiotic with a root bacteria that fixes nitrogen for them, and the onion family (and particularly garlic) are all antibiotic, and therefore not very friendly to this bacteria.

The subject of companion planting deserves a book of its own, and there are several good companion planting books on the market. But a common complaint is that even those written in Australia are based on the experience and folklore of Europe and to a lesser extent, North America, where most of our food

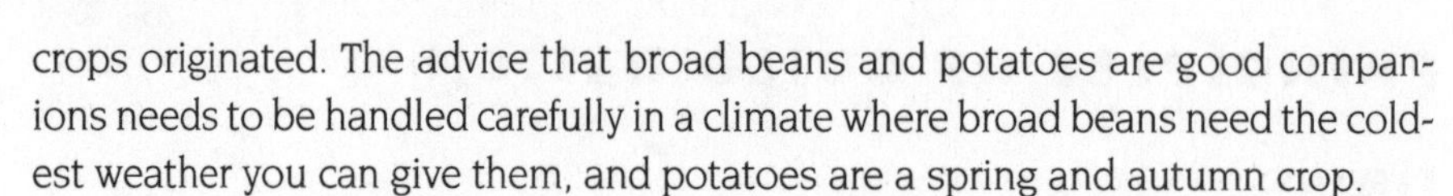

crops originated. The advice that broad beans and potatoes are good companions needs to be handled carefully in a climate where broad beans need the coldest weather you can give them, and potatoes are a spring and autumn crop.

The classic companions of sweet corn and beans or cucumbers have never worked for me, despite several tries at varying the timing and spacing. The corn just swamps anything else. Perhaps it is because I use Balinese corn – a particularly tall, vigorous, southern hemisphere variety. The only really reliable source of companion planting information is your own diary!

But don't be too intimidated by it all. The effects of companion planting are usually quite subtle and, provided the rest is right, making a mistake will only mean the difference between a good harvest and a superb one.

ROTATING HEAVY AND LIGHT FEEDERS

Heavy feeders, especially crops like leafy greens that use a lot of nitrogen, are preceded by either chooks or legumes and followed by lighter feeders (like most fruiting or root crop plants) or legumes. Very heavy feeders like potatoes are preceded and followed by chooks. The main idea is to avoid planting two plants that have high requirements for the same nutrients straight after one another. Section 5, 'Alphabet Soup', will give you a few hints about the dietary preferences of individual species.

I like to include some legumes in every planting to capture nitrogen from the air and keep the soil levels of this essential nutrient high. I plant them in a different spot each time to make sure every part of the bed gets a share.

MELANGE NOT BLANCMANGE

Plants are mixed up to the maximum degree feasible, in space and in time. No two plants of the same family are planted next to each other or directly after each other. Leaf shapes, colours and scents are disguised by neighbouring plants so as to make it difficult for pests to pick their specific host out of the melee. Different plants have subtly different nutrient needs, so neighbouring or succeeding plants aren't competing for the exact same menu.

With experience, and good diary records, an anarchic jumble will give way to a subtle pattern of good and bad companions. But initially, avoiding anything that resembles a monoculture is more vital than proper companion planting. Corn is the only vegetable that actually needs to be planted in a block, because it is wind-pollinated and the corn will not set unless pollen from another plant blows onto it. With everything else, if in doubt, mix it up!

PLAN(T) TO MINIMISE SOIL COMPACTION

This means planning your planting pattern to minimise the number of times the bed needs to be stepped on. The row closest to the path is planted with 'pick and pick again' vegetables and herbs like silver beet, parsley, basil, spinach, leaf lettuces, endive, kale . . . I include celery for home consumption in this category, as I find the best way to harvest it is a stalk at a time picked from the outside over a couple of months. I also include broccoli for home consumption, choosing the sprouting varieties that yield good value in side shoots over several months.

The next rows in are planted with vegetables that bear over several weeks – tomatoes, eggplants, capsicums, beans, peas . . . They can usually be picked from the path, perhaps just with one foot on the bed for balance.

Vegetables that are picked once only – potatoes, leeks, cauliflowers, cabbages, hearting lettuces, beets, turnips – are concentrated in the inside rows. The worms don't like heavy feet tramping around on their roof.

GOURMET GARDEN

The yield is small quantities of a large variety spread over a relatively long time so as to avoid kitchen and market gluts, or shortages. If you don't like brussels sprouts, don't plant them! If you only use a few potatoes, plant less. But don't fall into the trap of being forced to eat lettuces ad nauseam to prevent them going to waste, especially without tomatoes, cucumbers, celery and herbs to go with them!

PUTTING GUILDS TOGETHER

With careful guild planting, a single mandala can supply you with a varied, balanced, abundant diet, all year round. Climates and tastes vary so much that every garden will be unique, but as a starting point, Figure 19 (see page 104) represents an idealised version of one of the rotations I use.

The chooks move clockwise around this mandala, spending a fortnight at each station. In the warmer months, the chook stations are extra-heavily mulched and the extra used to make compost on the adjacent sites.

The chooks will complete a rotation of a single mandala in three months, so they will need to go elsewhere for the next three months, until it is time for them to do their next circuit. In this plan they go elsewhere between the end of September and the beginning of January, and between the end of March and the beginning of July. If you are working two mandalas, they simply move on to do a circuit of the adjacent mandala.

On each station, the chooks are followed by a combination of guilds that lasts six months. In the warmer months, Guild One is combined with Guild Two to give a six-month planting schedule. (Guild One is the top circle and Guild Two is the bottom circle in Figure 18.) When it is not possible to use the standard Guild Two because of encroaching cooler weather, you can use a modified form I have called 'Guild Two B'. It is like Guild Two, but for planting following Guild One in autumn and early winter, when the weather is too cool for beans,

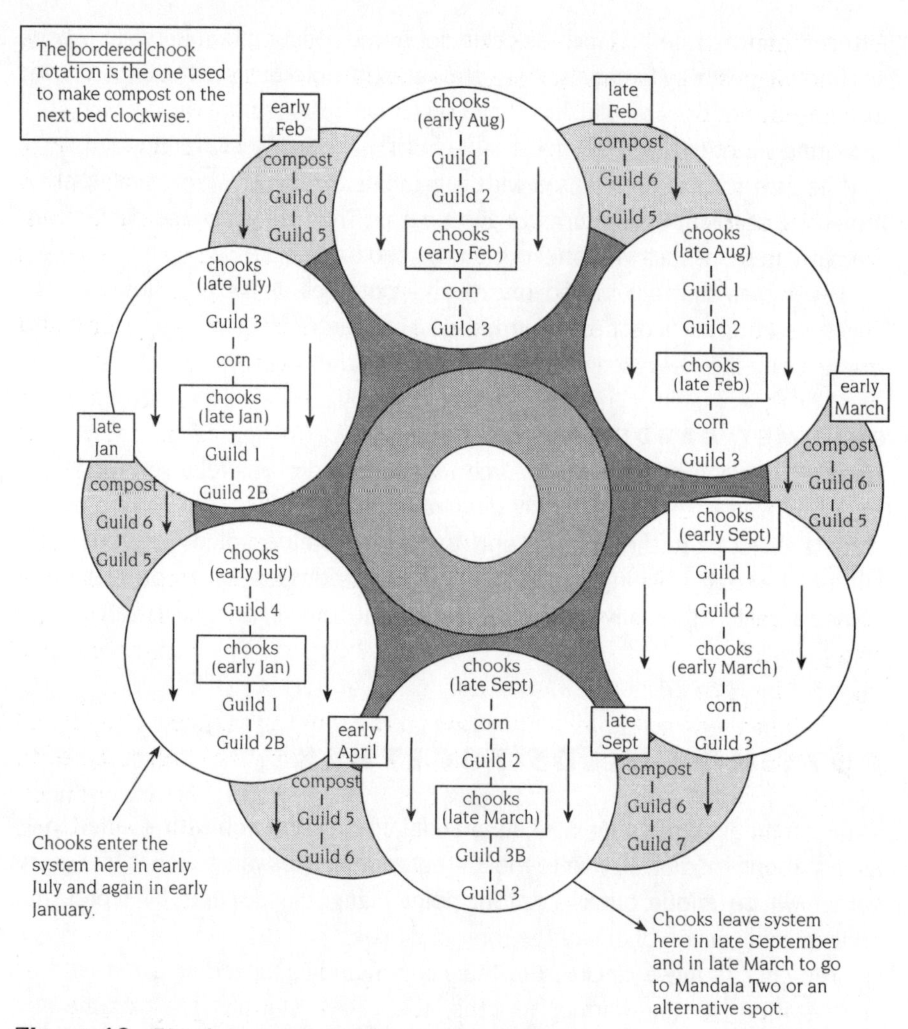

Figure 19 Plan for an annual guild-planting rotation.

tomatoes, eggplants and capsicums. Simply substitute peas for beans, and turnips and cauliflowers for tomatoes, eggplants and capsicums.

Guild Three is illustrated in Figure 20. It is a cool-weather guild lasting about three months. It can be paired with corn planted in spring or late summer or with itself in winter, to give a six-month rotation. However, if two 'Guild Threes' are planted straight after each other, one of them should be modified so as to observe the rule of never planting two members of the same family in succession. Guild Three B is the modification I use. The positions of the peas and the cauliflower group are reversed, so that the peas are in the inner row and the caulis, beetroot, lettuces, cabbages, dill and turnips are nearer to the path. This modification is useful to avoid planting the same family in the same spot and to spread the nitrogen-fixing benefit of the peas. It is also useful for planting in late summer when cabbage moths are still active and the brassicas (plants from the cabbage family) need to be checked regularly, since in this modification they can be reached without stepping on the bed.

Corn is a guild all on its own, as it needs to be planted in a clump of at least twenty plants to pollinate. It is a very heavy feeder, so should usually follow chooks or, at a pinch, a very legume-concentrated planting. A good double handful of compost per plant may be needed if it follows any other crop. Leafy greens following corn may appreciate extra compost or worm castings too.

Guild Four is illustrated in Figure 21. It is a six-month-long guild for planting in midwinter. It starts with 'pick-and-pick-again' vegetables (silver beet, celery, parsley, broccoli . . .) along the path edge, and alternate rows of broad beans and the lettuce–cabbage–beet combination filling the rest of the bed. All are planted as advanced seedlings, as soon as the chooks are moved off the bed.

As the lettuces, cabbages and beets come out in early spring, they are replaced with potatoes. When the broad beans have finished bearing in late spring, the spent plants are used to mulch up the spuds, and the Chinese cabbage–mustard–cress–radish combination is planted in their place. This is a tricky way of achieving the broad beans–potatoes companion planting, while allowing for their different climatic preferences.

The remaining guilds are for planting on the compost pile sites. They are all quite simple guilds, occupying only a few square metres each and designed to make the most of the eleven and a half months available between compost piles. They concentrate on long-season crops that would not reach maturity in the six months available between chook rotations.

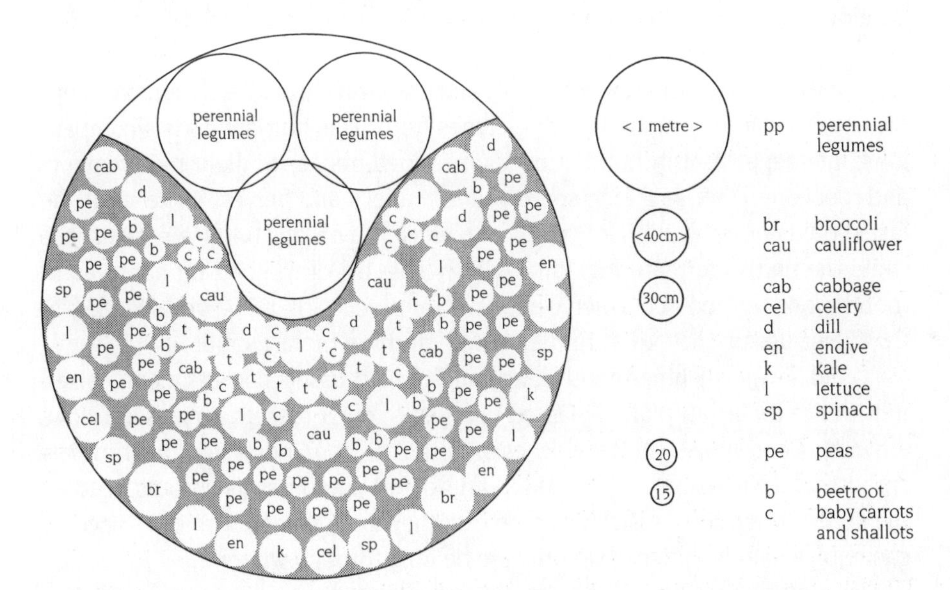

Figure 20 Design for Guild Three.

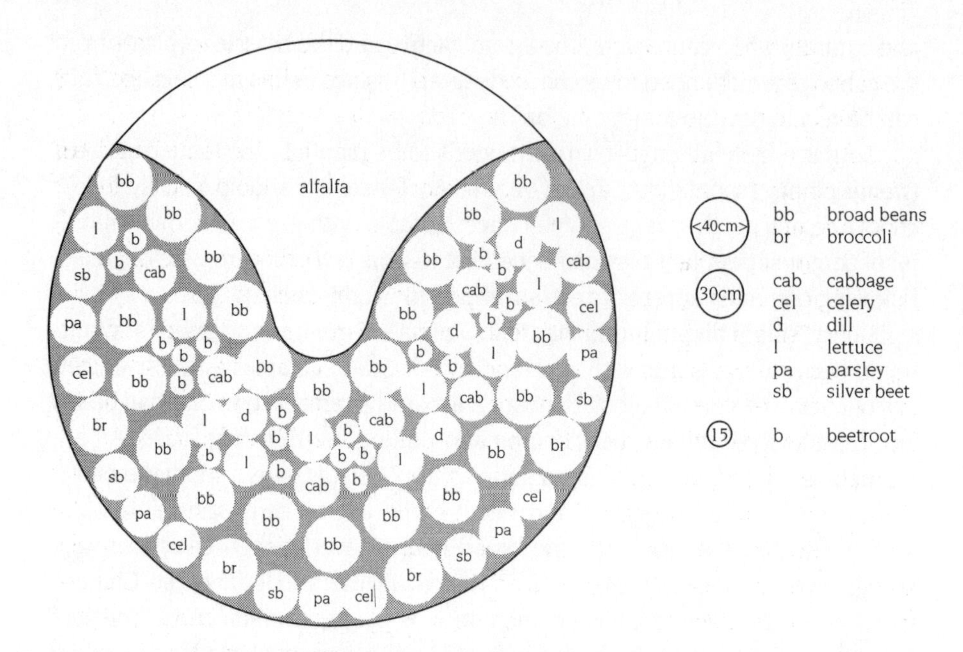

Figure 21 Design for Guild Four.

Guild Five is one plant each of zucchini, squash and bush cucumber, interspersed with four sunflowers. I prefer to keep all these out of the main beds as they use up so much space. They do very well immediately following a compost pile, since they like warm ground and can cope with very 'raw' nutrients. Sunflowers are the benign overlords, taking their light and nutrients at a different level and deterring cucumber beetles.

Guild Six is alternate rows of carrots and onions. This is where your main supply of onions for drying and storing comes from. This pair are classic companions, interdependent in nutrient needs, pest deterrence, sunlight requirements and root zone. Choose a long-season carrot variety, and harvest as needed. The last should come out in plenty of time to allow the onions full use of the space while the bulbs are maturing. This guild needs use of the bed for about eight months, and not too rich a diet. Guild Five pairs well with it. The gross feeders in Guild Five use up the excess nutrients in their three-month sprint.

Guild Seven is a nine-month-long guild of six brussels sprouts plants mixed in with five capsicum plants, planted in midsummer. Brussels sprouts are slow-growing. Capsicums will provide early disguise from pests for the brussels sprouts, and will come out in late autumn before the brussels sprouts need all the space. When the capsicums come out, they are replaced with dill to do the same job while the brussels sprouts are bearing through winter.

This rotation is particularly suited to people working a single mandala. It is designed to give you a good supply of varied vegetables all year round, with no seasonal gluts or shortages. You should be able to pick a different breakfast, lunch and dinner out of the garden every day of the year. The table on pages 108 and 109 shows the yields you should expect from this rotation. These yields are quite conservative, and don't include any of the perennials. The table illustrates two of the chief virtues of guild planting – very high yields, and a well-balanced, varied menu.

If all this seems very complicated and bewildering, take heart. Guild planting is not simple, but neither is it really that difficult. Like natural systems, it gets its vigour and stability from its diversity. Simple systems are much too vulnerable to be stable, and natural forces will always work to turn a simple system into a stable, complex one. If you design for simplicity, you are ignoring one of the prime design rules: it is smarter to work with, not against, natural forces.

If you are being lazy about using your creative intelligence, natural forces will work their hardest to overwhelm and undermine your inadequate design. The tools they will use are the species we call 'weeds', 'pests' and 'diseases' – species that are actually strong medicine for an unwell ecosystem. Like many medicines, they are not pleasant to take! It is much easier to go for diversity and complexity by design and choice than to be dragged to it fighting all the way.

Guild planting is, however, much less challenging than it might appear in writing. You are very *well* adapted for this kind of work. Your instincts will serve you well. Willingness to enjoy your garden, some contemplative time in it, and confidence to exercise your creative intelligence are all the skills you need.

Planting Table Yields from an annual guild-planting rotation.

JAN	FEB	MAR	APR	MAY	JUNE
12 bunches silver beet	12 bunches silver beet	8 bunches silver beet	4 bunches silver beet	8 bunches silver beet	8 bunches silver beet
12 bunches parsley	8 bunches parsley	4 bunches parsley	4 bunches parsley	4 bunches parsley	4 bunches parsley
8 bunches shallots	8 bunches shallots	4 bunches shallots	4 bunches shallots	4 bunches shallots	5 kg peas
8 bunches baby carrots	8 bunches baby carrots	4 bunches baby carrots	4 bunches baby carrots	4 bunches baby carrots	spinach, endive
5 kg beans	10 kg beans	5 kg beans	5 kg beans	5 kg beans	2 cauliflowers
36 capsicums	27 capsicums	9 capsicums	15 capsicums	21 capsicums	6 capsicums
18 eggplants	18 eggplants	9 eggplants		6 eggplants	6 eggplants
3 bunches celery	4 bunches celery	4 bunches celery			3 bunches celery
6 kg tomatoes	12 kg tomatoes	6 kg tomatoes	6 kg tomatoes	6 kg tomatoes	11 turnips
12 leeks	12 leeks		6 leeks	12 leeks	12 leeks
2 kg broccoli		2 kg broccoli	2 kg broccoli		radishes, cress, mustard
60 cobs corn	60 cobs corn			60 cobs corn	120 cobs corn
25 kg potatoes			10 kg potatoes		10 kg potatoes
20 beetroot	40 beetroot	36 beetroot	16 beetroot		10 beetroot
		8 cucumbers	8 cucumbers	16 cucumbers	8 cucumbers
20 kg onions	20 kg onions	2 kg zucchini, squash	2 kg zucchini, squash	4 kg zucchini, squash	2 kg zucchini, squash
9 lettuces	18 lettuces	12 lettuces	3 lettuces		3 lettuces
		2 cabbages	2 cabbages		3 cabbages
radishes, cress, mustard	radishes, cress, mustard	radishes, cress, mustard		1 kg brussels sprouts	1 kg brussels sprouts

JULY	AUG	SEPT	OCT	NOV	DEC
8 bunches silver beet	8 bunches silver beet	4 bunches silver beet	4 bunches silver beet	8 bunches silver beet	12 bunches silver beet
4 bunches parsley	4 bunches parsley	4 bunches parsley	8 bunches parsley	8 bunches parsley	8 bunches parsley
	15 kg peas	5 kg peas	5 kg peas	4 bunches shallots	4 bunches shallots
2 kg carrots	8 kg carrots	10 kg carrots	10 kg carrots	12 kg carrots	6 kg carrots
2 cauliflowers	6 cauliflowers	2 cauliflowers	2 cauliflowers	10 kg beans	5 kg beans
	spinach, endive	spinach, endive	spinach, endive	10 kg broad beans	18 capsicums
	4 bunches spring onions	4 bunches spring onions	4 bunches spring onions		9 eggplants
3 bunches celery	3 bunches celery	3 bunches celery	3 bunches celery	1 bunch celery	1 bunch celery
11 turnips	22 turnips	11 turnips	11 turnips	9 kg tomatoes	9 kg tomatoes
6 leeks				12 leeks	18 leeks
radishes, cress, mustard			2 kg broccoli	4 kg broccoli	4 kg broccoli
					15 kg potatoes
	30 beetroot	10 beetroot	54 beetroot	24 beetroot	
					8 cucumbers
			13 kg onions	13 kg onions	2 kg zucchini, squash
	9 lettuces	3 lettuces	12 lettuces	5 lettuces	
	9 cabbages	5 cabbages	6 cabbages	5 cabbages	
1 kg brussels sprouts	1 kg brussels sprouts	1 kg brussels sprouts	1 kg brussels sprouts	1 kg brussels sprouts	

11 FRUIT TREES

Fruit trees can yield an enormous quantity of food that is expensive to buy and lucrative to sell. Tree-ripened organic fruit is so delectable that it spoils you for the conventional sort! Yet very few people achieve the same yields, in quantity or quality, that commercial orchardists do. Why?

To yield well, fruit trees need much the same conditions that the vegetable garden does. They need protection from grass invasion, enough water and high-enough nutrient levels. They need an ecological balance between populations of things that eat fruit, and things that eat the things that eat fruit. They also need that elusive something that happens when people talk or play music to their plants. Perhaps it is vibrations, or perhaps just that little bit of extra attention that leads to closer observation and better meeting of needs. Whatever it is, fruit trees, like house plants, respond to it.

Perennials last much longer than annuals, and take much longer to show signs of neglect. Where time and energy are limited (and when aren't they?), tending the trees often ends up at the bottom of the priority list. It is likely to be one of those jobs that keeps being put off. The lettuce seedlings will keel over if they are not watered today, but the trees will survive another day or two without mulch, water, weeding, fertilising, checking . . . Growing fruit *and* vegetables usually means dividing your time and energy between the garden and the orchard – and the orchard, with its little bit more stoicism, often misses out.

Yields that are disappointing in quantity and quality are usually simply the evidence of neglect. They are the nearly inevitable result of the usual practice of planting isolated fruit trees scattered around a lawn or grassy paddock. In this situation they are usually lucky if they have a metre-wide ring of mulch around the trunk, and they will only rarely be noticed, usually not until something is very wrong.

The answer, as with everything else, is not to work harder or longer, but to work smarter – to put a little more into design. Why divide your time and energy? Why not integrate the orchard and the garden and let the chooks do most of the work for both?

WHY PUT THE ORCHARD IN THE GARDEN?

1 TO MINIMISE THE JOB OF GRASS-CLEARING

Fruit trees and grass are very bad companions. If you do nothing else for your trees but keep the area at least out as far as the drip line clear of grass, yields will improve dramatically.

Conventional orchardists bare the ground between and around their trees with herbicides. Organic orchardists use ground covers and mulch to keep grass clear. However, even a medium-sized tree needs at least *10 m*^{2} kept clear of grass. If you are attempting to beat the grass by mulching it out, it takes only a few trees to give you a full-time job. If you are using ground covers, you still have to find a way of stopping the grass from overrunning them.

Too little mulch is worse than useless. If it is spread too thinly it will not drown out the grass but merely fertilise it. That metre-wide ring of mulch around the trunk does more harm than good. The tree is not feeding there, but at its root tips – out beyond the edge of its canopy. Mulch around the trunk is more likely to foster fungus diseases and shelter pests than do anything else.

A little bit of circle geometry provides the solution to the dilemma. Grass spreads occasionally by seed but mainly by runners. Either way, once it is cleared from an area it reinvades *from the edges*. Six isolated fruit trees scattered around a lawn or a paddock, each with a canopy 3 metres wide, create an incredible 67 metres of 'edge' to protect from grass invasion!

Now plant those same six trees in one clump. Each tree still has the same amount of space, but there is only 27 metres of edge to patrol and protect. The work involved in making sure the fertiliser and water you provide goes into fruit, not grass, has been cut by nearly two-thirds. But to add 60 m^2, enough for six fruit trees, to your garden area, you need only increase the edge by 7.5 *metres*. The geometry of circles means that you can add six fruit trees to your garden area, and keep them all clear of grass, for less effort than just one tree planted separately.

2 TO MINIMISE THE JOB OF PEST CONTROL

Many of the pests of fruit trees are, like vegetable pests, very species-specific. They like only one kind of fruit, or its close relatives, and when they find it, they breed up very quickly to take maximum advantage of the food source. They are also very well adapted to survive the gap between one fruiting and the next, even if that gap is eleven months. Their pattern is short flushes of very high populations while their food source is in fruit, then none at all for months and months.

Fruit pest predators are usually not nearly as fussy as the pests. They have a much more varied diet, but they cannot survive eleven months without food. All animals need proteins for growth and reproduction, and sugars for energy. Insects provide protein, but many insect-eaters also require nectar for sugars and energy. They need a year-round supply of both insects and flowering plants as a food source. They are also usually much slower breeders. Their pattern is a much more stable population, choosing as a home a place where there are varied and constant food sources.

With conventional monocultures or isolated fruit trees there is no alternative source of food to keep predators around between fruitings. By the time predators locate your flush of rapid growth in a pest population, and breed up enough to balance it, the fruiting season is over and the damage done.

But in the garden there is always something in flower and in fruit. Nectar and insects are always available, and there is (or should be) a strong, stable resident population of predatory insects, birds, frogs and reptiles. The flush of pest-breeding that happens as a tree comes into fruit never has a chance to get off the ground before the predators move in on it. Pest problems are nipped in the bud.

At the same time, the trees provide nectar, vantage points and nesting areas for insectivores that hunt in the garden.

3 TO DELEGATE MOST OF THE ORCHARD TASKS

Chooks have much the same symbiotic relationship with fruit trees that they have with the vegetable garden. The fruit not suitable for human consumption is valuable as chook fodder, and is converted automatically into eggs. Chooks are good weeders, and chook manure is a matchless source of high-phosphate fertiliser.

Chooks are insect predators. The pests attracted by the fruit are much better at sensing the presence of a predator than they are at sensing the presence of wire in between it and them. Some are deterred by the proximity of predators. Some become high-protein, high-calcium chook food, and are in turn converted into human food. The remainder do me what I consider a good deal. They get a small percentage of the fruit, and in return they breed up just enough to sustain my populations of predatory insects, birds and reptiles, and to keep a supply of high-quality chook food coming next year.

Moving the chooks under a tree just as it finishes fruiting is good orchard hygiene. The chooks clean up all the spoiled and fallen fruit, and scratch up and eat any pests that have gone dormant underground, so breaking their breeding cycle. The scratching does some damage to very superficial roots. But if the chooks are supplied with plenty of mulch and only kept in one spot for a fortnight, the damage is minimal. The fertilising, pest control and weeding more than compensate for it.

The garden worm population is also capable of competing successfully with insects, bacteria and fungi for the spoils of fallen fruit. A high worm population will dispose of remnants of spoiled fruit before the far less desirable 'pest' species get a chance to use it as a breeding ground. At the same time the worms are fertilising your trees for you.

4 TO AVOID DIVIDING YOUR FOCUS

With the orchard in the garden, you escape the trap of dividing your time and energy. Watering, weeding, feeding, checking and harvesting fruit trees *and* vegetables are all part of the same process. It is much easier to let the sprinkler run a bit longer to water the trees as well as the vegetables than it is to finish watering one then start on the other. It is much easier to provide a bit of extra mulch to the chooks to allow some for the trees too than it is to mulch two different places. It is much easier to check on the trees as part of your garden rounds than to finish the garden then start the rounds of the orchard.

Having the orchard in the garden circumvents the common temptation to do the garden tasks, run out of time, and skip the orchard.

5 TO KEEP ALL THE DAILY TASKS TOGETHER

The trees that are not in fruit are on the perimeter of the garden, so on the perimeter of your field of attention. The tree that *is* in fruit is next to the chook dome, so it is shifted to the centre of your field of attention, without having to shift the tree! You can allow fruit to ripen on the tree, picking it daily at the same time as you collect the eggs. Everything that needs daily attention is concentrated in the one place. Two tasks are turned into one task.

WHAT TO PLANT AND WHERE

The trees that are most suitable for including in a garden system are smaller trees that are high-yielding but require a lot of attention. This includes those that are particularly prone to pest attack or that require a lot of fertilising to bear well. If you love stone fruits but live in a fruit-fly area, the only place to plant the trees is in the garden.

The ideal mature size is a tree less than 3 metres tall, with a canopy about 3 metres wide. For many fruits this will mean choosing a dwarf or semi-dwarf variety. This is hardly a restriction, however, since dwarf trees have a lot of other things to recommend them, and in most cases are my first choice in or out of the garden. They usually reach bearing age much younger – you can probably begin eating fruit within a couple of years. They bear more fruit per square metre than their larger cousins. They take up less room, so you can plant more varieties in a given area. Being more compact, they are less prone to wind and storm damage. And picking, pruning, inspecting and thinning fruit can all be done with your feet firmly on the ground.

Which trees you choose will depend mainly on your tastes and your local climate. The true art is in designing the *sequence*. Unless your garden slopes north on a very sunny site, the trees on the north, north-east and north-west sides should be deciduous to allow maximum sunlight in winter. Those on the east, west and south sides can be evergreens, providing some shade in summer when it is needed.

It may seem almost too clever, but the ideal arrangement is one where a chook dome comes around to each tree just as it finishes fruiting. This means designing a sequence of trees in order of fruiting season around the mandala. One of the prime benefits of this kind of sequence is that you can create a steady, year-round supply of fresh fruit for eating.

The same variety of tree will fruit at different times in different local areas, so each sequence will be unique. Golden Delicious apples may fruit in late February in my area, but not until early April in yours. To get the information you need to design a sequence, you will have to quiz every local fruit tree owner you come across, talk to local nursery people and be very observant.

Even when you have gathered all the information, it will probably take you several sessions with a pencil and a large sheet of paper to design a sequence for your local area that works. The impatient among you will no doubt baulk at this. But if you consider that it will save you years of picking up and carting spoiled fruit, and that it will make your pest control virtually automatic, the investment becomes more attractive!

There are two kinds of sequences that work. You can design a sequence with each tree fruiting two weeks later than the one immediately before it. Since most trees fruit only once a year but the chooks do two circuits of a mandala each year, this will mean that all your fruit production is concentrated in one half of the year. In their second circuit the chooks will be moving around non-fruiting trees.

To spread your fruit production more evenly over the whole year, you can design a sequence where every *alternate* tree is in fruit in each circuit. This will mean that each tree fruits a month later than the one two places back. Run that past you again? Figure 22 represents an example of this kind of sequence. It is one that works in my area, but please, before you adopt any part of it, check for local suitability of the variety and for local fruiting times.

Figure 22 represents a large garden using three chook domes. Each chook dome rotates around a double mandala system twice a year. The domes move in the direction indicated by the arrows, occupying each station at the times of the year marked. The month in **bold** printing is the one in which the adjacent tree will be fruiting. If you examine the figure you will notice that the chook domes

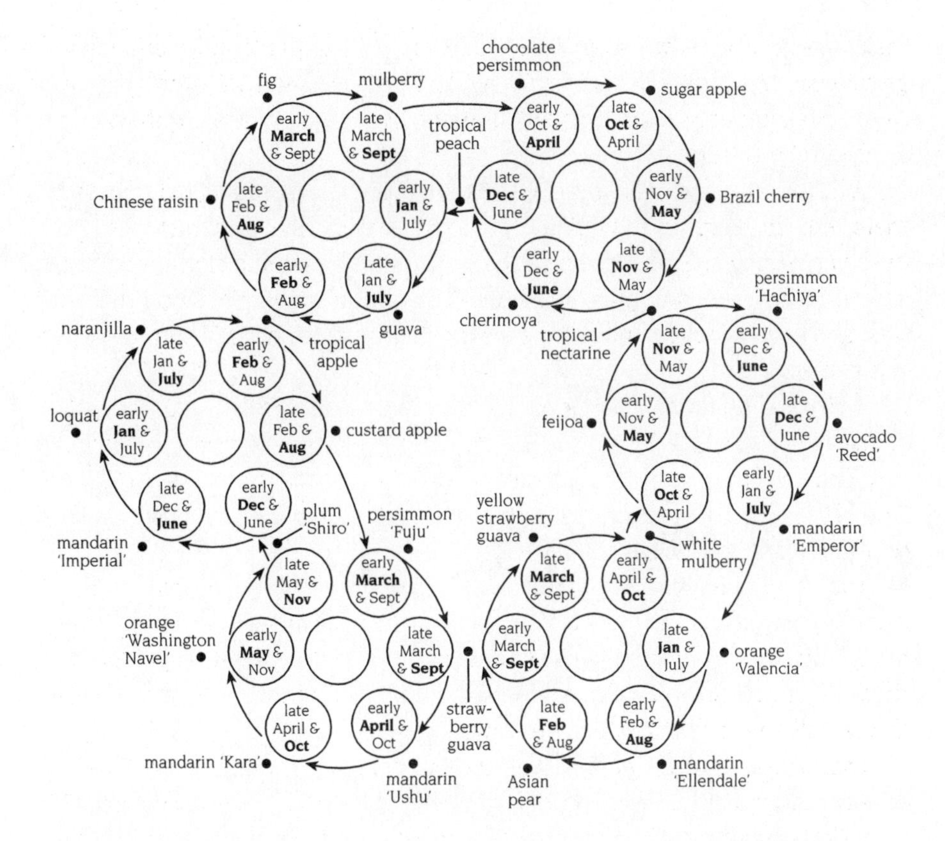

Figure 22 Example of a sequence of fruit trees in order of fruiting season.

are moving one place each time, alternating between trees that are fruiting in this circuit and ones that will be fruiting next circuit, in six months' time.

This diagram is not meant to be a prescription. Fruit trees are too finicky about their climatic requirements, and people are too specific in their tastes, for that! I hope it will give you a few ideas and principles to use in designing your own sequence – but beyond that, you are on your own.

PART FOUR

MAINTAINING THE GARDEN

12 HUMANS AND OTHER PESTS

The golden rule of pest control in the garden is: if in doubt, do nothing.

A great deal of humility is in order. You are very badly adapted for hunting minute and microscopic creatures. You don't have the eyesight, deftness, agility or patience for it. You need to be very conscious that once you have a population explosion on your hands, *anything* you do will probably make the problem worse. If in the process of killing thousands of aphids you accidentally knock off one ladybird, or even her eggs or larvae, you will have gone backwards. You will have done more harm than good.

If you only consider pest control once you have a problem, the cure is nearly always worse than the complaint. It can gobble up extraordinary amounts of time, energy and money, for negligible or even negative results. It can become the ultimate in make-work. Effective pest control has to begin much earlier in the process.

SELF-DEFENCE

As with humans, the first defence for plants against predators, parasites and diseases is general health and resistance. In some cases it is the *only* defence. Many insects do very little damage directly. It is by spreading viruses that they create havoc. We don't have vaccines for plants; natural immunity is the only defence. A weak or unhealthy plant, like an unhealthy person, will come down with everything going around. A strong, healthy plant can defend itself. Even our modern cultivars had many millions of years of evolution before human agriculture came on the scene. If they were as vulnerable as all that, they would have become extinct long ago.

In any life form, resistance to disease is a combination of 'nature and nurture': genetic inheritance and environmental development. Plants with the right genes for it, and enough nutrients to develop it, have a good chance of fending off most other predators except you!

SELECTIVE BREEDING

My first line of defence against pests and diseases is to choose plants with the most genetic potential for self-defence. Unfortunately, modern agricultural practices have imposed a triple handicap in genetic inheritance on our garden plants.

It is difficult to breed selectively for several characteristics at once. In selecting for yield, shelf life and visual appeal, and relying on chemical '-icides' for defence, we have bred out a great deal of natural immunity. Cherry tomatoes have greater pest and disease resistance than Grosse Lisse or Oxheart varieties. They are closer relatives to their wild cousins and have not been specially bred for size and appearance. In the process of breeding for large, glossy, transportable fruit, we have bred weaker plants.

At the same time, by growing these crops in massive monocultures we have laid out a banquet for those pests and diseases best able to capitalise on it. These insects have not had to adapt for versatility in food sources, but have been able to concentrate all their genes on getting past the defences of one specific crop. We have bred up varieties of insects that are perfectly adapted for feeding on one crop.

In a natural system any predator, parasite or disease that completely decimated its only host would quickly become extinct. Natural selection favours things that preserve their food source by causing it only minimal damage. In agriculture, by defending vulnerable hosts we save these pests from the consequences of overindulgence. We have bred more virulent pests.

Yet despite the triple whammy of more specialised and less restrained pests and less resistant plant varieties, even our mollycoddled garden crops have a much greater capacity for self-defence than the pesticide manufacturers would have us believe.

If a variety I plant is very badly attacked, I simply don't plant it again. I try another variety, until I find one that has a reasonable level of resistance. With carrots, for example, I had to try twelve different varieties before I found one from which the seed was really worth saving. Most of the other eleven yielded a crop, but they were too vulnerable in my conditions to local pests and diseases.

This is one of the many occasions when observation and diary records are invaluable. It is extremely frustrating to look through a seed catalogue and be unable to remember which varieties you have already tried and had no luck with, or which variety it was that did so well. Home gardeners, especially those of a couple of generations ago, saved seed with much more of an eye for pest resistance than modern seed companies do. A very disproportionate number of the varieties

I swear by came originally from heirloom seed, swapped or received as presents from other gardeners or bought from suppliers of non-hybrid heirloom seeds.

I look at pest attacks as opportunities to select the individual plant with the most resistance, and earmark it for breeding stock. It takes only a few seasons to breed up your own varieties with good defences against your own local breeds of pests and diseases. When I buy seed, I look for non-hybrid kinds so that I can breed from them if they perform well. Hybrid varieties do not breed true to type, so the seed from them is not worth saving.

Occasionally a mutant variety will appear, and even more occasionally it will be stunningly successful. Several years ago, before I fully appreciated how rare this is, I had one eggplant bush that bore an amazingly heavy crop with no disease problems at all. It kept bearing for nearly four months and supplied all the eggplants we could eat. I could kick myself now, but I didn't save the seed, and I've never come across another like it! Now I put a bright red stake in next to the most successful plants to remind me not to harvest them but to let them go to seed.

There is a danger of inbreeding if you stick too rigidly to your own saved seed generation after generation. But I find seed catalogues too tempting, and my own curiosity about new varieties is enough to keep me adding a wild card to the genetic deck often enough to prevent this. Unless you have an eggplant like mine, it is good practice to save and sow together the seed from at least four or five different plants. This avoids the lack of general vigour that is often the result of inbreeding.

CULLING

Like nearly all life forms, plants are most vulnerable in their infancy, before their natural immunities are fully developed. So infancy is a good time for selecting the strongest and culling the weakest. Plants attempt to out-evolve their predators by seeding prolifically. Seeds are relatively cheap, and if you save your own you will almost always have many times more than you can possibly plant. You can afford to waste lots.

I germinate two or three times as many seeds as I intend planting. Of these, I pot out about a third more than I intend to plant, choosing the strongest and healthiest. When they are about 15 cm tall, I discard the weakest and again choose the strongest and healthiest to plant out into the garden. Those that survive this two-stage selection are likely to be the ones that least need my help to survive and bear.

NUTRITION

No genetic inheritance will reach its full potential without the right nutrition. You can spend your time and energy much more productively improving your soil, particularly the supply of micronutrients, than in fruitless hunting of very small beasts. With the right nutrition, your plants can fend off the beasts themselves.

It is important not just *how much* plants are fed, but also *how* they are fed. Imagine that the only source of liquid available for you to drink was a highly concentrated sugar solution. Drinking it would only make you more thirsty and cause you to drink more. You would get very fat, but your resistance to disease and your reproductive success would be severely retarded.

This is a bit like what happens to plants if they are overindulged with water-soluble fertilisers. They cannot absorb water to replace what they use up and lose through evaporation from their leaves without making the concentration of salts inside their system too high. So they are forced to drink more to try to equalise. If the fertiliser solution is very nitrogen-rich, they put on lots of new growth and, at least in laboratory conditions, can appear to be doing very well. However, without the other nutrients necessary to construct healthy new cells, this new growth is made up of thin-walled, weak cells that are excessively vulnerable to pests (particularly sap-suckers like aphids) and diseases (particularly fungus diseases). They have a much lower nutrient value as food, and often convert the excess nitrogen into nitrosamine, the same carcinogen found in cured meats.

People don't normally die directly from malnutrition. They succumb to an otherwise small infection because of it. In the same way, malnourished plants succumb to diseases that healthy plants hardly notice. Micronutrients probably perform something like the same function in a plant's diet that vitamins do in a human diet. I have found that the best remedy for a number of plant ailments, especially aphids, is a good dose of seaweed brew. It doesn't kill the pest, but, probably because it is so rich in micronutrients, it increases resistance to the point where the pest is irrelevant.

Once it is past infancy, a well-nourished lettuce will be growing so fast that slugs can munch all night without significant damage. If it isn't growing fast enough, slugs are the least of your problems, and eliminating every single slug in the district still won't give you a good lettuce.

PREDATORS

Very often the solution to any problem lies in changing the way you see and define it. Often you are not getting the right answer because you are not asking the right question. 'What should I do about too many pests?' is the wrong question. If you change it to 'What should I do about too few predators?' the answer is very different, and much more useful.

 ***You don't have too many pests. You have not enough predators.***

For every creature you have in excessive numbers, there is at least one and probably many other creatures who would be delighted to relieve you of the excess, for free! In natural systems everything, alive or dead, is food. Aphids are only a pest from the point of view of the potatoes; for the ladybirds they are an opportunity.

If you focus on the inadequate numbers of predators instead of on the excess numbers of a pest, the easy solution is much more apparent. My second line of defence against pests and diseases is to foster a strong, stable resident population of predatory insects, birds, reptiles and even microscopic creatures. The first and most important rule for doing this is:

 ***Do not allow '-icides' of any form anywhere near the garden.***

There is no doubt that poisons of natural origin, especially of plant origin, are less of an environmental hazard than those of chemical origin, simply because *somewhere* there is something that will eat them. Chemicals are too recent for anything to have evolved to make use of them, so they do not cycle but persist in some form. Nevertheless there are several very good reasons why even 'organic' pesticides are a bad idea.

Firstly, they are expensive and a lot of work. Whether you buy them or make your own, pesticides cost you time and/or money, and applying them effectively takes an inordinate amount of time. The less toxic and persistent chemicals are even worse from this point of view, as they need to be applied more often to be effective. The water-soluble ones need to be reapplied after every shower or watering. If you followed the directions in many gardening manuals, you would be out there for several hours every day bundled up in protective gear busily pumping a spray-gun. Not the most exciting of occupations!

Secondly, 'organic' does *not* mean less poisonous. If you compare the toxicity data for organic and synthetic pesticides, you may get a nasty surprise. Several of the organic ones are actually more poisonous to humans than all but the most toxic chemical compounds available. You need to be just as wary of eating residues of them on your vegetables or taking them in through your skin while spraying. This means doing your gardening bundled up like an astronaut and washing everything before eating it.

Thirdly, very few biocides of *any* origin are really specific. Most of them kill beneficial creatures along with the target ones, and many actually concentrate higher up the food chain, doing more damage to the predators of pests than to the pests themselves. Remember that no matter how effectively you knock off thousands and thousands of aphids, if you kill one ladybird in the process the net result is more aphids than you started with.

Fourthly, most pest organisms are actually very *well* adapted to survive this kind of warfare. Most have a very short generation span, and lay thousands of eggs, counting on the survival of only a few. If even one or two survive they will very quickly build up immunity to whatever you are using. Insects have numbers, size, fast mutation and fast reinfestation on their side. You have intelligence on yours. It is not smart to fight on their terms!

Forget the pests. Concentrate on attracting as many predators as possible and persuading them to hang around. Besides not killing them off with poisons, there are a few other things you can do to make your garden their permanent address.

FOOD

By using poisons you are approaching the problem from the wrong end. If your aim is to lure in more ladybirds and get them breeding up, the very *last* thing you want to do is eliminate their food source. You already have one of the most effective lures of all – lots of aphids!

Predators breed up *in response to* an increased food supply. This means *after* it! There will be a time lag, and in this lag some vegetables may be rendered unfit for human consumption or even killed. But once the predator numbers build up they will do a much more effective job of hunting your pest than you ever could. Provided you can persuade them to hang around, they will never allow the population of that particular pest to get out of hand again. If you are lucky they will tackle some of your less troublesome pests for dessert.

Most insectivorous birds and predatory insects also need nectar as an energy food. Fruit tree blossoms, vegetables you let go to flower and seed, and some flowering perennials in your border will provide sources of nectar.

WATER

All predators need access to drinking water, and some of the best of them like living in water. Frogs are a very important part of any garden ecosystem. Water is a powerful bird attracter, lizards come down to drink and bask, and dragonflies hover over the surface. Even a very small pond in the middle of your garden will work wonders. At the very, very least you should supply a birdbath, preferably set low enough for lizards and frogs to have access.

I put a small, simple pond in the middle of the centre circle of every mandala. It is simply a hole dug in the ground, lined with a sheet of vinyl. You can even get away without digging by using something like an old tractor tyre as edging. Some rocks around the edge hold the vinyl in place and provide cover and a basking spot for lizards. I prefer to fill my pond with creek or dam water as this already has the seeds, eggs and spawn of water plants and animals in it. The kids happily stock it with tadpoles, snails and small fish for me and I plant it out with water chestnuts that provide a good little yearly harvest.

SHELTER

Predators also need places to nest, lay eggs, and shelter from *their* predators. Lizards are cold-blooded, so a few piles of rocks to serve as a heat sink will help them keep their body temperature stable and provide a place to hide from birds. Undisturbed mulch will provide a place for them to lay and hatch eggs.

Frogs need a pond to lay eggs and hatch tadpoles, with plenty of water plants for cover, and a vine-covered trellis over it to stop kookaburras, magpies and butcherbirds having too easy pickings. I have some bromeliads planted around my pond, and the frogs love to hide in the partly water-filled intersections between the leaves. A low-voltage light (or even a kerosene lamp or a candle in a jar) over the pond, lit for a few hours on the occasional evening, will attract insects and give frogs an alluring feast.

If some of your perennials are bushy shrubs, small birds may well nest in them and predatory insects are likely to use them as breeding places. I like to plant a few acacias, cassias and callistemon around the garden as well.

Spiders are prodigious hunters and should be welcomed. Early morning dew on a spider's web is quite spectacular, and reason enough on its own to leave their webs alone!

Insectivorous bats are an often unrecognised ally. They only emerge at night, and are so tiny and fast that it is easy for them to go completely unnoticed. But one bat can eat as many as 600 insects an hour. Providing a bat box attached to some structure in or near the garden may persuade them to set up residence. Insectivorous bats eat only insects, harbour no vermin, and are totally endearing little creatures.

SAFETY

Limiting the effect of the next step up in the food chain is a very important strategy. Piles of rocks, bushy shrubs, hollow logs and trellises will provide cover and effective escape from decimation by birds of prey. The main problem is cats.

I cannot overstate how much extra work a cat will cost you. No self-respecting lizard or frog is going to emerge to hunt where it is in danger of being pounced upon, or even where it suspects it *might* be in danger. Given a choice, it will take up residence as far as possible away from the territory of the nearest cat.

You might see the occasional bird your cat brings in and think it is only catching a couple a year. You won't see the frogs, lizards, geckos, praying mantises or dragonflies it catches, especially those it catches at night. And you won't see the ones it doesn't catch because they're too smart to come anywhere near.

If you have to have a cat, put a bell on it, preferably one weighing about 10 kg. Lock it in at night, try to keep it out of the garden in the day, and have it desexed so that it doesn't attract other cats. The National Parks and Wildlife office in our area leases cat traps, which are quite effective in catching stray and feral cats. A couple of trips to the pound might induce your neighbours to keep their cats at home.

IGNORANCE IS BLISS

A third major strategy of pest and disease control is one I call the 'Pollyanna Technique'. Just as a weed is a plant for which we haven't yet found a use, a pest is often only a pest because we have been taught it is. With a bit of unblinkered perception, you can just as easily see them as very valuable allies. Besides providing an opportunity to choose resistant plant varieties, and a means to build up the resident population of predators, so-called pests have a number of other positive functions.

A FREE PRUNING SERVICE

Many leaf and root-eating species are actually a free pruning service. This is particularly valuable where the fruit is the harvested part of the plant. Tomatoes, for example, respond to heavy root and leaf pruning by setting lots of fruit in an effort to reproduce themselves before it is too late. The same trick works for most fruiting plants. If you are lucky and wise enough not to panic and intervene, a 'pest' might do the job for you, perhaps less neatly but just as effectively and for a lot less effort.

The heads of cauliflowers and broccoli are the fruiting body of the plant. If you don't harvest them they shoot up to blown flowers followed by seed. Provided it doesn't come too early or too severely, I find that a good cabbage moth attack actually *increases* the size and vigour of the head, and causes it to develop earlier. After harvest, the chooks appreciate the leaves riddled with cabbage moth caterpillars even more than the leaves alone.

A HARVEST OF CHOOK FODDER

Chooks in the garden are a wonderful way of unblinkering perception. I used to regard chickweed and slugs as my biggest problems. Now I actually sow seed of chickweed, and look forward to finding a slug, anticipating the relish of the chooks! I prefer my tomatoes without fruit fly, but the chooks like theirs better with, and since I am growing to feed both chooks and humans, some tomatoes with fruit fly are a bonus.

Pest or high-quality chook fodder? The same creature can be either depending only on your perception. If the produce store sold bags of dried slugs, snails, grubs and weeds, it would market them as a high-protein, balanced laying mash, at a good price. Yet the same mixture, free in the garden, is usually unappreciated!

I even grow some crops specifically to attract 'pests'. Semposai is a kind of cabbage with very large, loosely packed leaves relished by slugs, snails and chooks. It is very fast-growing and hardy, and you can pick the leaves at the rate of two or three per day per plant. If I need to boost the protein level in the chooks' diet, or if I'm planning to plant something like lettuce or wombok that is particularly vulnerable to snails, I lay a dozen or so semposai leaves over a bed last thing of an evening after watering. First thing in the morning (the earlier the better) I gather up the leaves and feed them, covered in slugs, to the chooks. Semposai is the best plant I've discovered for this technique, mainly because it is so prolific, but wombok and pak tsoi also work well. All these varieties of Chinese cabbage also flower prolifically, and the flowers are very attractive to aphids, which in turn attract ladybirds. Unaffected flowers go wonderfully well in a salad, adding colour, flavour and lots of vitamins. Aphid-infested flowers are much appreciated by the chooks, after the ladybirds have had a go.

My strawberry guava tree yields a bountiful harvest of fruit fly larvae-infested fruit for the chooks. As my garden expands and my chook population increases, I plant more strawberry guavas specially to attract fruit fly!

In the afternoon I take a bucket of chook scraps and a basket for harvesting dinner down to the garden. Two tomatoes for the basket, one (preferably with grubs) for the bucket. A lettuce for the basket, the outer leaves, slugs and all, for the bucket. Some broccoli for the basket, and while I'm there I might try to find some cabbage moth caterpillars for the bucket. A few carrots for the basket and a few handfuls of the chickweed starting to overtake them for the bucket. The bucketful for the chooks and some eggs for the basket. The 'pests' are part of the harvest.

The third pest control tactic, therefore, is to make sure there *is* a negative consequence before you spend any time or energy. The 'pests' may actually be doing you a good turn, providing you with free pruning or an extra harvest. If you can't see any positive benefit, at least make sure there is a negative one. Very often the effect on eating quality of an insect attack is negligible or nonexistent.

Unfortunately, commercially saleable quality means virtually blemish-free. Blemishes sometimes affect holding quality and shelf life, but more often the reason is that consumers are not educated to recognise that a few holes in the outside leaves do not mar a cabbage. Even if you are growing to sell, however, it is usually easier to grow extra to allow for blemishes than it is to try to eliminate them. The extra chook food is a bonus.

BARRICADES

My final major pest control strategy is physical barriers. The advantage of this is that it doesn't kill the pests, so they are still available for predator food. It just prevents their getting at particularly vulnerable or valuable plants.

The height of the bench on which I raise seedlings is a physical barrier to crawling and ground-dwelling creatures like slugs, snails, cutworm and nematodes. When I plant out seedlings, I leave the pieces of plastic milk containers that serve as pots in place as miniature fences around the seedlings for a week or so, at their most vulnerable time. They are about 15 cm tall, open at the top and bottom, and pressed a centimetre or two into the ground around the seedlings. This prevents cutworm from getting at the seedlings, and although slugs could scale them, not knowing what's inside they don't bother.

The only fruit I bother to barricade against fruit fly are peaches. This involves using a plastic clothes peg to secure a little cloth bag over each set of fruit. This is a lot of work but probably no more so than spraying every fortnight, and worth it for the sake of pesticide-free tree-ripened peaches. I leave some fruit exposed as fruit fly lures, feeding the infested fruit to the chooks before the larvae hatch.

I used to have to barricade large tomatoes against fruit fly too, or grow only cherry or egg types that are resistant to them. But something must be working, because for the last few years I have been able to skip the bags, with only the odd tomato being affected.

OCCASIONAL STRATEGIES

There are a few other minor strategies of pest control that I use. Most of them tend to involve a lot of work, so I use them only occasionally, erratically, and when I'm in the mood to treat them as play!

THE GREAT CABBAGE MOTH DERBY

One year, lured by high prices, I tried to grow far too many cabbages at once, and of course ended up with an overpopulation of cabbage moths. A scoreboard and a badminton racquet were all that was needed to get every family member and visitor enthused about playing squash with cabbage moths.

The method was not a complete success. Too many enthusiasts played squash with the vegetables as well. I still keep the racquet in the garden though, and occasionally practise my hand–eye coordination on cabbage moths.

HUMUS AND WORMS

I have tried growing marigolds to deter nematodes, with no very obvious effect. Part of the problem is that while there might be no nematodes within the root zone of the marigolds, there is no room for anything else either!

I have had much more success by simply using the chooks and mulch to boost the level of organic matter. I suspect that the large quantity of relatively fresh vegetable matter tricks the nematodes into believing that there is living plant material available as food. At the same time it attracts predatory and scavenger organisms. The nematodes begin their breeding cycle prematurely on the strength of it, emerging to find no living food, but a lot of voracious predatory underground organisms instead.

It may just be that worms like the kind of conditions that nematodes don't, or perhaps the worms actually displace nematodes, competing for a niche.

Whatever the case, I've never seen healthy populations of both coexisting. The best way to get rid of nematodes is to breed worms.

WITCH'S BREW

In very humid weather I often make up a brew to stop fungus diseases like powdery mildew getting a head start. To my perennial seaweed brew I add all the stinging nettle, comfrey, horsetail and/or chamomile I can easily gather. The first three are very high in silica, which is water-retardant and so creates leaf surface conditions unsuitable for fungi. The chamomile is a mild fungicide.

I cover the added ingredients with water and let the mixture brew for just two days. Then I use the liquid, diluted 1:10, to spray zucchini, squash, cucumber and pumpkin plants. If I've been getting too much damping-off in germinating seedlings, I saturate the seed trays with the same brew, and use up any leftovers on anything else I suspect might be susceptible. The same mixture is a good foliar fertiliser too, so there is no penalty for overenthusiasm.

The catch-22 with this method is that the brew only works really well if you catch the infection very early and if it is used fresh – after no more than forty-eight hours' brewing. After this it is still a good foliar fertiliser or compost ingredient, but it doesn't work against fungi. So you really have to use your sixth sense to predict when, in two days' time, you will have an outbreak of fungal disease!

SELF-IMMOLATION

Every few years I get a plague of monolepta beetles descending on the garden. They are attracted to light, and coat the windows of the house at night so thickly that you can't see out. A small wood fire in a kerosene tin in the garden leads them to self-immolation on a large scale. I usually put a candle above the frog pond at the same time, to give the frogs a feast.

GRASSHOPPER JUICE

I haven't been troubled by grasshoppers since I put in the pond. However, before that I tried a number of control methods with variable success. The best was the macabre process of catching several grasshoppers and putting them in the blender with plenty of slightly soapy water, then spraying the mixture on their favourite plants.

The theory with this method is that it spreads virus and bacterial diseases that affect grasshoppers, but I suspect the mechanism is a bit more complex because I found that it worked best if I shook the grasshoppers up in the blender jug first. My guess is that they release fear pheromones that deter other grasshoppers.

The question is academic, anyhow, since frogs, lizards and birds enjoy catching and mincing grasshoppers much more than I do!

13 GREEN GATECRASHERS

Weeds are a special category of pest, but most of the pest control rules discussed in Chapter 12 apply here as well. Healthy plants are capable of self-defence against weeds. Most plants are allopathic to some degree, releasing exudates that deter the germination of potential competitors in their space. The stronger and healthier your plants are, the more they will be able successfully to compete with any weeds that do germinate. Healthy plants will defend their own territory.

However, weeds are usually very fast, vigorous growers. It is necessary to give your crop plants a bit of a head start to fend them off successfully. It is a bit unfair to expect seedlings to defend the garden alone! Planting advanced seedlings gives them the head start they need. If you mix adult and baby plants up in your guilds, plants big and tough enough to do it bear most of the task.

I try to keep every square centimetre of my garden occupied, delegating weeding to an army of productive plants that use allopathy and competition for light, water and nutrients as weapons. Any patch of bare, open ground is an unfilled niche, and nature will do its damnedest to fill it. But if you fill it first, with a healthy, well-nourished, suitable plant, there will be no vacant niche for weeds to occupy. The few weeds that survive may be susceptible to the Pollyanna Technique, where, instead of seeing them as pests, you try looking at them as potential allies. For example, weeds such as chickweed and fat hen make excellent chook fodder, providing easily picked prolific greens for the chook bucket. Weed seeds in mulch are also a good source of chook fodder. The chooks enjoy the hunting as much as the finding, and busily scratch up piles of mulch searching for the odd seed in it. The lure of a few seeds is enough to bribe them into doing most of my compost mixing and turning for me!

A few weeds in the garden also help keep pest and predator populations in balance. Weeds have their own native pests too. If you overreact and busily tear out all your weeds, you may just be forcing those insects to migrate into your crop plants. If you indulge in nonselective insect extermination you are just as likely to kill insects that are feeding mainly or wholly on your weeds. 'If in doubt, do nothing' is just as applicable to weed control as it is to pest control.

Many weeds are very good micronutrient accumulators. In some cases it is only your awareness of the nutrients being mined that is the difference between calling something a weed or a herb. I would never try to get rid of my stinging nettle patch. It is too valuable for compost piles and liquid brews.

Even dock and sorrel are susceptible to the Pollyanna Technique. They are both extremely deep-rooted and almost impossible to pull or dig out. They re-sprout from tiny fragments of root, and from under a foot of mulch, and they seed prolifically. Chooks like the leaves, but the roots re-sprout from the mulch, appearing like chickenpox all over your newly planted bed. But both plants thrive in heavy, poorly drained acidic soil. The deep, pugnacious roots go down several metres, breaking up clods of clay, creating drainage channels and mining subsoil nutrients. They don't do nearly as well in good, light, pH-balanced, well-drained soil. They tend just to disappear as the soil improves. Though I still pull off their leaves for the chooks, and remove flowers before they have a chance to seed, I am much more inclined these days to tolerate them. I figure that if they are thriving in a particular patch, I have bigger problems than weeds with that patch, and the weeds are actually helping to solve those problems.

THE EDGE GUILD

The edge guild is a special kind of barricade. The only weed to really worry about in the garden is grass. Grass is so widespread precisely because it is extremely competitive, strongly allopathic, very persistent and an arch-survivor.

Chooks or compost will clear grass, but the problem is keeping it away. Grass propagates itself mostly by runners that invade your garden from the edges. In spring and summer it will make almost daily incursions, and unless you set up a barricade to stop it, you will be stuck with neverending perimeter weeding.

The first barricades I tried were edging with timber, or rocks. The runners simply went over and under, the edges had to be patrolled almost daily, and it was difficult to mow right up to it. Then I tried mounds of mulch. This was a bit more effective, but still the runners found a way through. The mulch clogged up the catcher when mowing, and it took a huge amount of mulch to maintain.

I felt like Goldilocks with the third bowl of porridge when I discovered perimeter planting. I now have a three-tier living barricade right around the garden, and I never have to weed out grass. I can mow or weed-eat right up to and even over the edges without difficulty. The barricade plants have many other uses as well. They are extremely hardy and can be propagated very simply by root division, multiplying at least ten times each season. If you beg or buy an initial parent plant, it takes a surprisingly short time to surround your garden completely. To plant them you have first to clear the area of grass by smothering it under mulch, building a compost pile on it, or exposing it to the chooks. But after planting, the barricades require no maintenance at all.

SUGARCANE AND LEMON GRASS

The outer row is grass, either lemon grass or sugarcane – fighting like with like. I use a rare kind of black sugarcane, only because the canes are so beautiful, but I expect regular sugarcane would do just as well. Both these grasses have dense root masses that prevent other grasses getting through, but neither will itself spread by running, so they stay where you plant them.

To propagate sugarcane, cut a cane into about 20 cm lengths with at least one joint per length. Hollow out the mulch and lay the length horizontally on the ground, then cover with about 2.5 cm of compost. Sprinkle with mulch and water. Leave a gap of about 30 cm and plant the next length. Each of these will grow, within a couple of months, into a dense stand of sugarcane. But they won't send out runners, and unless you lay a cane down and allow it to root, it won't spread.

A second row of sugarcane planted about 30 cm behind the first and offset will make an effective wallaby fence. Chewing raw sugarcane is very good for your teeth, and my children enjoy the treat. You can also cut the canes and either pass them through a chaffcutter or mulcher, or mow them. This makes a mulch that the worms love, or a nutrient-rich compost ingredient.

To propagate lemon grass, dig up a clump and separate the stems, using a fork to lever them apart. Try to keep at least a couple of roots on each. Cut off *all* the green leaf. Make hollows in the mulch at about 30 cm spacings and fill each one with a double handful of compost or good soil. Plant a rooted stem in each. Within a couple of months each of these stems will have grown into a dense clump of lemon grass that you can, if you need to, divide again.

Lemon grass leaf, fresh or dried, makes good tea, especially mixed with chamomile or peppermint or even added to regular black tea. The tender bases of the stems are a pleasant vegetable that goes well in stir-fries, curries, fish or chicken dishes. Many Thai recipes call for lemon grass. Mowed or cut and passed through the chaffcutter it makes a prolific high-carbon compost ingredient or a mulch that is very long-lasting.

COMFREY AND HORSETAIL

The second row of the barricade is comfrey or horsetail. Both plants are very high in silica (as are many grasses), and I suspect that they form an effective barricade by competing successfully for this essential nutrient.

Both plants need to be propagated with care, as a new plant will establish from even the tiniest fragment of root and will be all but impossible to eradicate once established. To propagate, simply dig up a plant and cut or break the root into pieces. Even very small fragments will grow, but to give the new plant a good start I like to use pieces about the size of a small carrot or beetroot. Plant the pieces in a hollow in the mulch, covered with about 3 cm of compost or good soil, at about 40 cm spacings.

Comfrey is an extremely good micronutrient accumulator – a complete fertiliser in a plant. It is so rich in nitrogen that you can substitute it for animal manure in compost. The leaves fermented in water make a very rich liquid fertiliser. Because it is so abundant in silica, an infusion of it makes a good medicine for fungus diseases in plants. It is also particularly rich in calcium: its traditional name is 'knitbone', which refers to its effectiveness as a treatment for broken bones. I've never broken any bones, but I apply shredded leaves as a poultice on sprains or bruises, and use it as a source of calcium for the compost.

Comfrey is also useful as a nutrient trap. Planted around the bottom edge of the garden it will grow huge and lush and prevent any nutrients escaping by leaching out. Unfortunately it is also quite rich in natural toxic compounds called pyrrolizidine alkaloids, which can damage your liver. I wouldn't eat any except if prescribed by someone very competent, and even then only in small quantities. The chooks like it, but because I'm not sure about the effect of these alkaloids on their livers, I go very easy in feeding it to them.

MIXED HERBS

The third row is a mixture of perennial herbs. The basics are the herbs that spread by running, creating a dense carpet. They spread out to fill any gaps between and around the first rows, but are held in check on the inner edge by periodic exposure to the chook domes. I also plant bush-type herbs among them in any spots where the running herbs will not completely overrun the bushes.

At the bottom end of the garden, where the path-drains end, I use the mint family: peppermint, apple mint, spearmint and ordinary mint. In the very wet patches some volunteer cress holds its own against them. At the top end of the garden, where it is dry and exposed to full sun, I use the thyme family. Along the edges are marjoram, oregano, yarrow and chamomile, and towards the wetter bottom edges, nasturtium. Also in this herbal carpet are borage, lavender, bush basil, sage, rosemary, wormwood, tansy, curry plant and evening primrose.

Most of these herbs have culinary and medicinal uses, and whatever I pick for the basket, I also pick for the chook bucket. I have never had to worm the chooks, and I suspect this is because I add small amounts of yarrow and thyme to their feed regularly, with which they dose themselves against intestinal worms. Many of these herbs yield beautiful cut flowers that also attract bees, butterflies, honeyeaters and predatory insects. Some of the flowers are edible and make magical salads. Most of them have wonderful scents that add the dimension of smell to the garden.

Some – wormwood and tansy in particular – are insect repellents. All of these herbs accumulate micronutrients, and some are very good at it. I gather a bucket or more of prunings to add to the compost every time I make it, which distributes the micronutrients around the garden and prevents deficiency diseases.

The easiest and cheapest way to acquire herbs is by raiding the gardens of friends and acquaintances. Even perfect strangers are usually pleased to let you have a root or a cutting for the asking. Propagate it in a pot and, when well established, transplant into the garden.

WEEDING THE EASY WAY

1. When you are establishing your garden, work from a centre out, so that you have a single, minimum edge to protect from grass invasion. Start a barrier around the edge of your garden as soon as you reach it. Use chooks or compost piles, and mulch, to eliminate all the grass inside this barrier.
2. Process all plant material you import into the garden, either by composting it, using it in liquid brews, exposing it to wild birds, or throwing it to the chooks to get rid of all the seeds and stop it reproducing.
3. Make sure the chooks get plenty of mulch to scratch over, so that after you move them on, you are planting into a heavily mulched weed-free bed. If you are not using chooks, cover any bed or part of a bed with a good thick layer of de-seeded mulch before you plant. Plant advanced seedlings, and avoid creating seedbed conditions anywhere but in the shadehouse. This should eliminate any need for weeding in the first part of the cycle.
4. In the middle part of the cycle, as your plants begin to bear, harvest any weeds growing among them for the chook bucket, compost pile or worm farm. They aren't really weeds, just volunteer fodder. Keep your beds full, replacing spent plants as soon as they come out.
5. In the last part of the cycle, before the chooks are due on again, leave any weeds to spread, and if you don't have enough, plant more! Chooks have backbones much better suited to weeding than humans, and they will appreciate the task much more than you will. If you are not using chooks, it is best not to let weeds get too out of hand by spreading or seeding. But it is still good practice to let some grow and mature around your garden. Cut them off at ground level before they propagate, and cover the spot with a thick layer of mulch. The roots will decompose in situ, providing air and water channels and nutrients. The tops are valuable in compost, liquid brew or worm food.
6. Don't be too ruthless with weeds. Many of them are sheltering pest predators, decoying pests and improving soil. If there is no reason to remove them, leave them alone and watch.

14 WATER

A food-producing garden uses quite a lot of water, much more than a native garden or rockery. Merely surviving without irrigation is quite a feat in this driest continent on earth. Many native plants have evolved some very clever adaptations for it. Mere survival, however, is not enough in a food-producing garden. A silver beet plant that just survives is not much use. We need it to grow, ideally at very close to the fastest possible rate, so we can keep picking from it! A tomato plant that just survives is not much use either. We need it to produce fruit, ideally as heavily as possible.

Like all living things, plants are made up mostly of water, and like all living things, they die very quickly if they are dehydrated. But plants have a bit of a problem keeping their body moisture in and growing at the same time. Growing uses a lot more water than just surviving, especially with humans continually harvesting the juiciest bits! To grow, plants need to make themselves new cells. They do this by taking the hydrogen out of water molecules, the carbon dioxide out of air and dissolved molecules out of the water around their roots, and using light to turn them into carbohydrates. Every element of this process uses water.

Some is dismantled for its hydrogen, with the oxygen atoms eliminated into the air. Some is unavoidably lost in the process of taking in carbon dioxide. Plants don't have a diaphragm to breathe with. To get enough carbon dioxide, they have to open up not just one little pair of bronchi to suck air in, but thousands of stomata so it can diffuse in. A relatively large part of their insides has to be exposed to the outside, and to evaporation. At night there is no light for photosynthesis and so no use for carbon dioxide. The plants close their stomata to conserve water. But in the daytime they can only use the available light for growth if their stomata are open. Unfortunately enough light for the reaction usually comes in a package with enough heat to evaporate any moisture exposed to the air!

Some water is also lost in the process of getting themselves cool enough for the reaction. Plants have a few tricks for controlling their temperature, including light-coloured leaves, turning their leaf edges on to the sun, oiling themselves to reflect heat, and covering themselves in white powder. However, many of these tricks also make them inedible, or at least unpalatable, and most of our food-producing plants evolved in places where none of these tricks were necessary. The main means our garden plants use for controlling temperature is transpiration, which, like sweating profusely, uses a lot of water.

Even if it is cool enough, plants need to transpire some water. They don't have a heart to pump their circulation system. One of their main engines for drawing nutrient-rich water up from the soil is to let water go out through their leaves, creating a suction effect.

Very little of the water taken in actually ends up in the plant tissue. Most ends up evaporating into the atmosphere. Nevertheless every element of the growing process uses water. If plants are in danger of dehydrating, they stop photosynthesising, close their stomata, stop taking in nutrients and stop growing. Even if there is no tissue damage, it can take several days for some plants to start photosynthesising again. A few hours of water deficit will cost quite a few dinners!

Drought-tolerant plants are those better adapted to *surviving* dry conditions (not *growing in* dry conditions – even drought-tolerant plants stop growing in dry conditions). They can close their stomata tighter, excrete oils so as to lose less water through their skin, and tolerate higher body temperatures. But unless it is these drought-surviving mechanisms that we want to harvest (like aromatic oils in herbs such as rosemary), even drought-tolerant plants grow better with enough water.

SOIL AND WATER

How much water is enough water depends on your soil. Plants absorb the water they need from the soil through fine hairs on their roots. However, not all the water applied by rain or irrigation is available to them. Some runs off the surface or drains right through the soil into the water table, and out to streams and waterways. Only the amount that can be absorbed by the soil within your plants' root zone is useful. Clay soils can hold more water than sandy soils, but they absorb it so slowly that heavy rain just runs off the surface, taking soil with it. Organic soils absorb water quickly and hold nearly as much as clay.

At the other end of the scale, some water is held onto so tightly by the soil particles that plants cannot draw it up, and so wilt. Clay soils hold water more tightly than sandy or organic soils. They can be as much as 30 per cent water, and the plants cannot get at any of it. Organic soils can be sucked much more nearly dry. Sandy soils can be sucked down to about 3 per cent water before plants start to wilt. Soil with lots of humus and organic matter has the best of both worlds. It is more difficult to over-water, as well as under-water. It can hold lots of water, and it can be sucked quite dry. This water-holding capacity is its most important characteristic, even more important than its nutrient content.

TEMPERATURE AND WATER

On hot dry days, especially with a hot wind, plants can wilt even in well-watered soil. This is most noticeable in broad, dark-leaved crops like zucchinis, but applies to most crops. It is because the plants are using water to cool down faster than they can suck it up. Remember – they will stop growing long before they actually start wilting, so this is even more severe than it looks.

Shade and windbreaks help, but the best defence is a large, well-developed, deep root system to take in water as fast as it is needed. This is just like a large lung capacity for an athlete. Frequent shallow watering will train your plants to develop small, surface roots. On a hot dry day, no matter how much you water them, they will not be able to get sufficient water into them quickly enough.

The solution is to develop soil that can hold a lot of water, and then water the plants deeply and infrequently. Husbanding your worms and leaving the roots of spent plants in place will create channels that allow water to penetrate deeply. Heavy mulch will keep the water there. This will force your plants to send their roots down deep, which will stand them in good stead on hot dry days.

'Infrequently' depends on the weather and on just how good your soil is. I water the seeds and seedlings every day, and give a watering-can's worth to each seedling at planting out and again within three or four days. I use the sprinklers only when there has been no rain. If I have to use them more often than once a fortnight in winter, or more than twice a week in even the hottest weather, I know my soil is not good enough.

WATER TABLE

Frequent watering is one of those tedious, repetitious garden chores that do more harm than good. Applying more water than your soil can absorb and hold is useless. Plants cannot suck up water that is trying to drain down, saturation squeezes the oxygen out of the soil, and water draining away takes precious nutrients with it. If your soil is not absorbent enough, and your plants need very frequent watering just to avoid wilting, the cure is worse than the complaint.

The biggest problem is that all that water you pour on has to go somewhere, either up or down. If it is not evaporating through your plants back into the atmosphere, it is feeding down into that giant underground lake called the water table. The water table will gradually rise as a result of all the irrigation water you are pouring into it. Eventually, and not so far down the track that you can afford to ignore it, your plants will end up with their feet in an underground pond. Not only will the current generation of plants die, but the mineral salts dissolved in this underground water will poison every future generation as well.

To be on the safe side, it is wise to include some deep-rooted perennials, preferably trees, in your garden design. These can make use of rain or irrigation water that has drained down out of reach of your vegetables. They can cycle it back into the atmosphere to be purified and fall again, rather than let it disappear into the water table.

HUMIDITY

The more humid the air, the less water plants use, because less will evaporate from their leaves. High humidity can be an advantage, because plants can have their stomata wide open and be taking in maximum carbon dioxide without losing too much moisture in the process. However, high humidity can also be a problem. If the air is already highly saturated, water won't evaporate from the leaves very well. Plants have no way of cooling down or of sucking up soil nutrients. They can suffer from heat stress, even with ample soil water. They can stop growing because the leaf temperature is too high and too few nutrients are flowing in. Fungi are not so handicapped. In very humid weather, fungus diseases have the advantage over your crop plants.

In a cool, temperate climate, humidity can be very high before it is 'too high'. A very low rate of evaporation is enough to cool down, and high humidity usually only happens when there is cloud cover, and so there is not much photosynthesis going on anyhow. But even in these climates, *too* high a humidity can impede the process of drawing up nutrients and limit growth.

In hot climates, a much lower humidity level is 'too high'. The biggest problem happens when it is very still, very hot, very humid *and* very bright – which rarely happens naturally. But this combination can happen if you water heavily during a hot, bright day. The water evaporating from the ground, and even before it hits the ground, creates high humidity even in bright sun.

I never water once the sun is hitting my garden in hot weather. Apart from the humidity effect, water droplets on plant leaves can focus the sun, like a lens, and cause little burn marks. The best time to water is in the early morning, because this gives the best temperature control. If you get up late, however, it is better to wait until late afternoon to water unless your garden is bone-dry.

PART FIVE

ALPHABET SOUP

LEARNING YOUR ABC

There are literally thousands of varieties of edible plants. Many of them are too delicate ever to reach the supermarket shelves, and are known only to gardeners. My seed boxes contain over 100 different packets. I have chosen fifty of the most familiar and popular vegetables and herbs – the things I think of as essential and that most people will want to grow – for this section of the book. They are listed in alphabetical order for ease of reference.

One of the wonderful things about life is that every individual is unique. Getting to know your crop is a bit like getting to know people – no two are remotely the same, but whole families have some features in common, and they are all much more alike than they are different. The first four sections of this book dealt with the similarities; this much shorter section deals with the differences.

If you have been impatient and skipped ahead to here, you will have to retrace your steps. The standard propagation and seedling-raising methods to which I constantly refer here are those described in Chapter 9, 'Raising Seedlings'. Unless the plant is idiosyncratic in its preferred propagation method, I refer you to this standard method. And unless it is idiosyncratic in its fertilising requirements, I refer you to the standard mixtures for raising seeds and seedlings.

The only way you will really get to know what plants are like in your conditions is by exercising your own curiosity, and keeping diary records. My observations about the following selection in my conditions will, however, allow you to take a pretty good guess at how their cousins might behave at your place.

ARTICHOKES

Globe artichokes are so large and have such a low yield for the amount of room they take up that I used to wonder if they were really worth growing, especially since I had a great deal of trouble propagating them on my first few attempts. But I'm glad I persisted, because they have some wonderful redeeming features.

The most persuasive is that they are such glorious eating. Like many vegetables they go bitter if stored for too long, so the ones you get in shops are not a good introduction, even if you can afford to buy them. Fresh, sweet artichoke hearts in butter – for breakfast – are the kind of delicacy that reminds you how decadent gardening really is! The second redeeming feature is that the plants themselves are quite decorative and make a very effective windbreak, so it is not too difficult to justify the space taken up on the grounds of multiple uses. Three or four plants yield enough to share around a family.

Globe artichokes are semiperennial, lasting around five years, although you get the best return for space by renewing them every two or three years. They can be grown from seed but, once you have a few, propagation is most easily done by transplanting the suckers that arise from the base of the plant in spring. If you raise them from seed, skip the seed-germinating tray stage and sow them straight into a seedling-raising pot. The seeds are quite large enough to handle, and the long taproot is easy to damage while transplanting. Young plants are not frost-hardy, but mature plants can survive light frost. If you sow seeds in midwinter the seedlings will be ready to be transplanted out straight after the last frost, and will get a full growing season to establish before the following winter.

I plant them in the edge guild on the windy side of the garden. They cope quite well with dry conditions but they don't like poor drainage at all. They will survive poor fertility, but there is just about a one-to-one ratio between the number of handfuls of compost and the number of harvestable buds. Unless you are willing to devote a good half bucketful of compost or worm castings to each plant at planting time and again each spring, you might as well not bother with them. They also appreciate heavy mulching. Whenever the chooks are nearby, I steal an armload of chook-processed mulch for each plant.

Aphids are the only artichoke pest I have ever encountered. They can be hosed off the underside of the leaves, and an occasional spraying with seaweed brew allows the plants to resist them at other times.

ASPARAGUS

Asparagus, like artichokes, is gourmet gardening for which you resent the outlay of effort until the first time you taste it. Very little of my asparagus actually makes it as far as the pot. Not a lot even makes it out of the garden! Fresh raw asparagus tastes like the sweetest baby peas, and can be used to bribe children to clean up their rooms.

Asparagus is an exercise in deferred gratification, since it takes two or three years for plants to bear harvestable shoots. However, once established they will last for twenty years or more. My friend Rod tells a story about a long-abandoned asparagus plot in his childhood backyard that was overtaken by lawn. Every spring the shoots came up through the grass, and his mother sent him out to cut them from the lawn. It was only many years later that he discovered that this was not the standard way to grow asparagus!

If the idea of waiting a few years is too frustrating, you can buy two-year-old crowns, which give you a much quicker crop. However, it is far cheaper to raise asparagus from seed. Soaking the seed overnight speeds up germination, but seeds can still take several weeks to germinate. Sow them in a standard seed-germinating mix in early spring. When they are about 5 cm tall, transplant the individual plants into a standard seedling-raising mix, twelve to a tray. Leave them in the tray in a moderately sunny spot until the following spring. Since they spend such a long time in the tray, I topdress them with compost or worm castings, or feed them with seaweed brew or liquid worm manure every few weeks.

After the plants have been in the tray for a year you should be able to identify which plants are male and which are female. The females are much more spindly, and have tiny white–green flowers followed by red berries. The males are more vigorous, with thicker stems. The standard advice is to discard the females, but there are lots of little nectar-eaters that relish the female flowers, and (perhaps superstitiously) I believe all forms of life do better with the chance to reproduce. So I plant out a few females as well.

Since you are looking at tending the plants for twenty years, and the standard of seedlings is very variable, it is worth being ruthless about the quality of the ones you select for planting out. Feed any plants that are not *very* vigorous to the worm farm.

In early spring you can transplant the seedlings to their permanent spot. In late autumn the fern will die back completely, making you wonder if the plant is dead. Over winter the roots lie dormant, preferably under at least 15 cm of mulch. Come spring, however, new shoots start to appear daily through the mulch.

In the first year you should resist, as much as you possibly can, the urge to harvest. The following year you can cut every shoot that sticks its head up for about eight weeks, before letting the fern grow out to replenish itself. The year after, and every spring from then on, you can continue cutting for up to twelve weeks if your plants are well enough fed. Cut the shoots with a knife below the level of the mulch, taking care not to damage the upcoming ones, and you will get one or two shoots from every plant nearly every day – a feast well worth waiting for!

A permanent spot for the asparagus plants is a bit tricky. Each plant will grow into a very attractive fern about a metre tall, taking up a circle about 40 cm across. They should be planted near a path, since in their season they need to be harvested every day, and the sprouting shoots are easily broken off if accidentally trodden on while they are still hidden under the mulch. They do not need pollination except to yield fertile seed, so there is no real reason to plant in a block. Asparagus and tomatoes are good companions, and the ferns are effective disguise plants for members of the cabbage family, so there are good reasons for scattering them amongst annual crops.

It is also quite desirable to expose the dormant plants to the chooks over winter. From late autumn through to late winter the chooks will do no damage to the dormant plants, which appreciate a good mulching with the phosphates the chooks provide, and especially benefit from the calcium gradually released from shellgrit and cuttlefish. Grasshoppers love asparagus almost as much as chooks love grasshoppers, and the chooks will clean up the eggs and larvae. But the problem is that these beds are also scheduled to have chooks in late spring and summer in a twice-yearly rotation.

I solve this problem by planting the asparagus as path edge plants, about four or five to a bed, in beds that will be chooked in June, July and August. When I move the chooks onto these beds in December, January and February, I place the domes about 40 cm back from the path edge, so that the ferns are just outside.

BASIL

I am a pesto addict, so I grow lots of basil. This is one of those strongly aromatic herbs confusing to pests that forage by scent. It seems to particularly get up the nose of fruit fly, so it is a good companion not only for tomatoes but for anything that is prone to fruit fly.

There are two common kinds of basil – sweet basil and bush basil. Sweet basil is an annual and suitable for growing in the main beds, scattered among your vegetables. The bush basils are perennial and should be grown in the edge guild area and around fruit trees. The perennial basils come in several different varieties, including lemon basil that is wonderful in fish dishes and red basil that has spectacular claret-coloured foliage.

Sweet basil is propagated from seed. It has identical climatic and growing requirements to tomatoes, so I usually just sow some basil seed along with the tomatoes every time, propagating it by the standard method. Even if you are a basil addict, a couple of bushes is enough. They grow about the same size as a tomato or capsicum plant. Regular picking keeps them bushy, so pick some for the chook bucket too.

Perennial basil can be grown from seed, but most types are easier and cheaper to obtain by taking a cutting from a mature plant. They will grow quite well in partial shade, but the aromatic oils that give them their distinctive smell and taste are, for the plants, a means of protecting them from the sun. So you will get more flavour from plants grown in full sun. Basil has such an extensive root system that it will cope quite well with drying out, but not at all with water-logging, so keep it in a well-drained position in your garden.

BEANS

Bean seeds are easy to save, and you get so few to a packet when you buy them that they are worth saving. Simply leave the best plants in and let the pods fully mature and dry on the plant. When the pods are brown and the seeds inside are plump and hard, pick and pod them, dry them in a warm airy place, and store them in an airtight container. The ones you don't plant you can eat as kidney beans.

Bean seeds are large enough and reliable enough germinators to plant directly into the garden. If you raise the plants in pots to about 15 cm, however, the fast dwarf varieties will start to bear within five or six weeks from planting out. This means that you can fit another crop in between chook rotations. I leave out the seed-germinating mixture stage, and plant the seed directly into seedling-raising pots.

The most common cause of failure in propagating beans is keeping the seeds too wet, which makes them vulnerable to fungus diseases. Plant bean seeds into damp, shaded soil or seedling mixture, and resist the temptation to water them again until the shoots appear, which should happen within a few days.

Beans are legumes, producing their own nitrogen, so they are not too fussy about nutrient levels and can be planted at any stage in a chook rotation. Save any extra compost or worm castings for the things that like it. Too much nitrogen-rich fertiliser, especially in liquid form, will make them go all to leaf and set few seeds, and it will make them sappy and vulnerable to pests and diseases. But they do like phosphorus. Bird manure is a good source, so keep the plants within the chook rotation beds.

Beans do not cope with frost at all, or even with chilly weather. Windy weather when they are flowering makes them fail to set seed. In northern NSW I can plant seed from early August, provided I pick a warm spot, and get the first harvest in October, provided I give the plants enough wind protection. If I am willing to gamble on no early frosts, I can plant successive crops until late March and keep on eating beans until mid-June.

You need a few bean plants to pick enough for a meal, so I like to plant some together to make the job easier. But they are also well liked by mites and aphids, whose job I prefer to make tough! I compromise by planting about a dozen plants to a batch, which is enough to pick a good dinner for four from at a time. All the plants of the Umbelliferae family, which includes carrots, celery, parsnips, parsley, coriander and dill, attract hoverflies, especially when they are flowering. Hoverflies love aphids, so any of these plants are good companions for anything prone to aphid attack.

The variety I mostly use is a dwarf bean that is a descendant of Redland Pioneer. The plants don't need staking, but if planted fairly close together they provide some support to each other. I plant them at about 20 cm spacing in two short rows, with about 20 cm between rows and about six plants in each row. If you offset the rows in a diamond pattern, each plant gets its share of the space. Dry trash like corn stalks or spent basil plants, laid on the ground between the plants when they are first planted out, will help keep the beans up off the ground so they don't rot.

Climbing beans take longer to bear, and bear for a longer time. Snake beans are my pick of the annual climbers because they are very vigorous, resistant to disease, yield prolifically, and make good eating green or dried. But they need a strong support at least 2 metres tall.

Climbing beans go up by twining around a vertical support, so trellises with horizontal wires don't really suit them. They grow well up a tepee, but my favourite support for them is a maypole-like structure, with a central pole about 2.5 metres tall. Lengths of twine run from the top of the pole to short stakes arranged in a circle around it. The beans hang down inside and are easy to pick and, if the circle is big enough, the vines can be used to provide summer shade for lettuces and silver beet.

Some varieties of climbing beans are perennial, and do well climbing a fence or permanent trellis. I have Seven Year, Borlotti and Madagascar beans climbing all over and providing much of the shade in my shadehouse. They have beautiful red flowers.

Because beans are symbiotic with a root bacterium that fixes atmospheric nitrogen, green leafy nitrogen-lovers (like lettuce, cabbage, parsley and silver beet) do well around and following them. The bacteria are vulnerable to the antibiotic properties of garlic and onions, so these make bad bean companions. Beans help deter pests of the Solanaceae family (potatoes, eggplants, capsicums and tomatoes).

BEETROOT

Until I began growing them I had only ever tasted beetroot as slices out of a can. This is a sad story. Beetroot, like many vegetables, begin converting their sugars to starches as soon as they are picked. Fresh whole baby beets, lightly steamed or baked, perhaps with a dob of sour cream, are a real treat! Beetroot are very versatile. They can be grated into salads, steamed, boiled, baked, made into soup or pickled and preserved. The plants are fast-growing, high-yielding, easy to grow, and will grow almost all year round.

I grow almost exclusively baby beetroot, which I use – because they are small and fast-growing – as fillers for any gap in the planting. I include thirty or forty in just about every guild. The conventional wisdom is that they do not like to be transplanted. But I find that if I transplant them into individual pots when they are very small, and take care not to disturb the roots when planting out, they don't suffer at all even from this double transplanting.

Beetroot seeds are really several seeds in a tough, corky outer coating. Soaking them overnight before planting is a definite advantage. Plant into a standard seed-germinating mix and transplant each seedling into its individual pot in a seedling-raising tray as early as possible. Smaller pots, like yoghurt containers with the bottom cut out, turned upside down, can be used instead of the standard two-litre milk containers.

Although it is a root vegetable, beetroot likes much the same conditions as the leafy greens. It is best grown very fast in a very rich soil. If it does not directly follow the chooks or a legume, it may benefit from a bit of compost. Each plant needs only about 8 cm of space if the soil is rich enough, so you can get a very high yield from a small area. The leaves as well as the roots are edible. The only trouble I have ever had with them is that some varieties bolt to seed in the heat of summer, especially if they are a bit hungry or stressed for lack of water. You can minimise this tendency by saving seed for summer beets from those that are slowest to bolt.

BORAGE

Legend has it that the knights of the Round Table used borage for courage, and I have noticed that the flowers seem to have an uplifting, optimistic effect. Of course this could easily be simply due to their appearance. The bright-blue, star-shaped flowers reek of cheerfulness!

Borage self-sows easily, and I have not planted it in my garden for many years now. It is extremely hardy, growing in shade, sun, wet or dry, but the plants are easy to remove from places where they are not welcome, so it doesn't become a troublesome weed. The roots go down a good 2 metres, mining the subsoil for nutrients and adding organic matter. It accumulates silica and potassium, and is prolific enough to make a good mulch and compost ingredient. Strawberries love it, and the flowers are quite magical in salads.

Borage is an annual, grown from seed sown in spring and dying off before winter. Propagate it by the standard method the first time. You will probably never need to propagate it again, as the plants will come up of their own accord.

BROAD BEANS

Broad beans are very nutritious, with lots of protein and complex carbohydrates. They yield very heavily at exactly the time of year – late winter and early spring – when the garden is likely to be at its leanest. They also fix copious amounts of nitrogen in the soil for the succeeding crop.

This is all just as well, since, at least in my garden, they wouldn't rate inclusion on the grounds of flavour alone! It is always possible to make a hearty, filling, nutritious meal based on broad beans, but it takes some culinary skill to make a flavoursome one. You can eat the leaf tips as a green, the young beans, pods and all, like French beans, and the older beans shelled and steamed or fried in butter. However, to my taste the best way to use them is to let the beans fully mature and dry out, and store them for use (after soaking overnight) as a filler in soups and casseroles. That way you don't really taste them at all!

I plant broad bean seeds in May to allow companion planting with early spuds. They need short days and cool temperatures to set beans: in tropical and subtropical climates, where the winter days are warm and relatively long, you can get wonderfully healthy, vigorous plants that set very few beans. It is also best if the plants are fairly mature and have finished flowering before the onset of warm weather brings the aphids around, since broad beans are one of their very favourites.

As for French beans, I skip the seed-propagating mix stage and plant the seeds directly into seedling-raising mix. Germination is sometimes faster if you soak the seeds for a few hours, but, like beans, you can rot the seeds by overwatering before germination.

Broad beans fix their own nitrogen, and they will suffer from too much leaf and no beans, as well as from aphid attack, if they have a diet too rich in water-soluble nitrogen. They don't need pampering. Ironically, people who don't particularly like them often get the best yields because they don't overindulge them! The plants like soil that is fairly heavy but not too acidic, and they are prone to a disease aptly called chocolate spot if the potassium levels are too low.

The ideal way to plant them is into a seedling-raising mix made with compost with lots of comfrey, nettles, yarrow or cow manure for potassium, and lots of seaweed brew for aphid immunity. Then plant them out into a bed where the chooks have scratched in plenty of wood ash. Take care not to overwater them, and give them no liquid fertilising at all.

Broad beans are classic companions for potatoes. However, while the beans will tolerate quite severe frost, potatoes won't. I solve this by planting the beans out in two double rows with a 50 cm space between rows. In late winter, by which time the broad beans are three-quarters grown, I plant potatoes in this space. I use quick greens like lettuce, Sugarloaf cabbage and beetroot as space fillers in the meantime. Coles Dwarf is the best variety for this as it gives heavy yields without completely dominating the bed. Within the double rows, seedlings are planted at 20 cm spacing in a diamond pattern.

If you get an early warm spring, or you plant broad beans too late, they may be troubled by the aphids that are likely to arrive with the warm weather. They should be well grown enough not to mind. If you like you can pick off the tips where the aphids will be clustered and either wash the aphids off and eat the tips yourself, or feed them, aphids and all, to the chooks.

If your broad beans *do* mind the aphids, regard it as an early warning that your soil has too much water-soluble nitrogen, which should be corrected before the warm weather brings major pest and disease problems. Start giving the chooks a lot more carbon-rich mulch like hay or leaf litter, and spread it around the garden. Hopefully the soil life will be persuaded to take up the excess nitrogen in trying to compost it. Justify a trip to the beach on the grounds of topping up your seaweed brew, and give every new compost pile plenty of it.

BROCCOLI

The best way to eat home-grown broccoli is raw in a salad. A close second is to let the heads flower and eat the beautiful creamy yellow flowers in a salad. It seems a pity to cook the vitamin C out of this extremely rich source, and home-grown broccoli is so sweet and tender that there is no need to cook it.

Unfortunately the drawback with this is that broccoli is a bit difficult to grow in salad season. This is partly because at this time it tends to grow too quickly to produce good-sized heads, but mainly because this is also the season of the cabbage moth. I grow it right through summer anyhow. I just place it on the path edges so that any cabbage moth caterpillars are easy to pick off, and don't worry too much about the size of the main head. The side shoots give a better harvest anyhow, and one that lasts for several months. Green Sprouting Calabrese is a good variety for this.

Swatow broccoli, an Asian variety, is especially good for summer planting. It has no central head like conventional varieties, but instead yields a heavy crop of small side shoots that continue for months if they are picked regularly and not allowed to set seed. It is resistant to cabbage moth attack, and indeed everything else. The beautiful white flowers that follow the green buds have a wonderful hot–sweet flavour and dress a salad up to look like fairy food, especially combined with the brilliant blue of borage flowers. Just before the chooks are due I let it run to seed. The seeds yield quite a phenomenal supply of very high-protein chook food.

There is nothing tricky whatsoever about growing broccoli. The seed is planted in standard seed-germinating mix, and germinates reliably with no fuss. It transplants easily to a seedling-raising tray, and grows there quite happily to about 15 cm, when it can be transplanted out. Each plant will occupy a 40 cm wide circle when fully grown, the Swatow variety a little less. Broccoli likes rich soil and is quite partial to a variety of micronutrients. Boron and molybdenum are special favourites, so it benefits from seaweed brew or compost containing seaweed.

BRUSSELS SPROUTS

Brussels sprouts are one of the most difficult vegetables to grow in my area, since they are really a cold-weather crop, adapted to a long, cold, frosty winter. The buds become loose and flavourless, the plant is liable to bolt to seed, and cabbage moth, aphids and fungi take their toll as soon as the warm weather arrives. For years I planted them, along with other cool-weather brassicas, in mid-autumn. But brussels sprouts are real slowcoaches, taking six months or more to reach maturity. They would only just be starting to bear in mid-spring. The weather warmed up, the days got longer, and the plants routinely bolted after a measly yield of very unpalatable sprouts.

The earlier I planted them, the better the yield, until gradually, over the years, the planting time crept back to early summer. I have to plant the seed in late November and have seedlings ready to plant out in early January to get a decent crop before late August. It *still* feels very strange to be planting such a winter crop along with the corn and cucumbers!

But this means that they reach bearing age at the *beginning* of winter. Once mature, they will bear for several months if the weather stays cool enough and the days stay short enough. So this way I get a whole three months of picking from them, with the sprouts large and tight and well flavoured. Since they are a large plant, and take up so much space for such a long time, it is worth extending the bearing time as long as possible.

However, this also means that the young plants are at their most vulnerable stage right in the middle of cabbage moth and aphid season. If I didn't like lightly steamed brussels sprouts with butter, and brussels sprouts soup, so much, I wouldn't bother! If you live in a cool temperate climate, or even if you have a south-facing, coolish garden site that is prone to frost, brussels sprouts can be a real mainstay. They will yield a large quantity of very delicious sprouts right through late winter and early spring, and not mind the frost at all.

Brussels sprouts are easy to germinate and transplant by the standard method. They like rich soil, but as they are prone to sap-sucking pests and fungus diseases, it is especially important to keep soluble nitrogen fertilisers away from them. They are rich in micronutrients, so they benefit from seaweed brew. They also appreciate a heavy mulching.

They are a bit difficult to place in the garden since they require a growing season of longer than six months. I usually plant them in one of the compost beds, after a nitrogen-hungry plant has been used to take up the excess. I mix them up with capsicums in the early part of their growing season, and dill in the later part, in order to help protect and disguise them from pests.

As the sprouts start forming, the lower leaves and any loose lower buds can be stripped off the stem and fed to the chooks. The older varieties mature a few at a time, allowing you to work your way up the stem, stripping the leaves as you go. When you get to the top you can harvest the cabbage-like head, which makes a very fine creamed soup.

CABBAGES

With a little bit of variety selection, breeding and local experience, you can easily grow cabbages all year round, and there are so many varieties it is difficult to get bored with them. The basic concept to remember is that the heart – the part we want the plant to put all its energy into – is just its way of storing enough nutrients to stay alive until it is time to seed. Warm weather, lengthening days or any stress are signs that it has waited long enough.

Genetic predisposition is the other main factor to consider when growing cabbages. If you save cabbage seed, *don't* save it from those plants that are unsuitable for eating because they have bolted too early. Sacrifice a few of your best eating cabbages for seed. I grow four different kinds for different uses.

Sugarloaf is the smallest and fastest, maturing in as little as eight weeks, or five to six weeks from transplant. These cabbages need only about 30 cm of space and are excellent fillers for small gaps in space or time. Because they are so fast-growing, they can be sown pretty well any time of the year. The difference in temperature and day length from sowing to maturity will not be enough to scare them into a premature bolt. I consider them a bit coarse for salads, but they go very well lightly fried with butter and black pepper.

A descendant of Golden Acre is my main spring and summer variety. They are nearly as fast-growing and compact as Sugarloaf, more resistant to cabbage moth and slug attack, and make a better coleslaw. Only midwinter plantings are a bit risky. If I have time to plant Golden Acre instead of Sugarloaf, I usually do.

By far the best kind for yield, flavour and pest resistance in my area is the Savoy. These are much better eaten raw than cooked, and although they take a few weeks longer to mature and need a bit more room to grow, they yield almost double the weight. Unfortunately this slightly longer growing season makes them unsuitable for planting in winter. The warmer weather hits before they are mature, and causes them to bolt to seed without heading. The best Savoys are started off in autumn, so that the onset of cool weather causes them to slow down and put on weight before they start thinking about reproducing.

Red cabbage used to be used only for pickling, but to my mind it is the best cooking cabbage of the lot. It takes longer to cook, but there is little risk of turning it to mush. It also makes a very acceptable and unusual salad, especially dressed with white Swatow broccoli flowers and bright-blue borage flowers. I have a descendant of Red Dutch that matures in ten weeks and therefore is nearly fast enough to plant any time of year.

All the cabbages are ideal for propagating by the standard method. Since they are vulnerable to quite a range of pests and diseases, it is worth keeping them in pots on a bench until they are about 15 cm tall. That way they can be kept out of the way of crawling and soil-dwelling creatures and easily monitored for aerial ones while they are at their most vulnerable. Using the pot as a miniature barricade around newly planted-out seedlings is extra-good practice, since cutworms are very partial to cabbages.

I try very hard never to plant out two members of this family – which includes cabbages, broccoli, cauliflowers, brussels sprouts, radishes and Chinese cabbages – together or immediately following each other. Disguise, of their appearance *and* their scent, is their best defence. Tomatoes are a very good companion for disguise.

Cabbages like rich soil, so they do best following the chooks or a legume. Some extra compost is a good idea otherwise. They are so greedy for micronutrients that they don't share the supply with neighbours or leave enough for succeeding members of the same family. They will survive quite dry conditions, especially through winter, but water stress and warm weather combined is just the thing to signal a bolt.

CAPSICUMS

Capsicums are very definitely a warm-weather crop. They need a soil temperature of 20°C to germinate, and air temperatures of 30°C or more to ripen fruit. I have managed to get some winter ones by using the heat generated by a compost pile, and you can grow them out of season in a glasshouse. But this short-circuits one of the main pleasures of gardening – the spice of anticipation. Whether a year-round supply yields jaded tastebuds, or whether these out-of-season ones really do taste inferior, there is something about the flavour of the first capsicums of the year that it would be a pity to miss!

Nevertheless I am inclined to be a bit impatient. I start capsicum seed off in a seed tray under glass in late July, transplant to seedling pots in early August, and aim to have seedlings ready for planting out in late August and early September. These very early plantings take a few weeks longer to mature than those planted a month or so later. I do successive plantings through until early February, but after this they will not have time to mature before the cool weather will stop them fruiting – if a frost doesn't kill them first. By then I am looking forward to peas and cauliflowers too much to devote space to capsicums anyhow.

Capsicum plants grow into a bush about a metre high, and need about a 40 cm wide circle of space. They are prone to cutworm, so planting out mature seedlings and using the pot as a barricade is important. They are also prone to fungus and bacterial diseases that make the fruit rot on the bush, especially if the fruit is kept wet. Since they need quite a lot of water for the fleshy fruit, this is tricky. Ideally they would be watered from below through a trickle irrigation system, so that the soil but not the plant is wet. If you use sprinklers or a hose, it is best to water in the early morning so that the plant dries off quickly. I try to plant them so that their neighbours are all short plants (like lettuces, beets, cabbages, carrots etc) that will not shade them or hold in humidity. Heavy mulch cover reduces the need to water at all. If you get weeks of rainy weather, you may have to resort to spraying with a seaweed–comfrey–horsetail–nettle–chamomile brew.

Like most fruiting plants, capsicums go all to leaf with little fruit if they have a diet too rich in soluble nitrogen. Extra fertilising is wasted on them, and they can be planted any time in a chook dome rotation. Following a leafy green that has already taken up all the excess nitrogen is ideal. I haven't discovered anything that particularly benefits them as a companion, but they seem to be of benefit to lots of other things. I suspect that because of their close relationship to chillies they give off a scent that deters insects and mites. To make the most of the benefit, I spread them as widely as I can.

CARROTS

It took me a long, very frustrating time to learn how to grow carrots successfully. There are lots of little tricks to growing them, and missing even one can mean failure of the crop. However, none of the tricks are very difficult or time-consuming, and once you have the method down pat it works every time. Home-grown carrots are so different to bought ones, and their yield for space is so heavy, that it is worth getting right.

Carrots are one of the few plants that just don't transplant. They must be sown directly where they are to grow. Even thinning should be minimised, as any disturbance bruises and upsets them and attracts carrot fly. The seed is extremely tiny and quite delicate. It needs to be planted very shallowly, almost on the surface, and kept moist *constantly* until it germinates – which can be as long as three weeks!

Carrots are prone to only one insect pest – carrot fly – but this fly is distressingly common and can smell a disturbed seedling from several kilometres away. Carrots are also prone to a number of underground fungus and bacterial diseases if the soil is not *very* well drained. Too much mulch on the surface can cause the plants to rot at the neck where they emerge from the ground. And aphids carry a virus that can affect carrot plants that are not resistant to it.

As with cabbages, the part we want to eat is, for the plant, just a food store waiting for seeding time. The onset of warm weather and long days once they are grown up, but before the carrots are big enough to eat, will cause the plants to bolt to seed without bearing a worthwhile crop. Similarly, any stress like lack of water or starvation will make them try to seed before it is too late. Too much water-soluble nitrogen will lead to all leaf, no root, and what root there is will be such odd forked and contorted shapes that the carrots are difficult to wash.

Does it all sound too disheartening? There are simple tricks to overcome all these traits. On the plus side, I believe the notion that carrots need sandy, well-dug soil is a myth. I get fine yields from very heavy clay soil with no digging at all. Check the time to maturity of the variety you are planting. Don't plant it when the season will change from cool to warm before it is mature, as this will make it bolt. The reverse is fine – shorter, cooler days will make the plants slow down and store up food to survive until next spring – which is exactly what we want them to do, except that we will be eating most of them before then!

Very fast-growing baby carrots tend to work all year, as the climate doesn't change enough in their short lifetime for the bolting effect to happen. But the large carrots need to be planted from spring through to early autumn, depending on the speed of the variety. I tend to rely on baby carrots for most of my supply, and reserve the larger, slower sorts for companion planting with onions in autumn. The largest and slowest varieties go in earliest and the quicker ones later. If you get very heavy frosts, you will have to plant both your onions and carrots in early spring instead, and choose virus-resistant varieties to foil the aphid-borne carrot virus.

Companion-plant all carrots with something in the onion family. I plant baby carrots with shallots and larger carrots with onions. The onions are quite happy to take up any excess soluble nitrogen and prevent it leaching down to the level at which the carrots are feeding. They are a powerful deterrent for carrot fly, and tend to have antibiotic characteristics that prevent underground rotting.

For midsummer plantings, the carrot–shallot patches should be companion-planted and even partly shaded by something that is relatively tall and canopied. Because they suffer from water deprivation but cannot be heavily mulched to offset this, it is important that they be provided with living shade. Tomatoes, capsicums and eggplants all work well, provided each carrot–shallot patch is only about 40 cm across. The large carrots and onions will be growing through winter, when drying out is not such a problem.

Clear the mulch from the area you intend to plant, and smooth out and water the soil. Soak the carrot seed for a couple of hours and mix it in equal quantities with the onion seed. Scatter the mix *very thinly* over the area. With baby carrots and shallots, the aim is to have about one seed every 8 cm^2, or about forty seeds in the area of this page. With large carrots and onions, halve this number. It may help to mix the seeds with sand to aid in sowing this thinly. The less thinning you have to do, the less chance of letting carrot flies know where your carrots are.

Just cover the seed with sifted mature compost, no more than 3 mm thick. I find an old kitchen colander is a good tool for this. Lightly press it down and water with a fine spray. Then cover the lot with something to shade it, conserve moisture and prevent rain from unearthing the seeds. I use some bits of old hessian potato sacks, but old blankets or anything similar will do. Keep the seed moist by watering through the covering. Inspect under the covering after a week, and then every day or two. As soon as the seedlings start to poke their heads up, remove the covering.

For midsummer plantings of baby carrots and spring onions, you may have to provide the seedlings with some extra shade for the first few weeks. Otherwise they can dry out between waterings even if watered every day. I poke a leafy branch into the ground so that it stands up like a little tree in the middle of the patch, removing it when the babies are about 7 cm tall. If your germination rate has been very good, you may have to thin the seedlings at this stage. Give baby carrots and shallots about 4 cm in each direction between plants, and large carrots and onions about 8 cm each. Wait for a few weeks, then start eating them! If you have to store carrots, twist the tops off first or they will go soft.

Once you find some varieties of carrots that do well in your local conditions, select the best and save the seed. Not only are the flowers quite beautiful and wonderful attracters of predatory insects, but carrots are one of the vegetables most variable according to conditions. Your own saved seed will outperform bought seed every time.

CAULIFLOWERS

Cauliflowers are among the greediest of all garden vegetables, so greedy that you can use the standard of your caulis to gauge whether you are developing and maintaining your soil. If your soil is rich enough for caulis, then it is rich enough for anything else! They are also quite fussy about temperature and day length. A period of cold weather is needed to make them set heads, and they will survive and even benefit from frost. Like just about all members of their family, they will bolt to seed before they are ready to harvest if they are grown on from short days to long days. Aim at having all your caulis harvested before spring.

The larger varieties of caulis are very slow-maturing and to support their size demand very concentrated nutrients in one spot. I don't believe they are well suited to organic gardens, or worth the use of so much space for such a long time. The smaller, faster varieties are easier to grow, and yield a head that is a nice size for a meal. The variety I use descended from Phenomenal Early and Snowball both planted at the same time, so is probably a cross between them.

I plant cauliflower seed in the standard seed-raising mixture from late February on, aiming to have the first plants ready for planting out in early April. I do successive sowings until mid-May, planting the last out as quite large seedlings in July. Cabbage moths are the main pest, and they are not so active in winter, but with early or late plantings I try to plant the caulis within easy reach of a path. Even the smaller varieties need a good 40 cm wide circle of space.

Caulis do best immediately following chooks or a legume, and should never follow or be surrounded by other members of their own family. Disguise plants like dill and celery are ideal companions. If you have extra fertiliser for only one of your garden plants, it should go to the caulis. Seaweed brew or compost made with lots of herbs are extra good, since caulis complain very obviously over lack of boron or molybdenum. Even worm-casting tea is not wasted on them, and the more mulch the better.

As soon as a head begins to form, break off one of the outer leaves and lay it over the head to protect it from sunburn. The head will mature in a matter of days from when you first notice it.

CELERY

People do some amazingly silly things to vegetables, but celery would have to rate among the silliest. The kind you buy in the shops is blanched, which means that the stems are starved of light for the last few weeks before harvest. Of course this also means that the whole plant must be harvested at once. For years I diligently blanched all my celery, and coped with the low yield and the slug and fungus problems that are the inevitable result. Nowadays I can think of no earthly reason why celery should be blanched, except that it has become the fashionable way to grow and eat it. Unblanched celery is just as crisp, has a great deal more flavour and nutritional value, is much less susceptible to pests and diseases, and yields a lot more over a much longer time.

Celery is a relatively slow plant: slow to germinate and slow to mature. Like carrots (to which it is related), the seed can take up to three weeks to germinate, and the kind you buy is normally at least five months old. I raise the seed in a standard seed-germinating mix, taking care not to plant it too deep. Soaking for an hour or two before planting can sometimes help the seed germinate a little faster and more evenly. As soon as possible, I transplant the seedlings into standard seedling-raising pots. It usually takes a month or more for them to outgrow the pots, and I like to wait as long as possible before planting them out. This ensures the maximum length of harvest before the chooks are due again.

I plant celery out around the path edge of a bed, immediately following a chook dome, and mulch it heavily. Drying out is its biggest problem, yielding tough stringy stems that are only good for cooking. I harvest it like silver beet, a stem or two at a time picked from the outside of the plant. That way I can continue picking for several months, picking the equivalent of three or four bunches from the one plant, until the chooks finish it off.

Celery is not damaged by frost and ideally likes a cool climate, but I find that I can keep it going all year round. If a plant does begin to flower, I usually leave it to repel cabbage moth and attract predatory insects (which it is very good at), and harvest the seed to flavour soups and egg dishes.

Besides the high requirement for general nutrition that it shares with all greens, celery has a particular partiality to calcium. Without it, the stems tend to wilt very quickly after harvest – which may not worry you if you are eating them immediately but which is a problem in lunch boxes or for sale. Compost or tea made from comfrey, horsetail, stinging nettles and/or watercress is high in calcium. Shellgrit and cuttlefish supplied to the chooks helps keep the levels of this essential nutrient high, and bones gradually decompose to release their calcium to the garden.

CHILLIES

Chillies are closely related to capsicums, the main difference being that many varieties are perennial. They like a frost-free site, but even in the coldest climates you should be able to find a spot against a north-facing wall for them. They are so decorative that if your north wall faces the street, all the better.

I have three different chillies in my garden. The Bird's Eye chillies are the smallest and hottest. They usually come on a medium-sized perennial shrub with glossy green leaves, but a chance mutation has given me a small bush with stunning purple foliage and masses of little bright-red fruit for most of the year. These chillies are so hot that they can only really be used after they have been dried and crushed into powder. Unfortunately they look very enticing to young children!

The Red Cayenne Peppers are an annual variety that I treat in exactly the same way as capsicums. They are the best variety for cooking, with a nice strong chilli flavour that doesn't numb your mouth for hours afterwards. The long, narrow, bright-red fruit are also perfect for pickling. Pack the raw chillies into sterilised jars, cover with hot spiced and salted vinegar, seal, and leave for at least three weeks. A cold beer and a platter of pickled chillies, cheese and apple is something to look forward to on a summer afternoon.

My third variety is the lucky result of an unintentional cross between a perennial chilli and a capsicum. Such liaisons are very common, and are something to beware of if you are saving seed from your own capsicums. The usual result is a smallish, thin capsicum that is too hot to eat, on an annual plant. In my case, chance gave me a large perennial shrub that yields, all summer and autumn, masses of large, sweet chillies mild enough for the children to pack in their lunch boxes.

Perennial chillies need to be kept out of a chook dome rotation, but otherwise they can be raised and treated the same way as capsicums. Mine have never been bothered by any pests at all. They are so unpalatable that a chilli tea can be sprayed on plants to deter almost any pest, including humans!

CHINESE CABBAGES

I have lumped all the different kinds of Chinese cabbages – bok choy, pak tsoi, wombok etc – together since they have similar growing styles. I grow them all, mainly for the flowers to use in salads, but also for the greens and seeds, and the slugs they attract as chook food. So my methods are quite different to conventional ones, and probably all wrong if you actually like the leaf.

I find all the Chinese cabbages to be very fast-growing, very hardy under my usual garden conditions, very prolific in both flowers and seeds, and wonderful slug attracters, and also that they have a tendency to behave like weeds. They will draw in every slug from miles around, and can then be fed, slugs and all, to the chooks. A few leaves laid out over any bed the evening before it is due to be planted, then gathered up early the next morning, will clear the area of slugs.

These cabbages have a strong tendency to bolt to seed in warm weather, and, since I like the flowers better than the leaves, I have selected seed to enhance rather than diminish this tendency. Occasionally I pick some leaves to use in a stir-fry, but the parts I most often eat are the brilliant yellow, very beautiful, very prolific, hot–sweet flowers – in salads. Continuous picking will make them continue to produce flowers rather than set seed. Just before the chooks are due, or when the aphids discover them (whichever happens first), I leave the flowers to set seed. The chooks like the seed almost as much as the slug-infested leaves, and I suspect they are protein-rich since even the geriatrics start laying.

I have three methods of propagating Chinese cabbages. The first is simply to scatter a handful of mixed seed, along with fat hen, amaranth, chickweed, radish and mustard seed, in any gaps left in the bed as it draws close to chook time. The cabbages will still be quite small, but usually large enough for me to harvest some tender young leaves if I want them before leaving them to the chooks.

The second method is to raise them in seed trays and transplant to seedling pots by the standard method. If I keep them in pots until they are 15 cm tall, it usually takes only another three weeks or so for them to begin to flower. Again I plant them out as gap-fillers, harvesting the flowers until a week or so before chook time, and letting the slugs have the leaves and the chooks have the slugs.

The third method is to let some of the ones that inevitably come up wild all over the garden, including in the edge guild area, survive. Occasionally, more by good luck than good management and usually in winter, they will not immediately bolt and, in the case of wombok, will even heart.

CHIVES AND GARLIC CHIVES

Chives and garlic chives can be propagated from seed, and each plant will grow into a clump of bulbs. Once you have some, it is easier just to divide the clumps. They are frost-hardy, and I can grow them all year round.

Both chives and garlic chives are usually regarded as perennials. But propagation is so easy and they are so prolific that I plant them around the path edge in the chook dome beds anyway. The chooks like them, and there is always a clump somewhere in the garden in need of dividing to replant after the chooks have been. Chives are not good companions for peas or beans.

Harvest your chives by snipping the greens with scissors. In spring many of the plants will flower. The flowers are very beautiful – and edible too, adding a delicate onion flavour to salads. The seeds make good sprouts.

CHOKOS

For almost everyone, the question with chokos is not *how* to grow them, but *why*. A whole generation of Australians know chokos only as a watery mush that you were once obliged to eat before you got any dessert. Cooked very, very, very lightly, they are a different vegetable. Give them another chance! Not in the garden itself – the rampant vines take up far too much room – but over any unsightly fence, wall, trellis or shed.

Buy or cadge a choko in spring, pot it (broad end up) until well sprouted, then plant it out. Make sure the vine gets plenty of water, and give it a severe pruning in late autumn every year. Pick the fruit young and *don't overcook them*. Dig up some root tubers while you are at it: they are even better eating than the fruit.

CORIANDER

Coriander is a love it or hate it herb. I love it, but have learned over a succession of dinner parties that the extremely strong flavour is not to everyone's taste. However, even if you do not use it in large quantities, it is still worth growing for the seed (which is used as a spice) and to attract predatory insects, particularly tachinid flies.

Coriander belongs to Umbelliferae, the same family as carrots, celery and parsley. It is easy and fast to grow, and it flowers and seeds relatively quickly. Since the very beautiful white and pale mauve flowers are one of the main harvests and also extremely useful as a predator attracter, this is an advantage.

Plant coriander seed by the standard method any time of year. The plant will grow into something that looks a bit like parsley, but needs a bit more space. I plant it out along the path edge because I pick it so frequently. The leaf is used in salads and as a flavouring herb in cooking. Carrot and coriander cream soup is close to heaven for those with a taste for coriander. The flowers are magical in salads, and if picked frequently will keep coming for several weeks. The seed is essential to most Indian recipes.

CUCUMBERS

From time to time cucumbers (along with cherry tomatoes) become a weed in my garden. They are a very unruly plant, needing strict discipline! Cucumbers are outrageously easy to grow. The least touch of frost will kill them, but practically nothing else will. The flowers need to be insect-pollinated to set fruit, but if you have to resort to hand-pollination, you have much bigger problems than setting fruit on your cucumbers.

They like a fairly high nutrient level, and will cope with quite raw compost and hot ground. They also like plenty of water, preferably in the mornings so that the leaves and fruit dry out quickly enough to avoid fungus diseases. They need good drainage, and plenty of mulch since they have surface roots. However, their main requirement is space. I have had one cucumber vine completely overrun several whole beds, strangling everything else, and this in a matter of a fortnight. Never trust a cucumber while you go on holidays!

I tend to ban cucumbers from the garden entirely, using them on trellises for shade around the house and to tame weedy banks instead. However, I have recently discovered a Lebanese Burpless bush-type cucumber that is trustworthy. The bush takes up about a metre-wide circle and the yield is moderate, but the fruit is superb, eaten skin and all with not a trace of bitterness. If you decide to trust a vine type in the garden after all, give it a tepee to climb and lecture it daily about sticking to its own area.

Cucumber seed germinates quickly and reliably, so I leave out the seed-germinating tray stage and plant straight into seedling-raising pots. Be careful not to plant too many or you will spend all summer making pickles and new friends to offload them onto once your old friends start begging a reprieve. Just one of the rampant type (although I invariably forget to stop at one) and two or three of the bush type are enough.

Cucumber beetles will inevitably arrive with the first flowers. These are small orange–red and black beetles that look a little bit like ladybirds. They feed off the flowers and if you are lucky will restrict your yield a bit. If they restrict it totally, try putting some in a blender, diluting the mixture, and spraying it back on the cucumber flowers. In very humid weather the plants will get powdery mildew. I find that the mildew's only effect normally is to shorten the lifespan of the plant by a matter of a week or two – by which time you will be heartily sick of cucumbers anyhow. If you get a bad case in a young plant, a spray of seaweed, comfrey, horsetail, nettle and chamomile brew will help. It is probably just as easy to pull out the plant and replace it, and hope for less humid weather.

DILL

Dill is another love it or hate it herb. I hate it. But I grow some anyway because it is another good predator attracter and a good companion for members of the cabbage family, especially brussels sprouts. Propagate by the standard method, taking special care not to plant the tiny seeds too deep. The plants need about 30 cm of space.

EGGPLANTS

Eggplants are almost worth growing just for the decorative value of the plant. With their beautiful mauve flowers and velvety leaves, they have an aura of indulgence as potent as Turkish delight. I don't know whether it is the variety I use or the home-growing, but I have never had to go to the bother of salting my eggplant. Since so many vegetables start to turn bitter within hours of picking, I suspect it is having them close to home that stops the bitterness.

Eggplants are even more of a hot-weather lover than capsicums. Seedlings planted out in October will catch up with those planted in September, so you really can't get out of waiting until at least December for them. Their needs and growing habits are almost identical to capsicum, except that they are not quite so likely to be troubled by fungi. Instead they are subject to a little insect called a flea beetle that usually does only minor damage but can decimate the leaves of young plants. If the plant is fully grown before the flea beetles find it they do little damage, providing a free pruning service that just makes the plant more eager to set fruit. If a lot of them happen to find a young plant, there is not a lot you can do about it except hope that the beetle predators catch up before it is too late.

You can try catching enough flea beetles to make a bug-juice spray, but they are not easy to catch. A chilli-and-garlic spray makes the leaves a little less palatable, but is a lot of work that must be repeated regularly. I usually restrict my efforts to brushing, hosing or shaking off as many as I can last thing of an evening before I complete my rounds. This allows the nocturnal, ground-dwelling predators to have a good go at the beetles. If there are some good rocks handy, I pile a few up around the plant to encourage the lizards to congregate there.

The most important strategy in controlling this pest is spreading the plants around the garden so that if you lose one it is not a disaster. Flea beetles do not seem to range far in search of new plants. If a plant is affected, then I believe, contrary to popular wisdom, it is better to leave it there as a predator lure than to destroy it. Removal will only force the beetles to go looking for a new home.

ENDIVE

Endive is a kind of loose-leaved lettuce with slightly bitter, very prolific, light-green crinkled leaves. It is propagated by the standard method and, being a leafy green, likes rich soil. It is very hardy, and I can grow it all year round.

The conventional way to harvest endive is to blanch the plant for about a fortnight before picking by covering it with something like a large pot or some hay to exclude light. The whole plant is then harvested at once. This process does remove the bitterness, but in my opinion it also makes it taste like an inferior lettuce – and since endive is a slower grower than lettuce, why not just plant lettuce instead and be done with it?

Green, unblanched endive, in small amounts, adds a pleasant, mildly bitter, interesting flavour to salads. If it is picked a leaf or two at a time, it will last for several months and grow to 50 cm across before flowering. I pick some for the chook bucket too. Endive blooms are among the most beautiful of all vegetable flowers, rivalling anything in a flower bed, and are very attractive to nectar-eaters.

GARLIC

Garlic is closely related to onions, and requires almost identical cultivation, except that it is grown from cloves rather than seed. I save my best cloves for next year's crop, but for starters you will have to either buy seed garlic, or cadge some sprouted garlic from your local greengrocer. If you get spoiled vegetables for mulch and chook food, you will often find sprouted garlic suitable for seed in it.

Garlic is best planted in autumn, between March and May, although you may be able to get away with early spring planting in cooler areas. I start the cloves off in yoghurt containers, pointy end up, poking just out of the seedling-raising mix. When they are 15 cm tall I plant them out into the garden.

Each plant needs only about 10 cm of space, but about nine months of time. Therefore they are not suitable for placing in the chook dome beds. I plant them in compost beds, scattering them amongst everything else, but taking particular care to keep them well away from peas and beans. Garlic is strongly antibiotic, and knocks around the symbiotic bacteria that peas and beans depend on for nitrogen. They will be ready for harvest in mid to late summer when the leaves and stems begin to dry out. Pull up the whole plant and hang it in an airy place to dry. From each clove you will get a corm – but remember to save the best for replanting.

KALE

It astonishes me how few varieties of vegetables are available in the shops. Only a small proportion of the whole enormous range of edible plants has the shelf life, portability and popularity needed to be successfully commercialised. Kale is one of the ones that doesn't. I only discovered it when I succumbed to a regular temptation – to try out the seed of something I had never heard of.

Kale is a kind of tender, mild cabbage that grows and is picked like silver beet. It loves frost but will grow quite happily all year round. It is extremely nutritious, and a rich source of a compound that eats up free radicals, so it serves as a cancer preventative. The deep blue–green crinkly leaves are a wonderful salad green, and because you pick them a leaf or two at a time, it is always very fresh. Ornamental kale, with its variegated purple–green and cream–green leaves, is beautiful enough to belong in a feature flower garden, and edible too.

Propagate kale by the standard method, any time of year, and plant it out around the path edges. You can begin harvesting it, a leaf or two at a time from the outside, within a few weeks of planting out, and it will continue to yield for at least six months. Harvest any extra for the chook bucket.

Kale belongs to the cabbage family, and is subject to many of the same pests and the same warnings about growing several members of this family together. Like brussels sprouts, it will tell you very clearly whether your levels of trace elements, especially boron and molybdenum, are high enough. If your kale develops a black, rotting hollow in the centre of the stem, it is suffering from boron deficiency. Seaweed contains boron, so if you are using seaweed brew regularly, you should not strike a deficiency. However, if you do, the tiniest amount of powdered boron will correct it. Just a teaspoonful dissolved in a bucketful of water is plenty for a whole bed. Don't be tempted to overdo it, as too much boron is much more of a problem than too little.

LEEKS

Leeks run a close second to asparagus for my favourite vegetable. Vichyssoise, or potato and leek soup, is justifiably one of the world's classic recipes. I like it hot as well as chilled, and I add a teaspoonful of mustard seeds to cook with the potatoes.

I grow leeks with potatoes since they are both potassium-lovers, take about the same time to mature and have similar seasonal requirements, although leeks can cope with and even benefit from a bit more cold than potatoes, especially as they approach maturity. As leeks are members of the onion family, they should be kept away from peas and beans. They are slow growers, but have such a high yield for space and are so delectable that I don't resent the time they take.

I plant leek seeds in a propagating mix in July, with successive plantings through to December. As soon as they are well germinated, I transplant them to a seedling-raising tray, using smaller pots than standard. Small yoghurt containers with the bottom cut out are about the right size. When they are about 15 cm tall they are ready to plant out. The best eating part of a leek is the stem, so the object is to get the maximum amount of thick white stem per plant. The easiest way to do this is to plant out the seedlings very deep, so that the stem elongates to get the leaf up into the light.

With a thick, pointed stick, poke a row of holes 10 cm apart and about 20 cm deep. Pop your leek seedlings into the bottom of the holes so that only the top 5 cm or so of leaf is above ground level. Push a little soil and mulch down the hole after them but don't fill it up. Water well. The leeks will grow upwards and outwards to fill up the hole, and soil will gradually wash in around them. When they are tall enough, pull the mulch in around them. The leeks will take a further four months or so to fully mature, but if you are very impatient you can begin eating them as soon as you think they are big enough to be worth picking.

LETTUCES

Lettuce can be a very boring vegetable unless you grow your own. Only gardeners get to experience the wonderful variety of flavours, textures and colours available. The trick with growing lettuces is to grow them very fast, with no checks. Like cabbages, the part we harvest is the food store. Anything the plant interprets as a threat to its survival will cause it to skip the food-storing stage and go straight to the seeding stage, ready or not. Even if the threat is not severe enough to cause a bolt, the lettuce will develop a bitterness that no amount of care and attention can remove.

For successful growing, first choose the right variety for season and location. Only experience and your own selection, cross-breeding and seed-saving will give you varieties that are absolutely right for your local conditions. I use a descendant of a Great Lakes/Narromar cross as my main summer heading variety, and an Iceberg descendant in winter. In the loose-leaved lettuces, the mignonettes – brown and green – are good for summer plantings, and the cos and oakleaf varieties work well in autumn and winter. My current favourite is a red, frilly, loose-leaved lettuce called Lollo Rosso.

However, lettuce is a wonderful vegetable to experiment with. There is an enormous number of varieties, and as soon as you are confident enough you can begin trying them all out. Propagate by the standard method, but sow lettuce seed *thinly*, and transplant carefully. A setback even at this very early stage will affect them for life. In midsummer you will get a better germination rate by putting your seed in the fridge for a few days before planting it. Don't keep your seedlings in too deep a shade or they will become leggy, another condition that they won't easily outgrow.

Slugs and snails love lettuces, so it is wise to clear them from the immediate area before you plant out. Lay a leaf of a Chinese cabbage, or an outside leaf of an already harvested lettuce, on the spot the evening before. First thing in the morning, pick up the leaf, slugs and all, and feed it to the chooks. Use the pot as a slug, snail and cutworm fence for a week or so.

I always try to plant out lettuces on a drizzly day, or if this isn't possible, last thing of an evening. In sunny weather, summer or winter, I usually lay a ferny leaf (like a frond of asparagus) across the top of the pot for the first day or two. This protects the lettuces from losing too much moisture until the roots have settled into the new location. Plant midsummer lettuces out into a spot where they will get some shade from neighbouring plants, as they can suffer from sunburn and they look really silly with pink zinc on their noses! If nothing else is available, poke a leafy branch into the ground next to them to act as a miniature shade tree. Companion planting with the taller tomatoes, capsicums and eggplants is easier.

Lettuces should ideally follow either the chooks or a legume. If not, a good double handful of compost is necessary. Plenty of mulch helps save them from drying out and going bitter or bolting to seed.

MARJORAM AND OREGANO

These two closely related perennial herbs grow by sending out runners to form a dense mat. I use them as the third or inside tier of the edge guild on the drier, hotter uphill edge of my garden. They both need some hard sun to develop their full flavour, since their aromatic oils are produced as protection from sunstroke.

They are both so vigorous that you should have no trouble obtaining and striking a root cutting.

MUSTARD

Mustard is one of the green manure and chook food catch crops I use to keep beds filled right up until the chooks go on. It is very fast-growing and bulky, and the chooks love it. I plant it simply by scattering seed, usually mixed with Chinese cabbage, cress, radish, chickweed and amaranth seed, among the established plants as it draws near to chook time. As the food crops finish bearing, these green manure crops will take over the space, so that the chooks are moved on to a bed filled with greens. As a side benefit, there are always some mustard greens around for me to harvest for salads. To ensure a continuing supply of seed for planting, and for seed for use as a spice, I occasionally transplant a few seedlings into the just chooked bed next door.

NASTURTIUMS

Nasturtium flowers are an essential salad ingredient, and sucking the nectar directly from the flowers keeps children foraging happily for hours. The leaves have a peppery flavour that goes well with cheese, and the pickled seeds taste like capers. Nasturtiums are a good nectar source for wasps, bees, predatory insects and birds, and they are a good ground cover companion for fruit trees, especially those prone to aphid attack. If the nasturtiums start to become rampant, I feed armloads to the chooks. Nasturtiums accumulate quite a range of nutrients, including good levels of calcium.

I have red, orange, yellow and variegated nasturtium patches in the edge guild. They are perennial, extremely hardy, and require no real attention. They do best in the wetter bottom sector, but bear the most flowers where they are subjected to a bit of stress – either poor soil or little water. Grow them from seed in spring, or cadge a root cutting.

ONIONS

Onions are such a central part of our culinary traditions that very few people, even serious gardeners, grow enough to last all year round. Yet they are not difficult to grow and, although they are slow, they give a very high yield for the amount of space they take up. By using several different varieties that mature at different times, you can easily grow a year-round supply.

Onions are day-length sensitive. Since you have absolutely no control over the length of the day, there is no way of growing them out of season. If you plant the wrong type for the season, they will simply either bolt or just fail to develop bulbs. Since latitude determines day length, onions suitable for planting in Brisbane in May are not the same ones suitable for Sydney. It may take you a few seasons to refine your variety selections in tune with your exact latitude.

I start planting onions, companion-planted with carrots, in mid-April, choosing extra-early varieties like Flat White, Lockyer and Red Italian Torpedo. The early kinds are not usually suitable for storage, and are best eaten fresh or kept in the fridge, but Lockyer can be dried and stored. In May I switch to White Spanish for keeping and brown Odorless for eating fresh. By June I am switching to the midseason brown onions like Pukekohe that are my favourites. These keep well and are my main source of onions for storage. Sometimes I include some Red Odorless Globes for fresh eating as well.

I live too far north to get away with planting onions after June, so from then on I restrict my planting to spring onions and shallots, which do well all year round. The farther south you live, the more you will be able to experiment with planting later varieties. Onions take at least five months to mature, most taking more like six and a half to seven months, so I cannot expect to start seriously harvesting them until spring. I can continue harvesting fresh onions until late summer, but for autumn and winter use I must rely on stored onions or shallots.

Onions can be planted out as seedlings, but because I plant them mixed with carrots, and carrots cannot stand transplanting, I plant the seed direct. Since the thick mulch cover on chook station beds restricts direct planting, and since most types take more than six months to mature, I plant them in the compost beds, usually following gross feeders like cucumbers and zucchinis. See the section on carrots for how to plant them.

I have never had any pest or disease problems at all with onions, but I get fairly dry winters and very dry springs. If you get wet winters, you may have to spray your onions with the seaweed–comfrey–horsetail–nettle–chamomile brew to stop downy mildew. The carrots repel onion fly and help deter weeds. Don't give the onions any extra feeding, as too much nitrogen makes them all leaf, no bulb, and vulnerable to rotting in storage.

I have never been struck with it, but onions are susceptible to a disease called white root rot, which infects the soil and stops you growing onions in the same place for ten years or more. It arrives in your garden in infected onions or seedlings (not seed), and is encouraged by growing onions in the same beds every year. The moral of the story is to use seed in preference to seedlings, and rotate the beds in which you grow your onions.

If your onions begin to flower, you may be able to save them by pinching out the flower stem while it is still very small. Onions for storage should be left in the ground until they are fully mature, when the leaves will begin to fall over. The stalks are then bent over, and the patch allowed to dry out for a week or so. Hope for no rain. The onions are then pulled and fully dried with the stalks still on. Be careful that they don't get sunburnt in the process.

PARSLEY

Parsley is one of the most nutritious vegetables of all, second only to carrots for vitamin A, peas and asparagus for vitamin B1 and capsicum for vitamin C. Tabouleh (a salad made with lots of parsley, mint, cracked wheat, garlic, olive oil and lemon juice) is about the most delicious vitamin pill you could imagine.

Parsley is closely related to carrots and celery: like them, the seed benefits from soaking and can be slow to germinate. For midsummer sowing, a few days in the fridge can help. I treat parsley exactly the same as celery. The plant will continue to bear for much longer if it is picked a few whole stems at a time from around the outside of the plant. You know if you are doing it right if the little half-moon at the base of the stem comes away too.

I have never had any pest or disease problems, apart from a tendency of the root to rot in beds without adequate drainage when the weather is very wet.

PARSNIPS

I believe parsnips are not worth eating until a couple of good frosts after they are mature have persuaded them to convert their starches to sugars. After this they are so full of sugar that they caramelise in the oven. Parsnips are closely related to carrots and, if possible, even trickier to grow. They have all the same difficult traits, plus a couple extra – a long growing season (up to six months) and seed that loses its viability after six months or so.

I plant a row of parsnips next to the leeks in each Guild One bed planted in late January and February. The seed is planted the same way as carrot seed, using a long strip of hessian 10 cm wide to cover the row until the seeds germinate. I sow them a little more thickly to make up for the erratic germination, and thin the seedlings to about 10 cm spacings. Use fresh seed: planting last year's leftover seed is a waste of time. Once they are germinated, they are relatively trouble-free. They should be ready for pulling in July, just before the chooks are due again.

PEAS

I have only ever had one major pest in my pea crop. Every afternoon at 3.30 in pea season, a gang of children descends on them, and I am very lucky if even one pod survives the onslaught. It doesn't seem to matter how many I plant, the number of children just increases in response.

Peas are a cool-season crop. Although it is supposed to be possible to grow them all year round, I have never had any success with any planted after August or before April. But then I have never tried very hard either. There is so much else going on in the garden over spring and summer that I wouldn't know where there was a space for peas anyhow! One thing to remember is that although the plants are frost-hardy, the flowers are not. If you get heavy frosts, you may have to restrict your pea-planting to late winter and spring, so that the last frost occurs before flowering.

The main variety I use is a pod-type dwarf pea that is a descendant of Greenfeast. It has a very heavy yield of well-filled pods that resist diseases even so close to ground level. It hardly seems worth growing sugar snap peas in a home garden since the yield is much lower, and freshly picked Greenfeast are just as sweet. I do, however, also grow some climbing snow peas. I haven't yet found a dwarf variety of snow pea that has an acceptable yield and enough pest and disease resistance. I grow the climbing variety up a couple of small A-frame trellises about 150 cm tall, with wide-gauge chicken wire so I can reach through the holes to pick.

Peas are another large and reliable germinator that can be planted directly into a seedling-raising pot. Like beans, they are very prone to rotting before germinating if they are kept too wet. Once the seed has absorbed enough water to signal it to begin germinating, it does not need any more until the seedling emerges from the ground. Even if the soil dries right out, it is not a problem. Resist the temptation to water!

I plant four pea seeds in each pot, remove the weakest as soon as I decide which it is, and plant out the other three as if they were one plant. These groups of three are planted at about 20 to 25 cm spacing in a diamond pattern. This uses a lot of seeds. It is worth saving your own if only to get a decent quantity to plant.

Peas are a legume and produce their own nitrogen, so they do not need especially rich soil. However, they like a lot of phosphorus. Bird manure, fish meal, bone meal, bracken, comfrey, watercress and yarrow all accumulate it. Cow manure is only a moderate source, but it has twice as much phosphorus as horse manure. Peas are also very fussy about the texture of their soil, and will keel over or bear abysmally at the least trace of waterlogging. When I plant them out, I give peas an extra mulch with dry trash like corn stalks or small twiggy branches or spent basil plants. This helps create enough air circulation around the plants to prevent mildew, and keeps the pea pods up off the ground. Slugs and snails love peas, and the kids regularly collect a small feast of them for the chooks. If you have wet winters you may have to resort to the seaweed–comfrey–horsetail–nettle–chamomile brew to prevent mildew diseases.

Never shell peas with your mind on anything else. You will catch yourself with a pile of empty pods and a guilty expression!

POTATOES

The award for most marked difference between home-grown and shop-bought vegetables goes to the humble potato. Gardeners often skip potatoes because they are so cheap to buy. But although commercially grown potatoes *look* similar to the home-grown variety, the taste is completely different. Organic home-grown potatoes are tasty and nutritious enough to make a meal all on their own.

Potatoes are a spring and autumn crop. Frost will kill the plants, and very hot weather, especially with warm nights, will make them bolt to seed without setting a decent crop. I plant them from mid-August to mid-September, then again from mid-January to mid-February. In frost-free sites you could plant them all winter, and in cooler areas from spring well into summer.

Potatoes are not planted from seed but from tubers that you buy as seed potatoes. They are susceptible to an aphid-borne virus that does not affect the current crop but causes successively lower yields in each generation grown from saved seed potatoes. If you plant bought eating potatoes that have developed eyes, they are likely to be carrying this virus, and the yield may be disappointing. Certified seed potatoes means ones that are certified not to be aphid-affected and, if you use them to plant every time, you can be assured of maximum yield without worrying about aphids at all.

The biggest yield I have ever had from a single seed potato was by planting it in a bed of mulch in an old tyre. As soon as the greens reached above the tyre, I added another tyre on top, and filled that up with mulch too, forcing the plant to grow taller and taller. I ended up with a stack of five tyres filled with mulch, bracken, comfrey, manure and potatoes. Although this was the biggest yield per seed potato, it is really only a novelty way of growing potatoes, sensible only if you have very limited quantities of seed potatoes or space. By spreading this quantity of mulch out over five different seed potatoes, the total yield is higher for much less work. However, this method gives you an idea of the principles of potato growing.

I plant potatoes simply by making little burrows 30 cm apart, down through the mulch to the soil surface, immediately after the chooks have been on a bed. I lay the well-eyed seed potatoes on the surface of the soil and cover them with a double handful of compost or mixed soil and compost. Potatoes are very hungry, especially for potassium, so if I have any extra mowed cow manure, I add a handful of this for the extra potassium it contains. As the potato plants grow, I pull the mulch in around them, leaving just the leaves exposed. Mowed bracken fern added to the mulch provides even more potassium.

The potato plants will flower with lovely lilac flowers like miniature eggplant flowers, then set green fruit, then begin yellowing from the lower leaves up. From then on you can begin bandicooting, or stealing individual potatoes from under the mulch, without disturbing the plant. After about four months the plants will die off, and will have set all the crop they are going to. Potatoes grown by this method do not have to be dug, and can simply be collected, almost clean, from under the mulch. The true roots of the plant, however, have extended deep into the soil beneath, and growing potatoes is a wonderful soil-conditioning treatment for a new garden.

If I am intending to save potatoes for seed, I spray them regularly with seaweed brew to give maximum aphid resistance. Otherwise I don't bother. The aphids do negligible damage to the plant or current crop, and are a good early attracter for ladybirds. I have never been struck with the dreaded potato blight that killed millions of people in the Irish potato famines. But if you are, you will recognise it by black patches with white borders on the leaves. I doubt that you can save potatoes grown under mulch.

Make sure you store your potatoes in a dry, dark, airy place that is safe from rodents. Untreated potatoes go green very quickly on exposure to even dim light, and the green areas contain poisonous oxalic acid.

PUMPKINS

Pumpkins are even less trustworthy in the garden than cucumbers. They are not quite as fast at sealing the takeover bid, but they (or rather *it* – one plant is enough) do it even more thoroughly. I never plant pumpkins. I simply transplant the ones that come up of their own accord from the mulch in a chook dome. But I *do* transplant every single one! The one time I made the mistake of letting a pumpkin vine go, it turned my entire garden into a pumpkin patch.

Pumpkins like warm weather (for at least four months from transplant), warm mulch or compost, lots of water and *space*. I have a mulched area below the garden where I let all these rampant vegetables fight it out among themselves.

RADISHES

Radishes are the easiest of all vegetables to grow, so easy that there is virtually nothing to say about them. They are also one of the fastest, the small round red type taking only about three weeks to mature.

Radishes can be grown all year round. I nearly always have a few plants of different varieties flowering and seeding somewhere in the garden. I pick the seeds, clear most of the mulch layer off any area that needs a quick filler crop, and scatter them haphazardly. Scatter a bit of the mulch back over the top, water them and wait for the crop. There will probably be lots more than you can eat, but the chooks like them too.

To ensure a continuing supply of seeds, I transplant a few of the best plants to a location where the chooks have just been, to allow enough time for flowering and seeding. I am not enough of a radish connoisseur to value purity in the varieties. I tend just to enjoy the novelties and surprises that the work of the bees in cross-pollinating gives me – a new kind of radish with each planting! But if you have a favourite kind, you will have to keep it separate, since they are quite promiscuous.

Horseradish or daikon is ideal for breaking up very heavy clay soil, the kind of soil where dock can become troublesome. To keep the very long, thick roots, I like to save the seed when there are no other radish varieties currently being allowed to flower.

ROSEMARY AND SAGE

These are both flowering perennial herbs that grow as a low bush. It is the aromatic oils that they develop as sun protection that give them their flavour, and harsh dry conditions that make them flower. Best grown from cuttings, they like the hottest, driest, harshest spot you can give them, but preferably within your garden area since they repel many plant-eating insects and attract many predatory ones.

I grow rosemary and sage in 50 cm high lengths of hollow log, filled with a seedling-raising mix heavy on the sand, and surrounded by rocks. The logs keep them a bit drier than the surrounding area, and up out of the range of being overrun by the surrounding marjoram, oregano and thyme, while the rock piles absorb heat.

SILVER BEET

Silver beet is very adaptable and quite easy to grow. I include some in every planting so as to have a reliable year-round supply. Home-grown silver beet is fresh and crisp enough to use raw as the basis of a salad which will have a great deal more flavour and character than one based on lettuce.

I use several different varieties. The main one is a descendant of Fordhook Giant, and has very large, deep green, crinkly leaves. But it is such a heavy feeder, with such a voracious appetite for nitrogen, that it is only really suitable once you have built up the fertility of your soil. If you are starting a new garden on fairly starved soil, one of the new miniature varieties, or one of the paler green types, may serve you better initially.

I also use several different kinds of Rainbow and Ruby Chard. These are varieties of silver beet that have red, yellow, purple and pink-coloured midribs and veins, instead of the standard creamy white. Their main advantage is that they are so very beautiful, in the garden and on the table. They also seem to cope a little better with the very heavy soil at the bottom end of the garden.

Silver beet is propagated and planted by the standard method, germinates easily, and has no major pests or diseases. It has an almost insatiable appetite for nitrogen, though, and should only ever follow the chooks or a legume. Even then it appreciates extra feeding with compost or worm castings, and is one of the very few plants that can safely use liquid nitrogen. I plant it around the path edges, since it can be picked daily over a five-month season.

In very humid weather, such as we sometimes get in early autumn, the plants can be troubled with leaf spots caused by a fungus. In these conditions, however, I usually have the seaweed–comfrey–horsetail–nettle–chamomile brew out to treat something, so I use up any leftovers on them. In midsummer, the plants that get some shade do better than those in full sun.

SPINACH

I cannot grow spinach in my area – the weather just doesn't get cold enough. Any spinach I plant just bolts straight to seed. But if your frosts are too heavy for silver beet, you should be able to grow spinach instead as a winter green.

Spinach is a small, fast-bearing plant. Propagate by the standard method, and plant within reach of a path. Each plant needs only about 20 cm of space, and you will be able to begin picking leaves a matter of three weeks or so from planting out. Like all leafy greens, spinach likes a high level of nitrogen, and it is especially partial to manganese. Deficiencies show up as pale or transparent areas on the new leaves. Bracken, chickweed and seaweed are good sources of manganese.

STRAWBERRIES

I grow strawberries quite unconventionally, mostly because I think conventional methods involve fighting an uphill battle against the plant's natural inclinations. Strawberries are prone (especially when they are all grown together) to quite a range of diseases that can quickly become epidemic, and pests find a banquet laid out. The flowers need insect pollination, but they are such a good nectar source that there is no problem about pollinators finding them! So there is no more reason for a strawberry bed than there is for a tomato or lettuce bed. I plant strawberries as individual plants, scattered throughout the garden, no two together.

I also plant them in the chook dome beds, giving them a very short life span by conventional standards. Strawberries are a woodland plant. Their native habitat is in the leaf mould under trees. They have extremely shallow and quite small root systems: if you dig up a plant you will see just how shallow. They are adapted to feeding almost exclusively off the mulch layer on the forest floor, avoiding an unequal competition with the trees for soil nutrients.

Of course the limited supply of nutrients in a small patch of mulch is quickly exhausted, especially with predators like people carting off the berries. Strawberries solve this problem by going wandering. They simply take off via a runner to find a new patch of nutrient-rich mulch to inhabit. In the garden, a strawberry plant will have used up all the nutrients in its little patch of mulch within a few months. It cannot, as other plants can, extend its root system to find more. In its natural habitat, it would go wandering. But although this solution might suit the plant's purposes, it doesn't suit our purposes for it!

For the plants, fruiting is just a backup method of reproducing. Their preferred method is to send out runners, and if they can do this successfully, why fruit? Runners are clones of the parent plant, whereas fruits are pollinated and so genetically unique. A few fruits are worthwhile to the species as a way of keeping a modicum of genetic variety, but nothing like the quantities that we like to see produced. The only way to convince the plants to fruit vigorously is to prevent them from running *at all*.

The runners from a plant that has been fruiting are of no use even as new stock. Strawberries, like potatoes, are prone to an aphid-borne virus that does not harm the plant in the first generation. However, it drastically and progressively reduces the yield of the offspring of the infected plants. Good yields come from virus-free stock, preferably from a virus-resistant variety. If you are propagating your own, the only way to keep the plants virus-free is to keep them aphid-free. But the flowers are so attractive to aphids that if the plants are being allowed to flower and fruit, this is all but impossible without spending exorbitant amounts of energy on control measures.

I solve the problem of virus-free stock by raising some plants just for their runners. Although they come from the same parent, I differentiate between plants I am going to raise for runners as a supply of new plants, and those I am going to raise for berries. Plants to be used for stock are planted well away from anything that attracts aphids, and are treated to a cupful of seaweed brew every week or so. These plants are not allowed to fruit or even to flower. Any flowers are removed as soon as they start, as part of my daily garden rounds. Runners are regularly snipped off and removed to the seedling-raising area. The parent plant is left to the chooks after six months so as to minimise the chances of it carrying the virus.

Plants to be harvested for berries are never allowed to run. When I pick the berries, I pinch off any tendrils beginning to form before they get anywhere near rooting. I plant some in most beds straight after the chooks. By the time the chooks are due again, they will have used up their local supply of nutrients and yield will start to drop. Better yield for space is to be had from a new plant in a new patch of recently chooked mulch. I find that by keeping a couple of varieties going and planting continuously, I can get strawberries from late spring right through until early winter.

Being woodland-adapted, strawberries will grow quite happily in shade. Although the yield is slightly heavier in the sun, they do quite well enough as an understorey plant in the vegetable garden, around and underneath taller plants like tomatoes, capsicums, eggplants and borage (which is an especially favoured companion). Ramblers like peas and beans will swamp them, and they are not good companions to the cabbage family.

It is worth buying good stock from a nursery to start with. Runners from a friend's strawberry patch, particularly if it is a few years old, are almost certainly virus-infected. Choose your variety carefully. Red Gauntlet is the main commercial variety, but it is bred for long, heavy yields of large, uniform fruit with a good shelf life, not for flavour. I use Tioga and Redlands Crimson, but different varieties perform well in different localities. Ask for virus-free stock.

I plant strawberry runners into seedling-raising pots filled with pure compost and watered with seaweed brew. I plant them out individually, in any chook dome or compost bed, at any time of the year. Each plant needs only about 15 cm of space, and I avoid planting two together. I plant most around the path edges so that the kids don't walk on the beds searching out the berries. However, I usually hide a few inside the beds so the adults get a look-in too. The chooks are quite partial to strawberry plants and to the various insects they attract!

SUNFLOWERS

Sunflowers seduced a spot in my garden as cut flowers – a single sunflower in a vase permeates the whole house with light. They earned an expanded space by getting the chooks to barrack so hard for them. The barter rate in sunflower seeds for eggs is very good! Then they clinched the deal as perfect companions for the cucurbits (zucchinis, squash and cucumbers). Sunflowers are phenomenally attractive to bees, luring lots of them into the cucurbit patches. This ensures the pollination that is essential for this family to fruit, but it also has another benefit. I'm not sure of the reason, but lots of bees seem to strongly deter the cucumber beetles that are the major pest of this family. My theory is that the cucumber beetles are after the pollen, and if the bees beat them to it, the plants lose a lot of their attractiveness.

Giant Russian is the sunflower variety I use, and I plant some of them every time I plant zucchinis, squash or cucumbers. They are raised by the standard method, and do well in the same kind of conditions as their companions. The only competition I have ever had for harvest is from rosellas, and they pay for their supper so well in visual delight that only the chooks hold a grudge!

SWEET CORN

It is an old story but a true one: the way to cook sweet corn is to have the water boiling, then pick the corn. As soon as it is picked, corn begins converting its sugars to starches, and loses its sweetness. Sweet corn in the shops is not sweet, and is not worth buying.

Unfortunately, sweet corn takes up a lot of room for its yield. You will get about sixty cobs from a bed, excluding the chook fodder area. The main advantage of the new super-sweet varieties is not that they are sweeter, but that they maintain their sweetness for longer – which is not really relevant if you are growing your own. They pay for it by having even lower yields. The highest-yielding corn is the maize type, and when picked young and eaten very fresh, it is almost as sweet as sweet corn.

Corn is wind-pollinated. The flowers on the top of the plant contain the pollen, which must be blown onto the silks emerging from the cobs of neighbouring plants. Inadequate pollination will cause the seeds not to develop and fill out. For effective pollination, corn must be planted in a block, not in a row or as isolated plants. Corn is the only crop I give a whole bed to itself. Giving the plants a bit of a shake around midmorning also helps to release and distribute the pollen.

Corn is a hot-weather crop. Even if you can manage to grow it in winter, it takes so long that it is not worth it. I plant the seeds in mid-August, ready for the first planting in early September, and stop planting it in late March. You can plant the seeds directly into the garden, but raising them in pots gives you an extra few weeks' head start, which allows you to get another crop from the same bed before the chooks are due again. Corn seeds are large enough and reliable enough to skip the seed-tray stage and plant directly into seedling-raising pots. Like most of the seeds large enough to do this with, they can rot before germinating if they are kept too wet.

Corn is a fairly heavy feeder, and to get decent yields for the space they take up, I like to plant them very close together – at 30 cm spacing in a diamond pattern over the whole bed. At this close a spacing their demand for fertility and water is high. When the plants are about half grown, I steal some mulch from a chook dome and give them an extra mulching. This helps feed them a bit extra, conserve moisture and buttress them against the wind.

For home consumption, corn has no real pests to worry about. Corn ear worms nearly always appear, burrowing in through the silk end into the cobs. But they rarely attack until the cobs are due to be picked anyway, they don't eat much, and the grubs can simply be added to the chook bucket along with the husks. If they become a problem, they can be foiled by cutting the silks off with scissors after the cobs have been pollinated. In humid weather, corn can get a fungus disease called smut, which causes the seeds to turn into grossly swollen, black sooty things. I have only ever had the odd plant affected, never enough to bother trying to find a treatment or preventative.

Corn is ripe when the silks have turned completely brown or black. If you are not sure, peel back some of the husk and check. This will do the cob no harm so close to harvest time, and if it is not ready, just defer the feast for a few days.

TOMATOES

In Queensland and northern NSW the familiar large red tomatoes are one of the hardest of all vegetables to grow organically. They are prone to that least co-operative of all insects – the fruit fly. Short of bagging every set of fruit, there is no sure way to discourage fruit fly enough to get even a share of your crop, and it takes a very well-developed predator breeding system to impose some sense of fair play on them.

I was only able to harvest most of my tomatoes without fruit fly after my garden had been established for about four years. I did not vary my method, and can only assume that the predator population was finally high enough to keep them in balance. Meanwhile, however, if you live in a fruit fly area and you really do need to grow the beefsteak varieties of tomatoes, then you will probably have to resort to bagging every set of fruit for a few years. There is a much easier way.

I can't see any good reason why it should be so, but both cherry tomatoes and the Roma variety of egg tomatoes are fruit fly resistant. The odd one is affected, but with even a rudimentary predator control system, the cut is acceptable. Both of these are very fine tomato varieties, suitable for salads, sandwiches, snacks and cooking. The egg tomatoes are firmer and less acid, but the cherry tomatoes are so sweet and flavoursome that kids eat them like lollies.

Cherry tomatoes are so hardy that they can become a nuisance in the garden, popping up all over the place and looking so healthy and beautiful that you don't have the heart to weed them out. Go away for a week and you are likely to come back to find a rampant, prolific vine-like plant that has climbed all over the lettuces and carrots. Egg and beefsteak varieties are much more domesticated.

Tomatoes are insect-pollinated and extremely genetically variable. A bit of selection will give you a variety that yields many times better for the space it occupies – that is, provided you have been ruthless enough with the volunteers to prevent their genes constantly dominating the pool. I am quite unrelenting about planting the cherry tomatoes I *choose*, and weeding out every one that plants itself.

Choose your tomatoes, of whatever variety, from three or four different plants to prevent inbreeding. Squeeze them onto a sheet of kitchen paper, and leave the paper to dry in the sun. In mid-August, plant the seeds, paper and all, in a seed-raising tray, and pot the seedlings into standard seedling-raising pots. I can continue planting successive crops through until early March. The egg and the beefsteak varieties will be killed by the first frost, and will stop fruiting with the arrival of cool weather in any case. The cherry tomatoes are semiperennial, and planted in spring will continue bearing, at a lower level, but well into the following winter. If you have bottled some for cooking while the crop was plentiful, they will keep you going right through.

Cherry tomatoes need a lot of space, and do better as a rambler than they do staked up. If you are not short of room, then choose a spot with easy access where each plant can have at least a 1.2 metre wide circle of space. If you have limited room, then erect a wide-gauge wire fence about a metre high and 60 cm wide around each plant to contain it. Egg and beefsteak tomatoes use less space. Give them a 40 cm wide area, and tie each plant to a firm, two-metre-high stake in the ground beside it. Old pantyhose are ideal for tying. Be careful not to bruise, squeeze or damage the plant when staking, as even minor injuries make it much more prone to disease. For the same reason, I do only very minimal, if any, pruning of tomato plants.

Tomatoes are prone to a host of pests and diseases. By separating the plants, avoiding growing them again on the same spot for several years, planting well-advanced seedlings and fostering insect predators, most of these pests and diseases (except fruit fly) can be ignored.

The classic companion for tomatoes, improving pest and disease resistance, yield and even flavour, is basil. This is very opportune, since basil and tomatoes are perfect companions in everything from a pizza to a salad. All the Umbelliferae (celery, parsley and carrots) attract hoverflies to prey upon tomato pests, and feed at a different root zone from a different menu, so they are good companions. Tomatoes provide worthwhile summer shade and protection for lettuce, silver beet and especially carrots.

Tomatoes are very acid, so they are easy to bottle and preserve. They also preserve well by drying, and it is not difficult to make for yourself those wonderful sun-dried tomatoes that are so outrageously expensive to buy.

TURNIPS

Turnips and swedes are closely related, and almost identical in their growing habits. The main difference is that swedes take four to five months to reach maturity, whereas turnips take only two or three. In northern European climates, where there are several months of the year when nothing grows, swedes are a useful crop, since they store well. But in my garden I stick to turnips.

Turnips have a strong flavour and are a bit of an acquired taste. If you have never tasted really fresh, home-grown ones, it is worth giving them a chance to acquire you. They are surprisingly sweet, very nutritious, easy to grow and very heavy-yielding. They are a cool-season crop, and ones grown into summer tend to be tough, stringy and bitter, if they don't just bolt to seed.

I plant turnips in the same guilds as peas, sowing the first ones in seed trays in mid-March for planting out in April, and the last in early July for planting out in August. They are propagated in standard seed-germinating trays, and transplanted to seedling-raising pots until they are about 15 cm tall, when they are ready for planting out. Since each plant needs only about 15 cm of space, the smaller yoghurt containers are more suitable for raising them than milk containers.

Too much soluble nitrogen will make turnips very leafy, with small tubers. Their main nutrient requirement is boron. Turnips are an indicator crop, giving you a clear and unequivocal measure of whether the levels of this element are adequate. While it is difficult with most crops to diagnose whether boron deficiency is the problem, turnips develop a very distinctive brownish-grey core that will rot out. Use seaweed brew or, if you have to, a *very* small amount of dissolved borax (one teaspoonful per bed), to cure it.

ZUCCHINIS

Zucchini cake, zucchini pie, zucchini soup, zucchini–egg bake, zucchini fritters, zucchini casserole, zucchini au gratin . . . Zucchini is a feast or famine vegetable. If you grow it at all, you very quickly acquire an encyclopedia of zucchini recipes.

Zucchini seeds need warm soil, at least 20°C, to germinate, and they cannot cope with any frost at all. I start raising the seedlings in early September, keeping the pots on the warmer northern side of the shadehouse. I plant the last lot in early March. The seeds are large enough to skip the seed-germinating mixture and plant directly into a seedling-raising pot. They are very quick to germinate and they outgrow the pot in a matter of ten days or so.

Zucchinis take up at least a metre-wide circle of space each. They have large, aggressive surface roots that extend over an even bigger area, so they are not suitable for companion planting with anything that is not willing and able to share its nutrient and water supply. They will starve out lettuces or cabbages. They need a fairly high nutrient level to sustain their very quick growth and prolific production, but they can get it from quite raw compost and mulch and are very able to go looking for extra nutrients. So provided the bed is well mulched, extra fertilising is wasted on them. I steal an armload of mulch from a neighbouring chook dome bed for each compost pile site, and plant them in that.

Sunflowers are wonderful companions for zucchinis: they are aggressive enough to compete for nutrients and tall enough to get their share of the light. They attract masses of bees that raid the zucchini flowers while they are there and so pollinate them, which is essential if the fruit is to set. I also suspect that enough bees can remove so much pollen that the cucumber beetles that are the major pest find it not worth their while, and go off looking for a patch to themselves.

Zucchinis, along with most of the other members of their family, are prone to fungus diseases, especially downy mildew, which shows up as powdery white patches on the leaves. These diseases are more likely to be a problem if the weather is humid and damp, and less likely to be a problem if the plant gets plenty of water to the roots but *not* on the leaves. If you water with a hose or sprinkler, try to do it in the early morning so that the leaves get a chance to dry out quickly. The seaweed–comfrey–horsetail–nettle–chamomile brew sprayed on the leaves regularly also helps to prevent these diseases.

Pick zucchinis young, and if you run out of recipes, feed young ones to the chooks. Once a plant has succeeded in producing a fruit that is mature enough to have viable seeds, it seems to give up caring whether it produces any more, or even whether it lives or dies. You might as well pull up the plant, since the yield from then on will be dismal, and the plant excessively prone to diseases.

INDEX